DEVELOPMENT STRATEGY AND MANAGEMENT
OF THE MARKET ECONOMY

VOLUME I

Development Strategy and Management of Market Economy

VOLUME I

Edmond Malinvaud
Jean-Claude Milleron
Mustapha K. Nabli
Amartya K. Sen
Arjun Sengupta
Nicholas Stern
Joseph E. Stiglitz
Kotaro Suzumura

CLARENDON PRESS · OXFORD

Published for and on behalf of the United Nations

1997

Oxford University Press, Great Clarendon Street, Oxford OX2 6DP

Oxford New York

*Athens Auckland Bangkok Bogota Bombay
Buenos Aires Calcutta Cape Town Dar es Salaam
Delhi Florence Hong Kong Istanbul Karachi
Kuala Lumpur Madras Madrid Melbourne
Mexico City Nairobi Paris Singapore
Taipei Tokyo Toronto Warsaw*

*and associated companies in
Berlin Ibadan*

Oxford is a trade mark of Oxford University Press

*Published in the United States
by Oxford University Press Inc., New York*

*British Library Cataloguing in Publication Data
Data available*

*Library of Congress Cataloging in Publication Data
Data available
ISBN 0–19–829212–0*

1 3 5 7 9 10 8 6 4 2

*Printed in Great Britain by
Bookcraft (Bath) Ltd, Midsomer Norton, Somerset.*

FOREWORD

This volume is the outcome of deliberations of a group set up by Jean-Claude Milleron of the United Nations to review some of the key questions that arise in formulating strategies for development in the contemporary world. The original idea for the Group emerged from discussions between Jean-Claude Milleron and Arjun Sengupta of the Indian Planning Commission. Deliberations in the group resulted in focusing on some basic understanding of the nature of the problem, and we may briefly comment on this approach in this Foreword.

(1) Public policy discussions should begin with the recognition of the essential role that the markets play in the efficient allocation of resources. International openness, as well as free domestic movement of goods and factors of production, are crucial. Many of the mistakes in earlier development policies arose from an inadequate appreciation of the role of markets. However, in some cases, markets either do not exist or fail to operate effectively—because of imperfect information, structural rigidities, insufficient infrastructure, or far-reaching externalities. Moreover, demands of distributive equity may end up being neglected in market allocations with unequal resource endowments. Deficiencies of these kinds can be particularly pervasive in developing and transitional economies.

Instances of market failure do not imply that the use of markets should be abandoned, or that liberalization and deregulation policies are unnecessary in those economies which have tended to cramp the effective operation of markets. On the contrary, they highlight the need for public policies to be informed by rigorous analysis, particularly of the nature and causes of likely market failures. Nor should we assume that governments can always eradicate market failures through intervention. Development experiences point to a wide range of government failures as well, especially when the measures aim at supplanting market signals rather modifying them appropriately.

(2) Development is a long-term endeavour. Nevertheless, many success stories demonstrate that substantial progress can be achieved within comparatively short periods—even one generation. The enhancement of human capabilities, in the broadest sense of the term, is a key ingredient of successful development policies. Besides growth of output and employment, attention has to be paid to basic health and education, the existence of sufficient safety nets and food security, equitable access to social and economic opportunities, development of an adequate infrastructure, and protection of the environment. These are crucial features of the pursuit of overall objectives of development policies.

The recognition of the basic objectives of development does not imply that the process of development has to be geared to some grand social welfare function, nor that a unique index can be found to measure the extent of progress in development. Moreover, it does not specify the kind of government involvement that is most likely to lead to fulfilment of development objectives. Nevertheless, market economies may require some well designed planning by governments, as well as by other significant economic and social actors, which aim at making sure that these objectives are met. Proper investment in human resources should improve the primary distribution of economic and social means, and thereby contribute to the long-term objective of distributional equity.

(3) A serious danger to the sustainability of any development process is macroeconomic instability. Such instability—in particular high levels of inflation—not only upsets the signals that the market provides for both the current and the intertemporal allocation of resources, but it also generates adverse expectations that may lead to insolvency and a cumulative economic crisis. In the long run, policies have to be, in general, guided by budgetary prudence and external payments constraints. This implies that development strategies should incorporate—rather than violate—conditions of macroeconomic stability.

This does not, however, entail that one should make a fetish of such simple rules as "fiscal deficits should be eliminated", or "the debt-GDP ratio should not be allowed to increase". But it does indicate the centrality of financial prudence and macroeconomic stability despite the importance of long-term development objectives. Credibility of development policies can be deeply undermined by the use of soft budget constraints by central governments and local authorities, often associated with ineffective tax policy or extravagant and unproductive expenditures.

These general ideas served as the point of departure for our examination of the appropriate combination of the government and the market in the construction of development policies. There is much complementarity between these two fundamental components, and it is sensible to think of a partnership between the government and the market in the formulation and implementation of successful development strategies. We have tried to explore and scrutinize the nature of that partnership.

Edmond Malinvaud
Amartya K. Sen

PREFACE

These two volumes are the result of the work of a High-level Group of Experts established by the Secretary-General of the United Nations at the end of 1993 to analyse key aspects of development policy in the light of the new thinking on economic and social issues that has evolved over recent years.

The Members of the Group were Professor Edmond Malinvaud (Collège de France, Paris), Jean-Claude Milleron (Under-Secretary-General for Economic and Social Information and Policy Analysis in the United Nations, New York), Professor Mustapha K. Nabli (University of Tunis, Tunisia), Professor Amartya K. Sen (Harvard University, Cambridge, Massachusetts), Arjun Sengupta (Member of the Planning Commission of India), Nicholas Stern (Chief Economist, European Bank for Reconstruction and Development, London), Joseph E. Stiglitz (Chairman, Council of Economic Advisers to the President of the United States) and Professor Kotaro Suzumura (Hitotsubashi University, Tokyo). Yves Berthelot (Executive Secretary of the United Nations Economic Commission for Europe) and Gert Rosenthal (Executive Secretary of the United Nations Economic Commission for Latin America and the Caribbean) also participated actively in most of the meetings of the Group. In addition, Peter E. de Jánosi (Director, International Institute for Applied Systems Analysis, Laxenburg, Austria) and Mihály Simai (Director, World Institute for Development Economics Research, Helsinki, Finland) participated as *ex-officio* Members of the Group. All Members served in their personal capacity.

The Group elected Professors Malinvaud and Sen as Co-chairpersons, while Jean-Claude Milleron and Arjun Sengupta jointly headed the secretariat of the Group.

The Group held five meetings between 1994 and 1996. In addition to the contributions of the Members of the Group, background papers for these meetings were prepared by John Bonin, Willem Buiter, Thomas Hellmann, Ricardo Lago, Bozena Leven, Kevin Murdock, Andrés Rodríguez-Clare, Richard Sabot, István P.

Székely, Vito Tanzi, Geedreck Uswatte-Aratchi and John Williamson.

Financial support for the Group was provided by a grant from the Government of France. The International Institute for Applied Systems Analysis (IIASA), the World Institute for Development Economics Research (WIDER), and the European Bank for Reconstruction and Development (EBRD) acted as hosts for the Group's meetings, with Shari Jandl, Lorraine Telfer-Tainvainen and Kerrie Quirk respectively playing key roles in taking care of the logistics for these meetings.

Both volumes were copy-edited by Ilyse Zable. Support for the Group, including in the preparation of these two volumes, was mainly provided by members of the United Nations Department for Economic and Social Information and Policy Analysis (DESIPA): Florence-Marie Anyansi, Joyce Ashie, Binta Dieye, Judith Goss, Marcela Guimaraes, Samuel Jan, Leah McDavid, István P. Székely, Marie-Esther Van Note, Alicia Villarama, Li Wang and Nikolai Zaitsev. Valerian Monteiro prepared the camera-ready copy. Ian Kinniburgh, with the assistance of Béatrice Frankard-Little, played an essential role in supervising the finalization of the two volumes. This group benefitted from the extensive cooperation received from those working directly with the Members of the Group and other contributors.

It is apparent from the foregoing that these two volumes resulted from a cooperative international effort. It is hoped that they will enjoy an equally international response.

CONTRIBUTORS

Edmond Malinvaud
 Professeur Honoraire au Collège de France, Paris

Jean-Claude Milleron
 Under-Secretary-General, Department for Economic
 and Social Information and Policy Analysis
 United Nations, New York

Mustapha K. Nabli
 Professor, University of Tunis, Tunis

Amartya Sen
 Lamont University Professor and
 Professor of Economics and Philosophy
 Harvard University, Cambridge, Massachusetts

Arjun Sengupta
 Member, Planning Commission of India

Nicholas Stern
 Chief Economist, European Bank for
 Reconstruction and Development, London

Joseph E. Stiglitz
 Senior Vice-President and Chief
 Economist of The World Bank,
 Washington, D.C.

Kotaro Suzumura
 Professor in Public Economics
 The Institute of Economic Research
 Hitotsubashi University, Tokyo

CONTENTS

1

Introduction: an Overview of the Exercise

A R J U N   S E N G U P T A

The United Nations High Level Group on Development Strategy and Management of the Market Economy was set up to review the role of government in designing and implementing development strategies and managing a market economy in the current (and future) economic environment. The Group members met several times in New York, Vienna, Helsinki and London, holding extensive discussions among themselves and with other experts. Several background papers were prepared to further these discussions, some of which are being published as Volume II. Volume I is the core of the exercise. It consists of eight chapters, including this introduction, which reflect mainly the views of the individual authors. The themes of the chapters and their broad contents were discussed extensively by the Group as a whole, but no attempt was made to develop a uniformity of views. However, the discussions did evolve towards a rather broad consensus, This introductory chapter tries to capture that thematic continuity. It provides an overview of the whole exercise, not just a summary of the papers included in this volume. It elaborates on the arguments made in the individual papers by drawing on points made in the discussions at the different sessions, the background papers that were considered by the Group and the references to other studies listed in those papers.

CHANGES IN THE INTERNATIONAL ECONOMIC ENVIRONMENT

The world economy of the 1990s is very different from the world economy of the 1950s and 1960s—the most important change has been the extent of globalization. In many developing countries foreign markets now absorb a substantial share of domestic production. Similarly, in most of them imports account for a significant share of domestic spending. There has also been a large increase in gross flows of international financial capital, as asset holders have been increasingly looking for international diversification and risk-sharing opportunities.[1] For many developing countries net flows of foreign capital have become a major source of financing domestic investment, both as direct investment and as portfolio capital. Consequently, most countries have to change domestic financial regulation and supervision, as well as monetary and exchange rate policies.

Multinational business has also become increasingly "foot-loose". Production plants, research and development (R&D) and other supporting establishments are able to relocate more and more freely outside of corporate headquarters' national boundaries to take advantage of lower costs for producing goods and bringing them to market. As a result, the production capacities and organizations of many countries are becoming increasingly integrated. Higher levels of education and training in developing countries, falling transportation and information costs, and large differences in wages have also led to increasing migration of young people to industrial countries, despite restrictive immigration policies. Developing countries have benefited from increased remittances of their earnings, as well as the technology and management know-how that they help to transfer. But developing countries must also cope with the implications of increased integration of the world market for skilled labour and the cost of brain-drain.

Such an increase in globalization would, in any case, call for a re-examination of the applicability of the earlier development policy paradigm, which was motivated by an inward-looking approach based on export pessimism and limited exposure to international finance. A major element of that paradigm, formulated in the 1950s and 1960s, was import substitution. It grew out of the premise that the prospects of exports from developing countries were very limited. It was believed that traditional exports consisting mostly of primary commodities could increase only slowly, because their income elasticities of demand were low, and at increasing cost, because of a secular decline in the terms of trade. In addition, the exports of non-traditional manufactures would be limited, on the demand side, by tariff and non-tariff barriers imposed by industrialized countries, and on the supply side, by lack of productive capacity in developing countries. Given this situation, import-substituting industrialization would have captured the productivity gains associated with industrial growth and relaxed the foreign exchange constraint on imports essential for sustaining income growth (Prebisch, 1964).

The development paradigm related to balanced growth also maintained export pessimism as a basic underlying premise. The version of the theory associated with Rosenstein-Rodan (1943) called for the simultaneous development of a number of industries showing increasing returns to scale in at least some of those supplying inputs to others so that enlarging their markets could create income that could become a source of demand for other industries. The crucial assumption of this paradigm was lack of access to export markets—only then would individual industries face small markets for their products, even with economies of scale, which could be exploited by simultaneous investment programmes in a number of industries.[2]

Likewise, the most influential planning model for economic development, known as the Mahalanobis two-sector model (Mahalanobis, 1953), assumes stagnant export earnings. In an economy with two sectors, one a light industry producing consumer goods and the other a heavy industry producing capital goods for itself and for the consumer goods industry, the model shows that long-run growth in both sectors, and therefore in the entire economy, rises if the share of the output from the capital goods industry reinvested in that industry is increased. The implicit assumption was that exports of consumer goods, which could be used to increase imports of capital goods, could not be raised.

Another model, which influenced policy-making in both national governments and international financing agencies, was the two-gap model of Chenery and Bruno (1962). Crucial assumptions in that model held that exports were exogenous and that neither exports nor imports could be changed by altering exchange rates or relative prices. The amounts of imports of machinery and equipment, intermediate inputs and other essential items needed to sustain a level of output and investment, and therefore a rate of growth, were fixed. Thus, even if enough domestic savings were available, the rate of growth could not be raised if the minimum imports required to sustain that growth could not be financed by the exogenously given export earnings. This model was used to show that an extra dollar of foreign aid would relax the binding import constraint and activate unutilized potential savings to raise the rate of growth.

The increase in globalization and the substantial growth in developing-country export earnings during the past 30 years undermined the development paradigm and policies that assumed stagnant export earnings. Overall, exports from developing countries grew at 4.9 per cent during 1963–73, 4.7 per cent during 1973–80 and 4.4 per cent during 1980–86. Exports of manufactures from these countries, however, grew at 11.6, 13.8 and 8.4 per cent during the same periods (Stern, 1989). Stern (1989) has examined empirical studies of exports from developing countries, which suggest that the demand for agricultural products has been income-inelastic and the demand for commodity exports has had a low short-term price elasticity. Thus, if developing countries had depended mainly on primary products for their exports, their pessimism would probably have been justified. In fact, most of the export growth came from manufactured products rather than primary commodities, and this was true for both low-income and middle-income developing countries. While some of this growth must be attributed to successive rounds of trade negotiations, which reduced protective barriers, most occurred in countries that adopted active export promotion and outward-oriented policies. In other words, the growth of manufactures exports from developing countries was the result of deliberate policy changes that were not in line with the earlier development paradigm.

Note, however, that the countries that successfully applied the outward-oriented, export-promoting policies were not following entirely free market policies. The many studies that document the experience of the east Asian countries, which have been most successful in implementing such policies, indicate that the governments of these countries used trade protection, selective credit subsidies, discriminatory export subsidies, physical export targets fixed at the level of individual firms and, often, price controls to build up the productive capacities of export industries and encourage them to increase their export supplies to the world market. Simultaneously, they also made substantial investments in the development of human capital and social infrastructure, which effectively complemented their policies of "governing" the market. [3]

By the 1980s, and markedly by the 1990s, many developing countries had changed their policy stance to favour free-market operations, price liberalization and deregulation, and an export orientation, even if all had not made equal progress in those directions. This change of stance was most likely the result of developments in the world economy in the 1980s. The combined impact of the world-wide recession, the debt crisis and the scarcity and high cost of international capital flows to developing countries created crisis conditions in many countries, particularly those in Latin America and Africa. A number of them came to the International Monetary Fund (IMF) and the World Bank for financial assistance. There was also a change in the financing method of these Bretton Woods institutions. The IMF, which was essentially a provider of stabilization assistance to take care of short-term balance of payments problems, shifted its emphasis in lending towards structural adjustment assistance through its Structural Adjustment Facility (SAF), Extended Structural Adjustment Facility (ESAF) and Extended Financing Facility (EFF) windows. The World Bank, which primarily lent for development projects, also started providing substantial structural adjustment loans (SALs) to national governments. These structural adjustment finances were frequently made conditional on market-oriented reforms.

The Bretton Woods institutions, which were used to negotiating separately with borrowing countries, established procedures for cooperating among themselves so that the policy conditions that they laid down were consistent when they lent to the same countries. The dialogues that these countries had with the Bretton Woods institutions on development policies, and the conditionality associated with their lending almost uniformly included liberalization of markets and better use of free market prices and private initiatives, privatization of public enterprises and reduction of the role of the state in productive activities, together with greater export orientation and policies to attract foreign investment. Many developing countries that sought accommodation by these institutions dismantled the barriers that they had earlier erected. And as a result the world economy and the economies of the developing countries in particular have become much more market-oriented than even 10 or 15 years ago.

These changes—increased globalization, increased marketization and the different stance of policy-making—are positive changes and are unlikely to be reversed. But there has been another recent change in the world economy that may not be very positive for developing countries: a declining trend in the savings rate of the major industrial countries and an associated sharp increase in real interest rates (Buiter, Lago and Stern, 1997, tables 3 and 4). The average rate of net saving in the G–10 countries was 14.3 per cent in the 1960s, 12.6 per cent in the 1970s and 8.51 per cent in the 1980s. And between 1990 and 1993 it fell from 8.3 per cent to 6.3 per cent.

Long-term interest rates have also increased quite sharply in most major industrial countries. The average real interest rate of France, Germany, the United Kingdom and the United States was only 1.7 per cent during 1956–73, and it dropped to near 0 per cent between 1974 and 1980. But between 1981 and 1993 the real rate of interest in these four countries averaged 5.1 per cent. These changes imply that the cost of funds in industrial countries—funds that could be transferred to developing countries—has increased substantially in the recent period. Without a substantial rise in the rate of saving they are not likely to come down significantly in the near future. This means that a large increase in foreign aid offered at concessional terms may not be feasible unless an international consensus emerges for redistributing world income in favour of poorer countries. Developing countries that want to supplement domestic savings with inflows of foreign savings will have to compete for the scarce resources on market terms. They will have to play the market game as fully and as efficiently as it is played in industrial countries in order to attract international capital.

THE OBJECTIVES OF DEVELOPMENT

Tinbergen, in his pioneering study *The Design of Development* (1958), suggested that we organize our thinking on development policies in terms of objectives, constraints and policy instruments. There may not be much scope for a grand development design or for a comprehensive plan based on optimization models in market economies with imperfect information, uncertainty and lack of full control. It may not be possible to assign objectives uniquely to particular instruments. But it still may be useful to think of a development strategy as composed of a set of consistent policies that can satisfy developmental objectives as best as possible.

To do so there must first be a consensus about developmental objectives. In the traditional development literature economic development usually meant much more than growth of per capita real income (See Srinivasan, 1994), although in practice and especially in public discussions of development policy, the focus has been mostly on increasing per capita GNP with some possible corrections for distributional objectives. Nicholas Stern and Joseph Stiglitz (chapter 8) set forth the objective of development strategies as "raising living standards" beyond the simple increase in per capita income. Amartya Sen (chapter 2) puts this goal more explicitly in a welfare theoretic context to bring out the social choices involved in evaluating development strategies.

Development should be seen, Sen argues, as "the expansion of the capability of people to do the things they have reason to value and choose". The constituent elements of such development are diverse and include health care, education, social security, environmental and social development, and any activity that improves the quality of life, in addition to real income. There is an inescapable problem of having to value these elements relatively, because their importance varies with changing circumstances. For example, the weight on longevity of a country with low life expectancy and high infant mortality may be much greater than that of nations with high life expectancies, irrespective of the levels of per capita income. There is no simple rule for applying weights or attaching priorities to social goals except through open discussion and public evaluation.

This problem is not avoided by using only real income or GDP as the index of development. The weights used in the construction of GDP—implicitly, through the market valuation of commodities—may not be appropriate for judging development. For example, GDP puts the same weight on each dollar, whether spent by a rich or a poor person. It puts zero weight, given the value of GDP per head, on concerns such as longevity and the quality of life. Since the connection between GDP and these human achievements, as Sen puts it, is far from tight, relying exclusively on GDP per head would leave out "some of the basic concerns of human beings and citizens of a modern society".

Sen recognizes the difficulties of obtaining a complete ranking of all options, such as the one produced by simple indicators like GDP per head, from an evaluation system covering different elements of human development. "The thing to look for is not some grand 'social objective function' which generates a complete ordering of all attractive social states, but the presence of sufficient agreement that points to partial orderings based on agreed priorities". Such agreements can be generated by discussion and political participation, and even a limited consensus can be the basis of public policy and provide general direction for development strategies.

There are two major implications of this approach. First, social development programmes (such as education, health care, women's development, nutrition, child welfare, anti-poverty schemes and so on) become crucial elements of any development strategy or programme. They have a direct impact in expanding capabilities and enhancing well-being, and an indirect impact that works through raising productivity and incomes (with increases in real incomes serving to further expand capabilities and well-being). Social development programmes, then, must be valued as means and as ends of any strategy that enhances economic development. Additionally, in developing countries that have low labour costs and high labour intensity in the social services, these programmes can be carried out at comparatively lower costs. In terms of cost-benefit analysis, resources used for social development are often more effective than those used for many other programmes promoting economic development.

The second major implication of this approach is that it assigns a major role to government in a development strategy. Although market forces may play a significant role in increasing the real income of developing countries, social development programmes will require well-designed, positive actions by government. Left to themselves, market forces can hardly be expected to provide these social services. Of course, the government may find it useful to include other agents from the private sector, international agencies or non-governmental organizations in designing, implementing and financing these programmes, and in delivering services. Market prices and incentives must be used appropriately in evaluating the cost of different segments of the programmes, as well as in their actual execution. But the government must ultimately be responsible for ensuring that these programmes are designed, financed and properly implemented.

MARKET FAILURE AND THE ROLE OF THE GOVERNMENT

Markets provide an incentive mechanism so that profit maximizing firms produce efficiently those goods that individuals value most. It is now recognized that markets are central to any modern economy, and they cannot be replaced or ignored by the government. Even when the government must play a critical role in promoting economic growth, it must act through markets, modifying their signals, not supplanting them. That the government should provide the legal framework to ensure the enforcement of contracts, property rights and security of assets, and an appropriate institutional infrastructure to facilitate the operation of markets is universally accepted. But whether the government should play any role beyond that or interfere with market forces have remained controversial.

Joseph Stiglitz has dealt with these issues extensively in chapter 3. The first fundamental theorem of welfare economics delineates the conditions under which markets yield Pareto-efficient outcomes. If those conditions are not satisfied, a market failure would ensue, either as an exchange inefficiency, in which a possible exchange of goods among individuals could make some individuals better off without making any one worse off, or as a production inefficiency, in which the economy is not producing as much goods as it could, given available resources. If markets failed, there would be potential for government action to correct the failures and improve the efficiency of the system.

There is an extensive literature on market failures, especially related to externalities and public goods, and the related government actions (taxes and subsidies) designed to correct them. There has also been extensive experience with governments' trying to enforce competition policies, since markets must be competitive to yield efficient outcomes. Stiglitz discussed three non-conventional examples of market failure that are particularly relevant for a developing economy. The first is innovation resulting from basic and applied research, in which the spillover benefits drive social returns above private returns, leading to underinvestment in those activities. This externality applies also to developing countries trying to adopt new technologies.

The second relates to information imperfections, because of which markets, especially those in developing countries, almost always fail. The presumption for this proposition has become very strong after Greenwald and Stiglitz (1986) showed that whenever information is imperfect, markets are never even constrained Pareto-efficient. As a result there is almost always some government intervention that, while respecting the limitations of markets and information, would be Pareto-improving.

The third example concerns missing markets. The competitive model assumes a complete set of markets because in the absence of markets prices cannot provide the signals necessary for market coordination. The most important gap in developing countries is the absence of risk markets or properly functioning capital markets, without which investments cannot be allocated efficiently. There may also be rigidities in the production structure and inflexible behaviour on the part of different agents that preclude the existence of an equilibrium with non-negative prices. The Keynesian theory of unemployment—especially the new-Keynesian extensions based on micro-foundations—are illustrations of labour markets failing to clear.[4] If we add to these examples of innovation, imperfect information and missing markets, the conventional cases of the presence of externalities, public goods, increasing returns to scale and natural monopoly, market failures become almost universal.

Such pervasive market failures do not, however, imply that government intervention will necessarily improve the situation. As Stiglitz claims, it only means that there is potential for government action in almost every sphere of the market. The purpose of policy would be to "identify areas in which market failures are most significant and government interventions are most likely to make a difference". Only by assessing the factors causing the market failures can a judgement be made about which government interventions are likely to lead to an improvement. The conditions that precipitate the market failure could also cause government failure. The problem of incentive incompatibility and the principal-agent problem would remain perhaps with greater force in the case of government operations. In addition, problems of rent-seeking or directly unproductive (DUP) activities arise when government controls and regulations encourage wasteful, resource-using activities to influence government behaviour. Furthermore, governments may be dominated by special interest groups pursuing their own narrow sectional interests and thus be prevented from following optimal policies.

In the discussions on market failures, arguments are restricted to market efficiency. A competitive market economy is expected to achieve Pareto efficiency, which implies a set of maximum output combinations that an economy can produce given its initial endowments of resources and technologies. But the first fundamental theorem of welfare economics does not ensure that an efficient outcome is also socially optimal, because the outcome will reflect the existing distribution of endowments and income shares —which may be highly unequal. To arrive at a socially optimal state, we may need to redistribute income or purchasing power among individuals and do so without creating any price distortions—through lump-sum taxes and subsidies, and then letting markets work. The second fundamental theorem of welfare economics establishes that the competitive market mechanism modified by lump-sum transfers can achieve virtually any optimal distribution (Feldman, 1987). The conditions necessary for the second welfare theorem to hold are more stringent than those for the first. But most crucial is the feasibility of lump-sum tax-cum-subsidy measures, as they are the only type of redistributive mechanism that does not generate any incentive-related losses.

The implicit assumption in these discussions is that if Pareto efficiency is achieved, but the second fundamental theorem does not hold, the economy has achieved its maximum potential welfare, leaving society to redistribute resources to achieve what it considers the optimum social welfare. But if there is no feasible redistribution that leaves Pareto efficiency untouched, an optimal social policy will have to consider comparing states of the economy that are not Pareto efficient. The question in such a situation is not whether government succeeds when markets fail, but whether society can find an acceptable optimal state of the economy and whether government, using markets and non-market instruments, can reach that state. Aside from the redistribution policies, the social development programmes necessary to achieve the developmental objectives that must be domestically financed, whether through taxes or borrowing, will affect market prices and incentives, the extent to which would depend on, among other things, the size of these programmes. In designing them, it would be desirable to minimize the violation of production efficiency conditions. But there is no escape from making judgements about the costs of such violation in comparison with the social benefits of these programmes.

Stiglitz discusses the policies aimed at improving both the after-tax-subsidy and the before-tax-subsidy distribution of income in terms of their effects on incentives, market prices and productivities. He also shows how governments could improve the efficiency of most of their policies by using market mechanisms. He pleads for a balanced approach to the role of government, which in any case is quite substantial. But government should do what it does in a way "that is most conducive to the efficiency of the private sector", and allow the market to do what it does best.

The debate on market failure versus government failure produces three broad conclusions. First, if the market fails, the government will not necessarily succeed. The outcome depends on the desired goal, the nature of failure, the reason for the failure and whether appropriate measures can be worked out. Second, whether the government's success depends on how these measures are implemented, taking into account all of the available information, the problem of interaction within the different government levels and the problem of incentive-compatibility. The government must use price and non-price signals in a manner that least violates the efficiency conditions of the market.

This would also mean that the effects of a policy designed for one activity on the outcomes of other activities must be taken into account—which may necessitate re-adjusting the objectives themselves. The third point is thus the need for planning and coordinating government policies. Solving the problems in one sector may create distortions in other sectors. According to the second-best theorems of welfare economics, when there are several distortions, removing one distortion may not necessarily improve welfare. And Stiglitz shows that policies that move an economy closer to free market solutions in one area may not be welfare enhancing if there are distortions in several other areas. With imperfect information and the possibility of adverse selection and moral hazard, credit rationing may be superior to deregulating credit markets. (Stiglitz and Weiss, 1981). McKinnon (1989) discussed how liberalizing financial markets in some of the southern-cone countries of Latin America in the presence of high fiscal deficits could not be considered welfare-enhancing. This was not to say that financial liberalization or interest rate deregulation was not desirable, only that the success of those policies required simultaneous or sequenced implementation of policies correcting other distortions in the system. Policies must be coordinated and planned both in terms of their magnitude and the timing of their application.

THE ROLE OF PLANNING

The recognition that government policies, even in a market economy, must be planned and coordinated does not mean that planning as an institution should play the same role today as it did in the 1960s and 1970s. Almost all developing countries in those years prepared development plans, and most donors insisted on the formulation of such plans as a prerequisite for external assistance. The philosophy of planning in some form or another also influenced the thinking about economic policies in the west. Malinvaud (1995) described this interest in planning in terms of a "shared awareness of market failures accompanied with confidence in planning as a tool for management of the economy in rich countries and promotion of development in poor ones". As he put it, "in Western Europe planners often had the experience of working in the public sector and were aware of 'government failures', but enlightened planning was perceived as the way for tackling these failures. For most Western European economists, the question was not whether planning was good, but rather which form of planning was best: authoritative or indicative? On quantities or through prices? On the whole economy or on the public sector?"

Many of the past mistakes of economic planning can be attributed to, as Edmond Malinvaud and Mustapha Nabli (chapter 4) put it, "overestimation of what planning could really achieve in a decentralized economy". Wrong choices were made concerning the structures of the economy or the long-term policies to be followed. Mistakes were made in trying to implement extensive plans, wholly prepared within the public administration. Still, we may not be able to do without planning if we intend to design a set of consistent and coordinated development policies with the goal of achieving social objectives (including efficient production of commodities), which market forces cannot achieve if left to themselves and which should not be jeopardized by "government failures".

Planning institutions, which should aim to enhance the long-term performance of the economy, must be well-embedded in the structure of each country and provide a framework for dealing with both government failures and market failures. Within the government, their main function is to enhance the efficiency of the decentralized decision-making process, which allocates resources outside of the market mechanism. In playing this role, planning institutions should help to insulate the government from pressure groups. They also must care about the long-run feasibility and sustainability of programmes, taking into account their impact on public debt and foreign debt. Publication of their independent policy analysis should also further their acceptability and credibility.

The information needs of private decision-makers vary widely. The extent to which these needs may be privately fulfilled depends on how developed are, not only markets and the information service industry, but also economic and technical education. But, everywhere, planning institutions can provide a useful service not only in scrutinizing the overall economic and social environment and establishing an objective framework for specialized prospective studies, but also in complementing private channels of information where they are deficient. Whether addressing the needs of the public or the private sector, planning must be viewed as interactive and involving "concertation" with interested parties.

Malinvaud and Nabli re-examine three traditional aspects of planning: the planning process, the planning institutions and the plans. The process of planning is establishing the set of rules and procedures through which planning functions are carried out. Planning functions include collecting, processing and diffusing information about economic, technical and physical environments. They also involve making projections about the exogenously given environments and the evolution of some basic prices, such as that of energy, raw materials, wage rates, interest rates and exchange rates, and then building up alternative scenarios about developments in the economy in response to changes in policies. To make such projections it is necessary to have enough information about the intents of economic agents, at least in major industries, sectors or regions, and their interactions. The planning process also involves consensus building on social objectives and their trade-offs, and concertation between different groups and agents. It thus involves coordination and collaboration between economic agents and sectors or departments to make decisions about public investment, spending and policies.

Planning institutions, which are the agencies in charge of carrying out planning functions, depend on the institutional history of the country concerned, and they must be patterned so as to ensure the effectiveness of the planning process. A prerequisite for success is close contact of planning institutions with operational units. All operations of planning institutions need not be located in one place. It is possible to apportion responsibilities for projections, policy analyses, cost-benefit assessments and diffusion of information to different agencies, including subcontracting them to private agencies, institutions and universities. Similarly, different operational departments or regions and subregions involved with developmental activities may have their own planning bureaus.

Planning institutions must be staffed with technical professionals who are not subject to special interests or political pressure groups and who take a long-term view of things, evaluating the alternatives on the basis of all available information and technical analysis of social costs and benefits. Their credibility depends on the objectivity of their exercises, so that value judgements regarding the choices of different policies and investment decisions can be made through a transparent process of political interaction.

Plans are documents that set the "main medium-term objectives and policies of the country". Although in principle one could conceive of a planning process that is not necessarily tied to any definitive plan, in practice it may be useful to prepare such documents periodically to effectively execute planning exercises. Concertation among various actors, discussions of policy options and challenges, and decisions about medium-term programmes will be easier to conclude if they are centred around an overall plan.

It should be clear from the above discussions that the role of planning being considered here—from the altered perspective of the economic environment of the 1990s—is much more limited than that of the earlier paradigm. There is no scope for a grand design of comprehensive planning, based on mathematical programming and optimal inter-temporal savings. There is now much better awareness of our limited ability to direct economic activities, limited information to make projections about the future and about interactions of different agents in a market economy, and limited confidence in estimating the effects of policy changes. Similarly, the scope of planning is now accepted to be much more limited, confined mainly to the explicit study and discussions of development trends, as well as to the management of public sector activities.

A closer examination, however, suggests that although planning in this new framework will have a more limited role than it had in earlier paradigms, in practice the importance of planning may actually increase, mainly because the comprehensive planning of earlier years did not work. It was a grand design in theory, but highly ineffective in practice. And as a result it was usually either irrelevant or counter-productive. In the new framework with greater recognition of how market forces operate, planning is expected to be more realistic. It must show greater flexibility in designing policies and awareness of the limitations of policy analysis. We need alternative scenarios of development based on changes in the environment and in policy. We are now aware of the shortcomings of macroeconometric models that should be seen only as providing useful checks of macroeconomic consistency requirements. Planners must use more judgement and economic analysis, taking into account all the information that is available from other sources. And they must be prepared to revise their estimates when situations change.

Similarly for making decisions about public investment and choosing between different projects, cost-benefit analysis is the most usable tool, although the theoretical basis of its operational rules is not beyond controversy. It imposes a discipline that could minimize the cost of mistakes, at least if it is applied free from the influence of sectional interests.

Finally, it should be noted that while planning is concerned with the medium term, governments are involved every year in budgetary exercises—in balancing revenues and expenditures, deciding on programmes and choosing how to finance those programmes. Clearly, these exercises must be coordinated, and the short-term budgetary exercises must be dovetailed to medium-term planning exercises. Financiability of government programmes and adherence to hard budget constraints imply that one of the most important elements of planning exercises would be the planning of fiscal and monetary policies in a framework of macroeconomic stability.

MACROECONOMIC POLICY

Macroeconomic stability depends on the level of government activity, the method of financing that activity and the level of macroeconomic balance between aggregate income and expenditure. Macroeconomic instability can, of course, be caused by factors beyond the control of governments, such as failure of international policy coordination, spillovers from policies of other nations or exogenous shocks that can be internalized only in the long run or with the help of other countries. But, generally, macroeconomic instability is the result of the unsustainability of a country's fiscal and monetary policies and programmes.

The symptoms of macroeconomic instability are reflected in a high and rising public debt relative to GDP, a high and rising rate of inflation and, in extreme cases, hyperinflation. They are all caused by macroeconomic imbalance—when aggregate expenditure exceeds aggregate income. But it should be noted that all macroeconomic imbalances do not necessarily lead to instability—only imbalances that are unsustainable. For the country as a whole that depends on the sustainability of the corresponding current account deficit, prospects for export growth and the terms of foreign capital inflows. For the public sector, if the government's total expenditure exceeds its revenue earnings, it must raise public debt at home or abroad or must create seigniorage (that is, issue base money). An increase in public debt will become unsustainable if it is not commensurate with an increase in the government's capacity to repay, achieved by generating a sufficient primary (non-interest) budget surplus in the future. The danger of potential insolvency becomes serious when real GDP growth falls short of the real interest rate (see Stern, chapter 5 of this volume; Buiter, Lago and Stern, 1997).

If the government tries to finance its deficit through seigniorage, the increased money supply will raise the rate of inflation. But that would not necessarily lead to instability, unless the rate of inflation keeps rising, and the high level of inflation generates an expectation for further rising inflation. The limiting case is, of course, hyperinflation, when the willingness of the domestic market to hold monetary debt issued by the government virtually disappears. However, inflationary financing of government deficits is highly inefficient and costly. Up to a limited rate, inflation can divert real resources from the private sector to the government, like a tax, as long as the public is willing to hold non-interest-bearing base money, even when its real value declines (because of inflation). But such an inflation tax ultimately falls when the rate of inflation becomes high. And even at a moderate level, it is highly regressive, lowering the real income of the poor, who cannot easily avoid this tax by switching their meagre savings portfolio to other domestic and foreign assets. It is also inefficient—all of the distortionary effects of inflation on the decisions of enterprises, workers, portfolio holders and consumers would be felt, even in the case of moderate inflation, unless they are fully anticipated and indexed. Further, moderate inflation rarely remains moderate, and when it becomes high, it tends to become uncertain, generating expectations of higher inflation.

Inflation also tends to make the country's balance of payments position unviable. If nominal exchange rates are not changed, real exchange rates will increase. The country will lose its competitiveness, widening its current account deficit. To finance the deficit, it would have to increase its external borrowing, encountering similar problems of sustainability of its debt-to-exports ratio and facing the risk of default on foreign debts and a balance of payments crisis. If the country attempted to correct the initial overvaluation of the real exchange rate (resulting from inflation) by nominal devaluation, the inflation rate would rise further, starting the process again as long as the basic cause of inflation remained.

The crisis comes when domestic and international markets become increasingly unwilling to absorb monetary and non-monetary government debt because of the growing perception that the government is becoming insolvent. At that point the country has no alternative but to adjust using emergency measures, which cause retrenchment of output and employment, slashing of public and private spending, an increase in taxes or the default of debt. The cost of these measures is so high that market agents at home and abroad raise the price for accepting government debts long before the crisis occurs.

The likelihood that this situation will occur depends on the rate of increase of the debt-GDP ratio and the debt-export ratio and how quickly moderate rates of inflation degenerate into high inflation. The government can run a limited fiscal deficit and still avoid precipitating such conditions if its policies are appropriately designed and its expenditures are essentially related to implementing those policies. For instance, if government policies increase the rate of GDP and export growth significantly, the debt-GDP ratio and the debt-export ratio may actually decline, even if there is an increase in outstanding debt. Similarly, there is now enough knowledge about policy instruments that the government can use to prevent moderate inflation from degenerating into high and unpredictable inflation. Although high levels of inflation trigger macroeconomic instability, there is no way to know how high the rate of inflation must be to create such conditions. There is some evidence suggesting that even with rates of inflation up to 15 to 20 per cent a year, it may not be difficult to sustain economic growth without much instability, assuming the inflation is anticipated and indexed (Bruno, 1994). But it may be prudent to not allow the rate of inflation to rise beyond a much more moderate rate because of its highly regressive nature and because of the difficulties associated with indexing and anticipation.

In considering the implications of fiscal deficit, it may be useful to distinguish between the revenue deficit, which is the difference between current revenue and current expenditure, and the overall deficit, which also includes net capital expenditures. If the revenue deficit is positive, that implies the government is borrowing to finance its current or consumption expenditures, which could set the country onto a path of insolvency. If social development expenditures are excluded from current expenditures, then there is a poor case for financing the revenue deficit with borrowed resources.

Social development expenditures are very similar to capital expenditures, as they expand human capital formation and, therefore, raise the future productivity of the economy. This, in turn, creates the potential for generating increased revenue from a larger tax base and thus the potential to repay past debts. The case for capital expenditures should be examined very carefully, taking into account the government's ability to identify activities that should yield a reasonable rate of return, which is at least higher than the rate of interest at which the government borrows funds.

The limitations on spending should also be enforced to limit the task of taxation. Tax bases should be broad so that marginal rates can be kept as low as possible to minimize disincentive effects and to simplify collection. The very low tax-GDP ratio in most developing countries suggests that total revenue could be raised—perhaps quite significantly (see Stern, chapter 5, this volume; Burgess and Stern, 1993). Governments should collect full charges for the services they render. The rates of return to public enterprises should be raised, as should the prices of some infrastructure services, not only to be commensurate with rising costs but also to include monopoly profits that the public sector may enjoy from providing these services. To this must be added removal of all wastes and reduction of subsidies. Privatization of public enterprises—that is, selling off of government assets in public enterprises—could also be a substantial source of finance. In most developing countries large investments in public enterprises have been sunk over a long period, and in most cases they earn a very low rate of return. If these assets were sold and the proceeds used to finance the government's new, more productive capital expenditures, the viability of the government's policy would improve.

There will often be a need to substantially increase public investment as an element of development strategy. First, in the infrastructure sectors, even when their production system can be unbundled and capital investment made divisible, it would take a long time before capital requirements could be satisfied by private investment from home and abroad. Second, the government must provide public investments in areas such as technology, research and development, irrigation, water supply and electricity, which are not public goods in the strict sense, nor infrastructures, but whose benefits are difficult to appropriate commercially to pay for private investments. Third, there are industries in which private investments could have been made if capital and risk markets were perfect or if government policies for sustaining economic growth were credible. In their absence (at the initial stage of development) public investment may have to act as a catalyst, eventually inviting more private investment. Public investment need not be executed only through public enterprises. It could take the form of capital subsidies or support in the form of long-term credit and equity participation in joint ventures with the private sector. The idea is to increase the rate of capital formation and provide finance for activities whose returns accrue only over a long period or whose social benefits exceed perceived private returns.

To this we must add expenditures on social development. Their design should include proper methods of monitoring and evaluation, as well as delivery at the grass roots level to minimize waste and make expenditures as cost effective as possible. In many cases these functions should involve active association of the beneficiaries of these services and programmes. For achieving development, as we have defined it in this exercise, such expenditures will be substantial and expanding, and provision must be made for their financing without impairing macroeconomic stability.

Thus the formulation of a development strategy would imply deciding on the appropriate value of a number of variables in an iterative manner, to make them consistent, within a framework of macroeconomic stability. These are: the level of social development expenditures and public investments; proceeds from privatization of public enterprises; projections of revenue earnings for the government and current expenditures including subsidies, interest payments and projections of the primary budget surplus over a period, prospects of flows of foreign savings and current account deficits over a period, projections of export and GDP growth and the debt-export and the debt-GDP ratios, projections of money supply, the velocity of money and the rate of inflation. The aim would be to arrive at a programme that satisfies social objectives and that can be financed in a non-inflationary way.

Stern's chapter focuses on the importance of macroeconomic stability for the effective functioning of a market economy. However difficult circumstances are, governments have a responsibility to deliver this stability. Aside from fiscal authorities engaged in fiscal management, monetary authorities must also have the strength and independence to take a stand against inflation and maintain a sound banking system. They will have to take account of the challenges posed by integrated capital markets and respond to international developments in working out exchange rate and monetary policies.

INDUSTRIAL POLICY

While macroeconomic policy in the context of a development strategy is related to the interactions of aggregative economy-wide variables, industrial policy is concerned with microeconomic and sectoral variables, taking into account macroeconomic constraints. Recognizing the possibilities of different interpretations of the concept and content of industrial policy, Kotaro Suzumura (chapter 6) begins by defining it as a microeconomic policy designed to improve the long-run welfare of a country, through intervention in the allocation of resources among industrial sectors and in the industrial organizations of specific sectors in the presence of market failures. Because market failures are widespread in developing countries, the scope of industrial policies may also be large, provided they are appropriately designed. They must pay careful attention to the limitations of government and the conditions needed to successfully implement those policies in a market economy.

Industrial policies may fail, just as markets may fail, and in practice they are very difficult to design. More realistically, they probably should try to correct market failures by improving the competitive operation of markets. Competition minimizes waste, because waste is unexploited profit opportunity, and inter-firm competition should be able to exploit all opportunities fully. Competition motivates firms to introduce new innovations that would give them a competitive edge against rivals. Competition also allows firms to make the most efficient use of dispersed information located in decentralized units that coordinate competitive markets through profit incentives and price signals. The best sectoral policy may often be to remove all the impediments to competition.

In promoting Japan's post-war economic growth, industrial policies went far beyond promoting competition and played a substantial role in complementing the market mechanism when and where market failures occurred. Capitalizing on that historical experience, Suzumura evaluates the government's industrial policy as a development strategy, looking at four categories. The first category consists of policies affecting the nation's industrial structure, including policies towards the promotion of industries of strategic importance and adjustment assistance to declining and ailing industries. The second category consists of policies designed to correct market failures associated with technology development and imperfect information. The third category consists of policies seeking to raise economic welfare by intervening in the industrial organization of specific industries, through, for example, entry and/or exit regulation, depression cartels, rationalization cartels and investment adjustment cartels. The fourth category consists of policies based on political considerations rather than economic considerations, such as voluntary export restraints (VERs) and other bilateral trade-restricting agreements. Of these policies, some are justifiable at least in principle, whereas others are not even in principle.

The policies that are justifiable at least in principle include infant-industry protection to the extent that market failures prevent firms from appropriating the benefits of learning-induced technological progress and accumulating knowledge capital; policies to help the economy escape from a low-equilibrium trap caused by coordination failures, which may occur when several industries are strategic complements to at least one of the industries that exhibits increasing returns to scale; adjustment assistance for declining industries to the extent that policy interventions facilitate resource shifts away from declining industries more effectively than the autonomous adjustment in accordance with market signals and profit incentives; and public assistance for efficient importation of intra-marginal (best-practice) technology and its smooth adaptation to local conditions. On the other hand, policies that are not justifiable even in principle include: administrative regulation of competition in the name of controlling excessive competition, and voluntary export restraints, voluntary import expansion and other bilateral agreements to deal with trade frictions.

Even when an industrial policy can be justified in principle, there is no a priori guarantee that it can be feasibly implemented. Because of a lack of accurate information, the government's inability to understand the causes and consequences of market failures, and a lack of clearly defined and unanimously supported social objectives, the problems faced by the authority in charge of industrial policy are not those of simple constrained optimization of a given social objective. They involve designing and managing a public mechanism for information exchange, coordination and dissemination, through which disparate and conflicting objectives held by private agents and government officials are made compatible, and all parties' voluntary compliance with the industrial policy is eventually secured. To make matters even more difficult, government failures have an ultimate cause. Government interventions—be they direct interventions, administrative orders or guidance, or incentive-providing measures—inevitably favour some industries over others, making room for corruption, opportunistic behaviour and rent-seeking activities. Suzumura emphasizes the importance of the following factors for successfully implementing justifiable industrial policies: transparency of industrial policy criteria and procedure, active interaction among government bureaucrats and private agents during the process policy-making and policy-implementation and the use of contest-based competition among private agents.

Throughout his chapter, Suzumura emphasizes the importance of procedural considerations with respect to outcome considerations in understanding and evaluating the role of industrial policy in economic development.

GLOBAL ASPECTS OF DEVELOPMENT STRATEGY

Increased globalization makes developing economies, like all other economies, more susceptible to changes in the world economy. So, in formulating national economic policies, countries must be able to properly account for changes in the global environment. Also, because their policies can also influence developments in the world economy, they must consider the impact of their actions taken as a part of the multilateral system. The multilateral system has an autonomy that is more than just the sum total of the actions of individual members, and it is necessary to examine the impact of the functioning of the multilateral system on the development policies of individual countries.

Jean-Claude Milleron (chapter 7) examines the policy options of different countries, first in terms of adjusting to external shocks. An external shock can be defined as a discrete, unexpected and, in general, sudden change in the international environment. A basic distinction must be made between temporary and permanent shocks. If the shock is permanent, it calls for careful monitoring, analysis and policy change. For example, a fall in the terms of trade interpreted as a negative gain must be allocated from the supply side to the demand side of the economy—and the main handle at the disposal of the government is fiscal policy. In case of a real adverse permanent shock, there is no miracle solution. The response must be to reduce absorption while trying to avoid myopic cuts in investment expenditures and possibly re-examining investment expenditures to make sure they are well-adapted to the new situation, taking into consideration equity aspects in order to avoid imposing most of the effect on the poorest citizens. The size of the overall effort must be examined carefully. In cases of an adverse permanent shock affecting a group of inter-related economies, there is a possible bias towards deflation—which means overadjustment—especially when any one country fails to adjust on time.

If the shock is temporary, and likely to reverse itself, the country need not in principle respond to it by making a permanent change in policy. But if the pre-shock state of affairs was not in equilibrium and if some policies were already operating to correct that state, even a temporary change in the international environment could require substantial reformulation of those policies. If no such policies had been adopted, the shock would increase the urgency of introducing those policy changes. It would also imply that the affected country has the wherewithal to sustain itself without changing its policies during the period when the temporary international shock works itself out to reverse itself. This may be the case for countries having a reasonable stock of reserves or having access to international borrowing, which most developing countries in a disequilibrium state prior to the occurrence of the temporary shock do not have.

The ability of developing countries to adopt appropriate policies depends on further developments in the international environment. For example, if the country is able to borrow in the international market at the right time and at reasonable rates or to maintain macroeconomic stability depends on the conditions of international capital markets. It may therefore be of interest to developing countries to join the cooperative game with other countries both developing and developed, and opt for strategies that would persuade other members of the world economy to build a multilateral system that tries to redress the problems of developing countries.

Milleron considers the possibility of working towards a cooperative game in the case of trade, management of global commons, provision of international public goods, issues relating to international inequality and redistribution, and macroeconomic policy coordination. In international trade of goods and services the process of forming bilateral and multilateral trade arrangements and negotiations should promote increased cooperation of all the countries. The developing countries, acting together either in groups of producers of particular commodities, of a particular region or of a particular trade block, are not only affected by changes in the framework of the game, but can also seriously affect those changes themselves. On the serious issue of international migration, as Milleron claims, "there is and there will be more and more pressure towards further migration because of persistence of huge inequalities between countries and because of cheaper transportation services". This problem can be dealt with only if developing countries from which such labour migration takes place actively participate in international discussions.

Difficult problems related to global commons and international public goods must be solved in the elaboration of a global development strategy. Because of the absence of property rights, no single nation is motivated to prevent the degradation of global commons. And because of the traditional free rider problem, the provision of international public goods falls victim to a fundamental market failure that typically results in underprovision of such goods (services for peace and order, basic non-patentable research, many global environmental resources). These problems raise essential institutional questions that still have to be addressed.

In the international efforts to design a cooperative game, three sets of issues should be examined carefully. First, a cooperative game requires that participants believe that the outcome of the game will be beneficial to each of them. In most cases these are positive-sum games, yielding substantial net benefits to be shared by the participants. But even in a zero-sum game some countries would be willing to participate to avoid a negative outcome. All such cooperative games need agreement of the participating countries to compromise some of their national sovereignty and agreement to coordinate the policies of the different countries. The compromise in sovereignty may be in terms of accepting certain international rules of behaviour, even if they are not of direct national advantage, and also agreeing to some international financial arrangement or taxation agreement that might violate the principles of "no taxation without representation".

Coordination of national policies, especially macroeconomic policies, could build up an international environment conducive to global development. If macroeconomic policies of (at least) the major industrial countries can be properly coordinated, it may improve the functioning of not only the world economy but also the economies of these major countries. The major concern is the free rider problem and the burden sharing of the cost, as well as the possibility that a mistake in the policy response could magnify itself if it is coordinated.

The other dimension of policy coordination is related to building a proper multilateral system. The Bretton Woods institutions were the result of such policy coordination. Similar coordination over time resulted in the development of other international agencies, the latest of which was the World Trade Organization (WTO). It may be necessary to re-examine the nature of these international institutions, their role and how they function, as well as their inter-relationships and their areas of competence.

Finally, the success of development policies often requires provision of financial support to developing countries at concessional terms. For quite some time a large number of developing countries, especially those with serious poverty and inadequate social and physical infrastructure, will continue to need a substantial amount of concessional finance to supplement their own domestic savings. Even those countries that may not need concessional finance still require access to capital markets. Quite a few require international insurances and guarantees, as well as collateral supports and complementing finance from international agencies in order to attract direct investment from industrial countries. Leaving it to the market entirely to decide the distribution of the flow of international funds may not satisfy the requirements of development for most of the developing market economies, even today.

Providing such financial assistance would imply diverting some savings from industrial countries without a concomitant market rate of return. For this there has to be an international consensus regarding the need for such diversion, which in effect translates into a global redistribution. Further, there must be a coordinated approach towards raising those resources and burden-sharing. The idea that the industrial countries commit some percentage of their GDP to foreign aid was put forward as an element of such a cooperative and coordinated strategy. The need for such commitments is still valid, given the large disparities in income distribution and the dismal poverty in large sections of the world. But the fact that actual contributions of such aid by several countries fell far short of commitments betrays not only the weakness of the process of building such an international consensus, but also the need to find other ways to raise such financing.

In today's changed international environment there are some possible alternatives. The Tobin tax is one example (Tobin, 1978), and there are other measures that may be equally effective. These may take the form of taxes or fees, often designed to correct distortions or rectify market failures. But such taxes can be levied only by national authorities, although they may be used successfully with a much greater impact if they are coordinated globally.

CONCLUSIONS

While this introductory chapter provides an overview of issues that were brought out at the different sessions, the concluding chapter by Nicholas Stern and Joseph Stiglitz tries to summarize the general consensus that emerged from these discussions, though there may not be full agreement on all the details.

In brief, formulating development strategies would involve defining objectives, setting an organizational design and identifying a substantive agenda. The objectives can be taken broadly as "raising living standards" or more aptly as "enhancing human capabilities", which would go beyond increasing GDP per capita to include promoting health, education, the environment, social security and expansion of income-generating opportunities. These objectives and the strategies to achieve them would emerge from a political process, which, in a democracy, should be carried out through extensive discussions.

The organizational design should be concerned with building up institutions through which strategies will be implemented. Stern and Stiglitz regard a functioning modern economy as a partnership between governments and markets—the organizational design must assign certain areas of responsibility to each partner and set the rules of the game. They recognize the inherent problem in this concept of partnership deriving from the unequal relationship between participants. Participants should be considered to be playing a dynamic game with "differing objectives and limited information and understanding of the pay-offs", in which the government can be thought of as attempting to change the parameters of the game. But in a democratic system the government has a responsibility to play a cooperative game to provide conditions for markets to operate as freely and effectively as possible and to allow other parties to benefit from its actions.

The institutions include legal systems, financial infrastructure and regulatory authorities promoting competition, protecting consumers and controlling infrastructure. They affect participants in a market economy through impacts on incentives, information flows and transaction costs, and their proper funding is essential to implementing development strategies.

The agenda of a development strategy embodies specific policies, both macroeconomic and microeconomic, covering monetary, fiscal and foreign trade areas, as well as which specific sectors to encourage or discourage, in which areas competence can be developed and competitive strengths can be maintained, and how information can be gathered and disseminated. In accordance with the notion of partnership, national strategies focus not on supplanting markets but on complementing them and intervening in areas where markets fail, where there are large spillovers or externalities and where capital market imperfections limit investment.

In designing institutions and development strategies, it would be necessary to explicitly account for the limitations imposed by uncertainty and lack of information. Earlier planning models attempted fine-tuned optimization under direct control and full information. They were later extended to principal-agent models, taking into account the problem of incentive compatibility. But over time lack of knowledge about the structure of the economy and the relevant parameters of the behaviour of market participants, as well as the limitations of the instruments for control in inducing firms and households to act in a prescribed manner, detracted substantially from their usefulness. It is, therefore, necessary to build strategies and institutions that will function well in a range of circumstances, given the limitations of information and capacity. In other words, looking for "robustness" would be an important feature of the designs.

In assigning responsibilities in the partnership relations, markets have primacy in the production and allocation of goods and services. But since markets often fail on their own to produce socially desirable outcomes, the government must play a role in helping markets to perform in pursuing its own development objectives. It has the central responsibility of providing institutional infrastructure, maintaining macroeconomic stability through proper fiscal and monetary management, preserving and enriching the environment, and providing a safety net and welfare services that cannot be supplied by markets. There is, in addition, a wide area of shared responsibilities in which the government must collaborate with private agents in markets—in providing education and health, in establishing the physical infrastructure, in developing technology and in pursuing appropriate industrial policies.

It would be necessary to identify areas in which the government basically provides finance, leaving production to the private sector, or in which it may directly produce and provide goods and services. One part of the development strategy must be to reorganize the system of making and implementing decisions within the public sector, taking into account incentive compatibility (which would mean that it is in the interest of those charged with implementing the policies to actually implement them) and dynamic consistency (which means that it is in the interest of those charged with implementing the policies to carry through what they had originally proposed to do).

It would be difficult in any circumstance to arrive at a consensus on the appropriate role of the government and on a development strategy. As Stern and Stiglitz put it, the arguments presented in this book go considerably beyond "the night watchman state". There is a need for development strategies to achieve, through a process of consensus-building, socially accepted objectives of human development. The market on its own cannot deliver many of the elements of that development, and the government, through a process of interaction with the market analogous to a relation of partnership, must be responsible for providing them. It often has to play an expansive role in that partnership, guiding markets, shaping their structures and operations, and setting the rules of the game. The limits on the government's activism are set by the knowledge of the limits of its capacity, which we have learned from experience. And in a democratic society both the objectives and the strategies to realize them will have to emerge from a political process of discussion, persuasion and social choice. As Sen puts it "a development strategy need not be particularly despotic, nor be a very grand and neatly designed scheme. It is mainly a question of what a government can sensibly do on a systematic basis, and what approach it should take in deciding on what it can sensibly do".

NOTES

1. "The average daily turnover in the foreign exchange markets worldwide is today around $1.3 trillion dollars" (Buiter, Lago and Stern, 1997).
2. See Murphy, Schleifer and Vishney (1989) for a formal treatment of Rosenstein-Rodan's model, bringing out the implicit assumptions. Ragnar Nurke, the other major proponent of "balanced growth", was more explicit about the limitations of export possibilities for developing countries. He called for a simultaneous expansion of industries to increase domestic demand as a substitute for the growth transmission mechanism that international trade provided in the nineteenth century but failed to provide, according to him, in the more recent period for developing countries (Nurke, 1961).
3. For a comprehensive treatment of such policies see Wade (1990) and Amsden (1989).
4. See "Symposium of Keynesian Economics Today" in the *Journal of Economic Perspectives* 7(1):3–83. Winter 1993, especially the article by Bruce Greenwald and Joseph Stiglitz, "New and Old Keynesians."

REFERENCES

Amsden, Alice. 1989. *Asia's Next Giant.* New York: Oxford University Press.

Bruno, Michael. 1994. "Inflation, Growth and Monetary Control: Non-Linear Lessons from Crisis and Recovery." In Paolo Baffi. *Lectures on Money and Finance.* Rome: Banca D'Italia.

Buiter, Willem, Ricardo Lago and Nicholas Stern. 1997. "Promoting an Effective Market Economy in a Changing World." In Richard Sabot and István Székely, eds., *Development Strategy and Management of the Market Economy.* Volume 2. Oxford: Clarendon Press.

Burgess, R. and N. Stern. 1993. "Taxation and Development." *Journal of Economic Literature* 31(2):762–830.

Chenery, H.B. and M. Bruno. 1962. "Development Alternatives in an Open Economy, the Case of Israel." *Economic Journal* 72:79–103.

Feldman, A.M. 1987. "Welfare Economics." In *The New Palgrave: A Dictionary of Economies* 4.

Greenwald, B. and J.E. Stiglitz. 1986. "Externalities in Economics with Imperfect Information and Incomplete Markets." *Quarterly Journal of Economics.* 101(May):229–64.

Mahalanobis, P.C. 1953. "Some Observations on the Process of Growth of National Income." *Sankhya* 12:307–12.

Malinvaud, Edmond. 1995. "How Frisch Saw in the 60s the Contribution of Economists to Development Planning." Proceedings of the Frisch Centennial Conference held in Oslo, March (to be published).

McKinnon, R. 1989. "Macroeconomic Instability and Moral Hazard in Banking in Liberalizing Economy." In P.L. Brock, M.B. Connolly and C. Gonzales-Vega, eds., *Latin American Debt and Adjustment.* New York: Praeger.

Murphy, Kevin M., Andrei Schleifer and Robert W. Vishny. 1989. "Industrialization and the Big Push." *Journal of Political Economy* 97(5):1002–25.

Nurke, Ragnar. 1961. *Equilibrium and Growth in the World Economy*. Cambridge, Mass.: Harvard University Press.

Prebisch, R. 1964. *Towards a New Trade Policy for Development*. Geneva: United Nations Conference on Trade and Development.

Rosenstein-Rodan. 1943. "Problems of Industrialization of Eastern and South Eastern Europe." *Economic Journal* 53:202–12.

Srinivasan, T.N. 1994. "Development Economics Then and Now." In Jan Willem Gunning et al. eds., *Trade, Aid, and Development: Essays in Honour of Hans Linnemann*. New York: St. Martin's Press.

Stern, Nicholas. 1989. "The Economies of Development: A Survey." *Economic Journal* 99(September):597–685.

Stiglitz, J.E. and A. Weiss. 1981. "Credit Rationing in Markets within Perfect Information." *American Economic Review.* June.

"Symposium of Keynesian Economics Today." 1993. *Journal of Economic Perspectives* 7(1):3–83.

Tinbergen, Jan. 1958. *The Design of Development*. Baltimore: Johns Hopkins University Press.

Tobin, James. 1978. "A Proposal for International Monitory Reform." *Eastern Economic Journal* 4 (July-October):153–9.

Wade, Robert. 1990. *Governing the Market*. Princeton: Princeton University Press.

2

What's the Point of a Development Strategy?

AMARTYA SEN

INTRODUCTION

Is a "development strategy" a smart thing to have? It looked like that when development economics was born as a new subject in the late 1940s. A state could do wonders, it seemed, with a well thought-out design of development. Many economists—Nurkse (1953), Lewis (1955), Baran (1957), Leibenstein (1957), Tinbergen (1958), Kindleberger (1958), among others—outlined their respective views of how to get development going. There were, of course, sceptics, too, such as Hirschman (1958), who saw development less as a planned than as a spontaneous process, often emerging from undesigned chaos rather than from designed order. But the balance of opinion in the circle of development economists was very definitely on the side of "strategists" rather than "anti-strategists".[1]

Things have moved on from there. Views have changed. Faith in government's ability to do good things has dwindled. The increased appreciation of the role of markets over that of governments also tends to make the reliance on public policy and development strategy deeply suspect. Indeed, development strategy has ceased to be an attractive term. It is often seen as the airing of Napoleonic ambitions by a bureaucracy with a solid record of bungling, blundering and botching.

We must scrutinize the rationale underlying the search for a sensible development strategy. This rationale can be examined at different levels. The focus of this chapter is on the welfare-economic issues underlying the subject. The implicit priorities of an "unfettered" system of market-based growth can involve serious neglect of significant human ends to which we have reason to attach importance. However, in arguing for a departure, we have to identify what these neglects are, why they arise, and how they may be addressed in the choice of a development strategy.

PUBLIC POLICY AND DEVELOPMENT STRATEGY

The need for a development strategy can be denied at two rather different levels. First, it could be argued that *public policies*, in general, do not actually facilitate economic development. Perhaps the government could do better by letting well alone, and by permitting people to pursue their private gains, without let or hindrance. The point is also made that the rich countries today were once poor too, and managed to develop without any fancy public policy for economic development.[2] Why can't the poor countries today do the same?

Second, even if it is thought that there is a reasonable case for having *some* public policies for economic development, it is doubted that these policies should take the form of a great design that the government imposes on the economy. The doubt here is not about the need for public policy but about presenting it in so grand a form that it could be called, without blushing, a "development strategy". An alternative would be to leave matters to rational microeconomic evaluation and cost-benefit analysis of individual projects—and to accept whatever overall pattern results from such evaluation and analysis. Scepticism of development strategies can combine well with an affirmative belief in governmental cost-benefit analysis (nicely illustrated by the classic manual of project appraisal by Little and Mirrlees, 1968).[3]

These sceptical questions are important to address. In responding to them, it is useful to note that a development strategy need not be particularly despotic, nor be a very grand and neatly designed scheme. It is mainly a question of what a government can sensibly do on a systematic basis and what approach it should take in deciding what it can sensibly do. In this context some points stand out as obvious.

First, what is the alternative? What would it be like to have no development strategy at all? No state can exist in a policy vacuum, and public policy in one form or another is inescapable (even if it takes the shape of only governmental non-interference). Even the rallying cry for more free trade in radical Manchester was a demand for a particular type of public policy—indeed for a specific type of development strategy—different from what was then in vogue. Adam Smith's (1776) *Wealth of Nations* outlines such a strategic departure in some detail.

Second, even the flourishing of profit-seeking private enterprises turns on an established set up of law and order. Indeed, big differences were made in the history of early economic development by governmental machinery that provided the security and stability needed for the efficient and confident functioning of business enterprises. Even if there had been no room for positive state activities in promoting economic development, there would surely have been a need for the supportive strategy of curbing economic insecurity related to the usurping, commandeering or vandalizing of useful assets and endowments.

Third, as a matter of fact, positive state activities have played quite a considerable part in the historical process of economic development. This applies even to early economic development in Europe and the United States, not to mention the later experiences of Japan, and more recently, east Asia, where the state has very actively assisted industrial development (for example, in the Republic of Korea).[4] States have participated not only through deliberate patronage of particular types of economic activities (sometimes through protection initially and then by assisting exports and providing cheaper finance, as in Korea), but also by providing the population with suitable social and economic preparation for seizing economic opportunities (for example, through the spread of literacy and education, land reform and so on, as in Japan and much of east Asia).[5] The question arises as to what we have learned from these experiences and what today's developing countries should do to profit from these lessons.

Fourth, in addition to favouring general economic development, any responsible state must consider issues of equity and disparity. Even very rapid economic development can neglect some groups, while others do extremely well. There is no escape from distributional issues. How distributional problems are to be tackled by the state, the civil society and social groups remains an important question—but the concern for social justice cannot be brushed aside in thinking about the promotion of economic development.

Finally, there are important questions of ends and means in defining the concept of development. Even though it is conventional to think of development primarily in terms of the growth of GNP per head, we need to think about what all this is for. This involves a scrutiny of ideas and strategies of development at a conceptual level. We cannot escape asking what criteria of development should guide our policies and strategies.

WELFARE ECONOMICS, DEVELOPMENT AND SOCIAL CHOICE

Traditional welfare economics is founded on the principle of assessing states and decisions in terms of individual preferences and values. Preferences can be seen rather narrowly as the desires that guide our day-to-day choices in markets (for example, when we buy commodity bundles for personal use according to our taste) or in very broad terms, including the role of citizens in deciding on the kind of society we would like to have. While there is a strong case for using broadly defined preferences as the basis of public judgements and decisions (on this, see Arrow, 1951), traditional welfare economics has typically focused on a narrower characterization of preferences.

Furthermore, given the fact that "utility functions", based even on these narrow preferences, are hard to identify in practice, standard welfare-economic analysis has tended to concentrate on market valuation of commodity holdings in assessing individual preference fulfilment and social welfare. The result has been the practice of judging economic success and failure in terms of movements of "real income", representing the valuation of commodities produced or consumed at constant prices—prices that reflect conditions in the market (or as they would be in some appropriately imagined market).

Indeed, for a given individual with given characteristics, a functional relation can take us from comparative statements in the commodity space to those in the space of achievements (or utilities, as the generic indicator of achievement is sometimes called). However, in comparing the achievements of different individuals or different communities, relying only on comparative holdings of commodities and their aggregate valuations in terms of real income can be very deceptive. Much depends on other factors that influence the person-specific correspondences between real incomes and individual achievements (and between commodity holdings and the capability to achieve).[6]

The relationship between commodities owned and the lives that people can lead may vary with individual circumstances (such as age, disability and proneness to illness) and social conditions (such as epidemiological situations, prevalence of crime and availability of social services).[7]

Variations in social conditions are particularly relevant for public policies because they not only influence real incomes, they also influence the conversion of real incomes into good living conditions. Comparisons of real incomes can thus be very deceptive in examining the quality of life—indeed, even the "quantity" of life in the sense of longevity. For example, compared with the people of China, Sri Lanka or the Indian state of Kerala, the inhabitants of the Harlem district in the prosperous city of New York have systematically lower chances of surviving to a ripe old age—as do African-Americans in general (figure 2.1).[8] And yet the residents of Harlem and African-Americans generally have many times higher levels of real income per head than the average Chinese, Sri Lankan or Keralite. The differences in survival rates stem from factors other than personal income, such as the nature of primary health care, the opportunity for basic education, the maintenance of local peace and order, and the quality of family life. These factors, too, are influenced by development strategies, and it would be a mistake to base a development strategy only on the enhancement of real incomes.

Figure 2.1: Variations in survival rates by
           sex and region in the 1980s

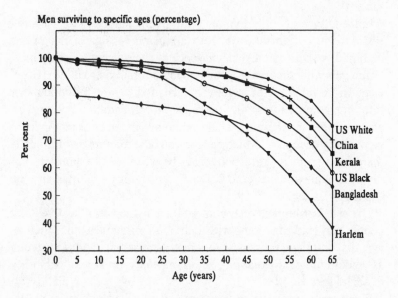

Men surviving to specific ages (percentage)

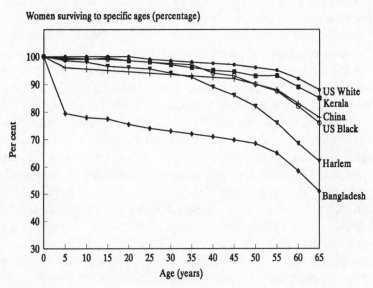

Women surviving to specific ages (percentage)

Source: See Sen (1993).

To take another example, consider the decadal growth of real GDP per head in the United Kingdom in each of the first six decades of this century and the decadal increases in life expectancy at birth in each of these six decades (figure 2.2). The two sets of figures are, to say the least, not close.[9] Even if the argument were made that life expectancy ultimately depends mainly on GDP per head with a decadal lag (a hypothesis that is not contradicted by this figure, but does not stand up well to further critical examination), we must still accept that the growth experiences of the respective decades differ depending on the variable on which we choose to focus. For example, whether a decade should be classified as high-growth or low-growth depends on whether we look at the growth of GDP per head or at the growth of life expectancy.

In fact, there are other ways to explain the variations in life expectancy. There is much evidence that the big upward jumps in

Figure 2.2: Decadal growth of real per capita GDP (United Kingdom) and decadal increase in life expectancy at birth (England and Wales), 1901–1960

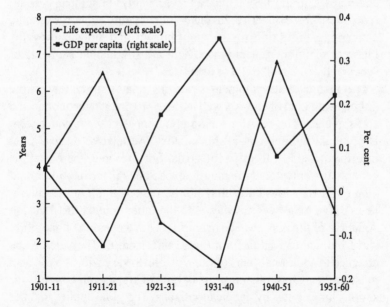

Source: The growth figures are from Maddison (1982) and life expectancy information is from Preston, Keylitz and Schoen (1972).

life expectancy in the United Kingdom during 1911–21 and during 1940–51 were connected with the increase in public distribution of food and health care in the war years—related partly to the culture of sharing that emerged during those beleaguered times.[10] Indeed, even though the average quantity of food consumed in the United Kingdom during the war years fell significantly, cases of acute undernourishment virtually disappeared in the same period because of the guaranteeing of minimal nutrition through public distribution systems.[11] Also, a better sharing of health care contributed to this outcome, and played a role in the ultimate emergence of the National Health Service in the late 1940s. Public health and nutrition are also "economic" matters, and since they do influence the variables that make a difference, why should that part of the story not be included in the development strategy, going well beyond the pursuit of fast economic growth?

Our interest in people's well-being and quality of life can scarcely be brushed aside in favour of no-nonsense growth of GDP per head, and this calls immediately for a broader discussion of development strategies. This discussion must be inescapably valuational. Normative questions also arise in many other contexts, for example, concerning protection of the environment and safeguarding the interests of future generations. There are irreducible elements of "social choice" in all of these exercises.[12]

The nature of development strategies relates ultimately to the public evaluation of ends, as well as the assessment of economic and social means. The case for seeing preferences in the *broader* form is particularly important in this context. We have to discuss what priorities to attach to different goals. For example, there may be general agreement that raising life expectancy is terribly important when it is very low, but it may not be seen as a top priority when people live long lives anyway.[13] In the latter context the focus on "quality" of life may even be in conflict with the length of one's life, since old age can be uncomfortable and painful. The value to be attached to additional years of life will tend to vary with age and also must be put against other aspects of human life, and all this calls for serious judgements by people as citizens. The same applies to other social goals, such as giving priority to the removal of poverty or the social commitment to preserve the environment.

Open discussion of public policies and governmental strategies remain crucial even in a world that is increasingly doubtful about bureaucracy and the efficiency and usefulness of the state.[14] Policy alternatives must be scrutinized and social opportunities assessed— and, ultimately, the market, as well as the government must withstand democratic critique.[15] Scepticism of governance is not sufficient ground for limiting public participation in the market.

HUMAN BEINGS AS MEANS AND ENDS

In recent years there has been a significant transformation in the analysis of economic growth and development—there has been a greater recognition of the role of human capital, as opposed to physical capital. This is, in many ways, a return to an earlier approach to economic development—an approach championed particularly by Adam Smith's (1776) *Wealth of Nations*. Focusing on the development of human ability and competence, and emphasizing exchange and economies of scale in supporting skill formation were among the central points in Smith's analysis of the expansion of the wealth of nations. That perspective was rather neglected in early models in the post-World War II revival of growth theory—for example, in the Harrod-Domar model—and even in early neoclassical analysis of the process of growth and trade (often in very Ricardian lines).[16] However, more recent works give more recognition to the far-reaching role of human skill, re-establishing an old tradition that had been temporarily overshadowed.[17]

By now, the importance of human capital in economic development is widely acknowledged. Typical readings of the experiences of the more successful east Asian economies—and, increasingly, of some south-east Asian economies—have tended to emphasize this causal relationship. Even the World Bank—not invariably the quickest to notice a fresh and innovative idea—has firmly come to terms with the new lionizing of human capital in the process of development.[18]

There is much to appreciate here. But we must ask whether simply recognizing the role of human capital is adequate for understanding the importance of human beings in the process of development. If development is seen as the expansion of the capability of people to do the things that they have reason to value and choose, the glorification of human beings as "instruments" of economic development cannot be adequate.[19] There is a crucial difference here between means and ends.[20] Seeing human qualities only in terms of their importance in promoting and sustaining economic growth, significant as it is, tells us nothing about why economic growth is sought in the first place, nor much about the direct role of enhanced human qualities in enabling us to lead freer and more fulfilling lives.[21]

If, instead, we take a less partial view of human beings in the development process, we must note that expanding health care, education or social security must directly count as "developmental", since they help us to lead longer, freer and more fruitful lives, whether or not that expansion also increases labour productivity or the actual production of commodities (reflected in such indicators as GDP). When human development is seen in this broader way, the *direct* impact (on human welfare and freedom) of public activities in health, education, and so on, must be taken into account, in addition to their role in the formation and use of human capital, raising productivities and expanding actual commodity production.[22] Indeed, even as far as the expansion of commodity production is concerned, it has to be borne in mind that it is valued, ultimately, not for its own sake, but as means to human welfare and freedom.

In this context it is important to discuss some fears that are understandably aired about broadening the criteria for success and failure. The constituent elements of quality of life are diverse, and there is no escape from the problem of relative valuation. In comparison, using such standard indicators as GDP per head may seem unproblematic. While there is also a problem of "weighting" different commodities, it has been pointed out that there is "an operational metric for weighting commodities—the metric of exchange value".[23] Important questions have been raised about whether a broadening of focus to take note of the achievement of some basic quality of life (or of the enhancement of human capability to live longer and better) would be "operational", and it has often been pointed out that value judgements would have to be made in accommodating such concerns.

There certainly is no escape from making explicit value judgements on the relative importance of various aspects of quality of life, or on the relative importance of various basic capabilities. But are such value judgements absent when we use GDP or real income? We must distinguish between the availability of externally given weights to *calculate* GDP and taking those weights to be appropriate in *judging* development, or in *evaluating* the economic or social progress of a nation. Just because some weights are simply *given* to us and are available for calculating market values (in the form of "the metric of exchange value"),[24] it does not follow that we must find those very weights to be just right for judging development. The need for an *evaluative* judgement is inescapable in this exercise, and anyone who values public scrutiny must be under some obligation to make clear that a judgement *is* being made in using the GDP (and the weights implicitly present in its construction).

For example, the GDP puts the same weight on each dollar of a person in great poverty as it does on each dollar of a millionaire. It also puts a *zero* weight—not any more than that—on the length of life and the level of education, *given* the level of GDP per head. Rather than brushing the whole issue under the carpet of a technical definition of *something else* (as many devotees of the GDP do, as if a technical definition of an exchange-value metric gives it automatically an *evaluative* status), we can explicitly present social judgements based on broader concerns, which can then be subjected to discussion and debate. As an approach it is much more open to public scrutiny. This is appropriate since the use of *any* indicator in judging development requires inevitably an evaluative judgement. GDP, which is not particularly plausible as an indicator of development (or of the quality of life), makes these judgements implicitly, and its ability to get away with severe imperfections (as an *evaluative* indicator) has much to do with this implicitness.

In any choice of criteria for evaluative purposes, there would not be only value judgements, but also some that many would question.

This is inescapable in making public policy. The real issue is whether we can use criteria that would have greater public support than the use of GNP alone, for evaluative purposes. If we do not insist on completeness, substantial agreements can be found around some specific judgements. Also, the process of public discussion and interaction can generate limited consensus, which can be the basis of public policy.[25]

The thing to look for is not some grand "social objective function" that generates a complete ordering of all alternative social states, but the presence of sufficient agreement that points to partial orderings based on agreed priorities (on this, see Sen, 1970, 1995). The fact that African-Americans have a lower chance of surviving to an older age than do the much poorer—in terms of income per head—populations of many third-world countries would be seen as a matter of serious concern by many. And this concern cannot be made to disappear simply by pointing to the alleged "operational" advantage of relying exclusively on income per head because it easily generates a complete ordering. The central issue is how far we can go on the basis of widely agreed judgements to derive some policy guidance. It is this problem of practical reason that must be our basic concern.

BENEFITS AND COSTS OF SOCIAL DEVELOPMENT

In the light of the preceding discussion it is useful to distinguish between two ways in which social development expands human capabilities:

- a *direct* impact of these social programmes in expanding personal capabilities and in enhancing well-being and effective freedom;
- an *indirect* impact that works through raising productivities and incomes, with the increases in real incomes serving to expand capabilities and well-being further.[26]

Traditional analyses of human capital tend to concentrate on the second impact, particularly income generation.[27] But these must be supplemented by analyses of direct impacts. The broadening that is needed is, in this sense, additional and cumulative, rather than an alternative to the human capital perspective.

This broader view of human development also permits us to include the far-reaching *distributional* impacts of expansion of education and health care that are lost in the aggregative perspectives. Expansion of education, especially at the most basic level, can be a major force in generating economic equality, in addition to its immediate role in enhancing educational equality.[28] Nutritional improvements can also influence productivity and earning power.[29]

Such distributional considerations apply to differentiations based not only on class, community and location, but also on gender. Indeed, greater education and health opportunities can make women's lives richer and also substantially expand their ability to seek and find employment and income. Furthermore, greater economic independence of women can, in turn, also reduce inequalities in power and authority within the household.[30] Thus the indirect route may involve several distinct steps, but the overall result for women (in particular, greater economic opportunity and independence, on the one hand, and a better relative position within the household, on the other) can powerfully reinforce the direct gain that is made in their welfare and freedom, deriving from their better health and education.

In addition to these considerations, attention must also be paid to the impact of health, education and other social achievements on fertility. Since frequent child bearing tends to have the most immediately adverse impact on the lives of young women, one effect of greater gender equality tends to be a reduction of the fertility rate. This pattern has been observed extensively in inter-country comparisons.[31]

The same relationship has also emerged very clearly in the inter-district contrasts within India, which has been investigated extensively by Mamta Murthi, Catherine Guio, and Jean Drèze (1995). When the comparative statistics from the different districts of India are analyzed, it turns out that among all the usual candidates for causal influence, the *only* ones that have a statistically significant effect in reducing fertility are female literacy and female labour force participation.[32] The importance of women's social and economic freedom emerges forcefully from this analysis, especially compared with the weaker effects of variables relating directly to economic development.

In the light of the Murthi-Guio-Drèze analysis, economic development may be far from the "best contraceptive" that it is sometimes described as. On the other hand, *social* development—especially women's education and employment—can be very effective. Many of the richest Indian districts in, say, Punjab and Haryana have much higher fertility rates than those in the southern districts, which have much lower incomes per capita but much higher female literacy rates and female job opportunities. Indeed, in this inter-district comparison, the level of real income per capita has almost no impact (once the effects of female education and female employment are accounted for) relative to the sharp difference made by women's education and economic independence. The importance of social development, particularly in promoting gender equality, can thus be crucial in the demographic transition to a low-fertility, low-mortality society.

I have been paying particular attention to the importance of social development, broadly speaking, within a development strategy, since social factors are often neglected in economic analysis. The point, however, is sometimes made that a poor country cannot afford much expenditure on social development because of lack of resources, and for this reason priority must be given to economic development first—to build up resources.

Is this argument sound? I do not believe it is for three distinct reasons. First, as I have already discussed, social development can be crucial for enhancing economic development—it is not a question of choosing one or the other, nor of deciding which to do first. We must integrate the analyses of development strategies.

Second, even when a country is poor, there is a need to worry about the welfare and freedom of individual members of society. Indeed, these concerns may be even more important when people are generally poor and deprived. Preventing terrible deprivation is not a luxury that can be easily postponed.

Third, when an economy is poor, its labour costs are lower—as are the real expenses of providing basic social services, including elementary education and health care, which are highly labour-intensive activities.[33] Indeed, this explains how poor economies with committed governments have been able to carry out quite ambitious programmes of social development, including broad provisioning of health care and basic education. Cost-benefit analyses of social development must take note not only of the benefits of social programmes, but also of the comparatively lower economic costs of running these programmes.

FINANCIAL PRUDENCE AND DEVELOPMENT STRATEGY

The point of noting the lower economic costs of social development in the poorer countries is not to dismiss the concern for financial prudence in early stages of development—far from it. The need for such prudence is a different issue altogether. The relatively low cost of social programmes at the early stages of development is a factor to be taken into account in assessing costs and benefits of different development strategies, but it is not an invitation to ignore the general constraints on resource allocation.

We may ask, however, why is financial prudence so important for determining development strategies? The answer relates to the likely effects of financial overspending. The basic issue that must be faced is the consequential importance of macroeconomic stability. The case for financial conservatism lies in the recognition that immoderate inflation brought on by fiscal indulgence and irresponsibility can exact a heavy price on the real economy.

In an illuminating critical survey of international experiences in this area, Bruno (1995) notes that "several recorded episodes of moderate inflation (20–40 per cent [price rise per year]) and most instances of higher rates of inflation (of which there have been a substantial number) suggest that high inflation goes together with significant negative growth effects". And, "conversely, the cumulative evidence suggests that sharp stabilization from high inflation brings very strong positive growth effects over even the short to medium run". But Bruno also finds that "the growth effects of inflation are at best obscure at low rates of inflation (less than 15–20 per cent annually)", and goes on to ask the question: "why worry about low rates of inflation, especially if the costs of *anticipated* inflation can be avoided (by indexation) and those of *unanticipated* inflation seem to be low?" (Bruno, 1995, pp. 7–8).

The real problem, in Bruno's analysis, lies in the fact that "inflation is an inherently persistent process and, moreover, the degree of persistence tends to increase with the rate of inflation". Bruno makes the lesson graphic with an analogy: "chronic inflation tends to resemble smoking: once you [are] beyond a minimal number it is very difficult to escape a worsening addiction". In fact, "when shocks occur (e.g., a personal crisis for a smoker, a price crisis for an economy) there is great chance that the severity of the habit... will jump to a new, higher level that persists even after the shock has abated", and this process can repeat itself (Bruno, 1995, pp. 8, 56).

The case for financial prudence must not, however, be identified with the demand for what I would call "anti-deficit radicalism", which is often confused with financial conservatism. The case made is not for eliminating the budget deficit altogether.[34] Nor is it for achieving zero inflation at any cost. Rather, the lesson is to keep in view the likely costs of tolerating deficits and their inflationary impacts in terms of the sacrifices that have to be made in eliminating deficits.[35] The critical issue is to avoid dynamic instability, which even seemingly moderate and stable inflation may create. But radicalism in the cause of zero inflation or a zero budget deficit does not emerge here as the appropriate reading of the demands of financial prudence.

In choosing development strategies, it is necessary to pay attention to financial prudence along with the far-reaching importance of social development. Financial prudence demands that we take note of both the identified economic costs of budget deficits and their likely inflationary implications, and long-run risks of macroeconomic instability. This can be done in assessing alternative choices of development strategies, paying full attention to the *direct* as well as *indirect* effects of social development, in terms of their overall impact in enhancing the lives of people. The costs associated with the budget constraint will apply to *all* alternative avenues of public spending, and the case for social development has to meet that test of doing comparatively well.

The point of a "development strategy" must not be seen as evading comparative scrutiny in resource allocation. It is possible to get useful indications of likely directions of success by looking at the history of economic development. Perhaps the most important strategic lesson that has emerged from the type of success that the east Asian economies have had—beginning with Japan—is the importance of social development both in facilitating economic growth and in directly raising the quality of life. All of these economies went comparatively early for massive expansion of education, and later also of health care, and this they did, in many cases, *before* they broke the restraints of general poverty. They have reaped as they have sown. Indeed, in the case of Japan, as Ishi (1995) has argued, the priority of human resource development applies particularly to the early history of Japanese economic development, beginning with the Meiji era (1868–1911). That focus has not in any way intensified—rather, the reverse has occurred—as Japan has grown richer. The development of social programmes is first and foremost an ally of the poor, rather than of the rich. Similar lessons emerge from the study of the other east Asian economies.[36]

CONCLUDING REMARKS

I will not try to summarize the chapter, but rather make a few general remarks. First, a government cannot avoid having a public policy or a development strategy (any more than M. Jourdain could escape talking prose). Whatever approach a government chooses to take reflects, in some sense, a "policy" and a "strategy", even if it is one of doing nothing much for anybody. Neither the idea of "public policy" nor that of "development strategy" need be inescapably "statist" or "militant". States do exist, and governments do some things and abstain from others, and there is an important need to decide what, if anything, they should do regarding development. The point of having a *conscious* development strategy is to subject implicit choices to explicit scrutiny.

Second, there is much to scrutinize. The apparent absence of a development strategy is often no more than a simple reliance on what the markets would deliver. But even the performance of markets may depend crucially on many public policies, beginning with the preservation of legal guarantees and support for orderly commerce, to providing opportunities for productive work, to "enabling" social developments (such as elementary public education) and building favourable institutional structures (such as land reforms). Considering the relationship between markets and governance is essential for making a reasoned assessment of public policies, even when markets are to be much used.

Third, the standard indicators of success, such as GDP per head, leave out many aspects of development that are crucial to people's well-being and freedom. There is a need to examine the ends, as well as the means that are implicitly promoted in different development strategies. There is a need for public discussion of priorities and values underlying policy decisions, including the values that are implicitly used in relying exclusively on GDP per head. That evaluative system puts zero weight on other concerns, such as longevity and the quality of life (given the value of GDP per head). Since the connection between GDP and these human achievements is far from tight, the result is to leave out some of the most basic concerns of human beings and citizens of a modern society. What is needed is not an alternative system of elaborate weighting procedures that would produce another complete ranking of all options (different from—but just as complete as—the one produced by crude indicators, such as GDP per head), but to use the social agreements that may exist—or may be generated by discussion and political participation—to guide the general direction of development strategies.[37]

Fourth, the role of programmes of social development has to be appraised in a broad welfare-economic perspective. The framework of "human capital" provides some insight, but leaves out others, since it treats people primarily as "means" (what they contribute to production as "capital") rather than as "ends" (what kind of lives they are able to live). Adam Smith voiced some grievance, in a different but related context, about the tendency to judge a human being by his usefulness, or—as he put it—for "that for which we commend a chest of drawers" (Smith 1790, p. 188).

The impacts of education, health care, social security and so on must be seen both in terms of their direct effects on human capabilities and their indirect consequences on people's lives through raising productivities and earning power, and through reducing the burden of high fertility and frequent childbirth. Issues of gender equity, as well as of demographic transition to low-mortality, low-fertility societies relate closely to social impacts of human development. And this takes us beyond the limited focus of instrumental concerns exclusively on the generation of economic growth (through the use of human capital).

Fifth, the need for financial discipline and prudence is not inimical to the broader evaluations advocated in this chapter. Social programmes must compete with other uses of public resources for comparative assessment. In making these comparisons note has to be taken not only of the scarcity value of public funds, but also of the lower cost of labour-intensive social programmes at early stages of development, and of the direct as well as indirect impacts of such programmes on the life and death of citizens.

Finally, there is much to learn from the successes and failures of different countries. But the most important motivating issue is an interest in human life, rather than only in indicators of commodity production and supply. The point of explicitly discussing development strategies is to promote discipline in our thinking about ends and means. We could do worse.

NOTES

[1.] Perhaps the most forceful theoretical analysis of development strategy was presented by Chakravarty (1969).
[2.] See Bauer (1972, 1991). Hirschman's (1958) scepticism did not follow this route. His doubts also applied to relying on the market, not just to relying on government, and he pointed to complex social and political factors that influence the process of development.
[3.] See also Dasgupta, Marglin and Sen (1972) and Drèze and Stern (1987).
[4.] On different aspects of public policy in the Republic of Korea, see Hong and Krueger (1975), Amsden (1989), Birdsall and Sabot (1993b), World Bank (1993), McGuire (1995), and the references cited therein.
[5.] Institutional reform, of which land reform is a pre-eminent example, is an important aspect of public policy for development. The underlying issues are discussed in Stiglitz and Mathewson (1986), Stiglitz (1988), Bardhan (1989), Stern (1989), Basu (1990), among other contributions. Another policy area relates to public policies that help to generate and sustain competition. On the importance of this factor in Japanese economic development, see Suzumura (1995).

6. The assumptions that would remove this parametric variability (making the commodity basis of real income more cogent for judging well-being) have been identified and examined in Sen (1979, 1985).

7. There can also be variations related to natural conditions, such as the physical climate or the likelihood of cyclones and flooding, over and above the influence that these factors can have on the volume of commodity production and the size of real incomes.

8. See Sen (1993), which also discusses the sources of data and the methods used.

9. See table 10.2 in Drèze and Sen (1989), which also gives data sources. The relevance of this comparative picture is also discussed in my presentation at the International Economic Association Roundtable Conference on "Economic Growth"; see Pasinetti and Solow (1994, pp. 363–8).

10. On this issue see Drèze and Sen (1989), chapter 10, and the literature discussed there.

11. See the references cited in Drèze and Sen (1989), in particular Hammond (1951). On this general issue, see also Winter (1986).

12. The theory of social choice had its origin in the systematic work done by French mathematicians in the eighteenth century, led by Condorcet and Borda, on social or group decisions. They were concerned with processes of election and the derivation of agreed decisions despite differences in preferences and interests. Over the last half century an extensive technical literature has developed in this field, following the pioneering work of Arrow (1951); see also Sen (1970, 1986) and Suzumura (1983). The subject of public participation in social decisions belongs solidly to this field, and a number of technical results have a clear bearing on what it is or is not possible to do in arriving at acceptable decisions despite differences in interests and judgements.

13. There is no need to assume linearity of a kind that would rule out variable weights on longevity, even though some rough and ready indicators (such as the Human Development Index of UNDP, 1990) have taken that simple route. The focus on longevity makes much more sense for countries with low life expectancy and high mortality rates at lower ages. It must not, however, be assumed that for rich countries in general, the problem of years of living is no longer a serious concern. It can be an especially serious issue when dealing with inequalities within the rich countries, for example, between blacks and whites in the United States, or even between the south and the north in Italy. However, the importance of life expectancy is clearly more central for low-longevity countries than for long-lived nations.

14. Systematic availability of information is very important for public discussion, and the broadening of evaluative concerns calls for regular reporting on phenomena in which citizens have reason to be interested. For example, Atkinson (1996) has cogently discussed "why we need an official poverty report."

15. On this general issue see Stern (1989).

16. However, one of the most influential findings of neoclassical growth theory was Solow's (1956) identification of how much remained to be explained, within the interpretative structure of that theory, after taking full note of the accumulation of capital and labour.

17. See, for example, Romer (1987), Lucas (1988) and Helpman and Krugman (1990). See also Jorgenson (1995).

18. See especially World Bank (1993).
19. This issue is discussed in Sen (1985).
20. On this, see also Anand and Ravallion (1993), Nussbaum and Sen (1993) and Desai (1995), among other writings.
21. There is some evidence that the effectiveness of economic growth in expanding basic achievements such as longevity depends on particular aspects of economic expansion, such as the increase in income going to the poorest people, and expansion of public health services. On this, see Anand and Ravallion (1993).
22. On this question, see Sen (1980, 1985), Streeten and others (1981), Stewart (1985), Behrman and Deolalikar (1988), Drèze and Sen (1989), Ramachandran (1990), UNDP (1990) and Birdsall and Sabot (1993a, 1993b), among other writings.
23. Sugden (1993, p. 239). See also Srinivasan (1994).
24. Even this is not fully the case, since "base" prices have to be selected for constant-price comparisons. Also, the prices and marketing conditions can vary with neighbourhoods and communities, even within a given country. (On the importance of taking note of such variations for welfare-economic analysis, see Atkinson 1995.)
25. On this, see particularly Knight (1947) and Buchanan (1954, 1986).
26. Another indirect effect (involving a different type of instrumental role) of social development relates to the impact of health care and basic education (especially that of women) on fertility rates. On this, see Drèze and Sen (1995) and the literature cited there.
27. For example, in World Bank (1995) there is plenty of emphasis on "the skills and capabilities of workers", but almost entirely in the context of commodity production and income earning.
28. For empirical analysis related to the Asian experience, see Mingat (1995), Gertler (1995) and Ishi (1995). See also the case studies of Japan, the Republic of Korea, Taiwan (province of China), Singapore and others. For a general discussion of the underlying approach, see the discussion of "growth-mediated" development processes in Drèze and Sen (1989) and also Birdsall and Sabot (1993a, 1993b).
29. See Bliss and Stern (1978), Dasgupta and Ray (1987, 1988), Behrman and Deolalikar (1988), Osmani (1992), Dasgupta (1993).
30. This last connection has been analyzed in Sen (1990, 1992). Land ownership can also be an important factor; see Agarwal (1994).
31. See the set of papers in Lindahl-Kiessling and Landberg (1994), especially the articles of Nancy Birdsall and Robert Willis which take up this issue. See also Easterlin (1980); Schultz (1981); Birdsall (1988); Caldwell, Reddy and Caldwell (1989); Barro and Lee (1993); Dasgupta (1993); Cassen (1994); and Sen, Germain and Chen (1994).
32. Murthi, Guio and Drèze (1995). The data they use relate to 1981, which is the last year for which adequately detailed statistics are available (from the 1981 census). The 296 districts covered in this study are all of those from the 14 major states for which data were available; the state of Assam missed out on the census of 1981 because of political turmoil. Those 14 states account for 94 per cent of the total population of India.
33. This issue is discussed in Drèze and Sen (1989).

34. The "clouding" of distinct issues is seen clearly enough in the ongoing debate on balancing the budget in the United States, with occasional "shut downs" of parts of the US government. While financial conservatism must demand a reduction of the budget deficit, this is not to be confused with the "radicalism" of eliminating budget deficits *altogether* within a few years, regardless of its social cost. There is no strong inflationary pressure in the US economy at the present time, and the level of the US budget deficit—the lowest among the G-7 countries—does not seem to be pressing the United States to the edge of what Bruno identifies as the prospect of "dynamic instability".

35. In the context of the European Union a different and partly political set of constraints is imposed by the agreed criteria of deficit reduction, laid down in Maastricht, as a part of the process of monetary union by 1999. I have tried to discuss elsewhere (Sen 1996) the problems of using such criteria, which are really arbitrary rules of thumb, without an adequate process of social choice involving participatory public discussion, including the importance of unemployment reduction (along with anti-inflationary precaution) and the need to scrutinize different types of public expenditures (military as well as civilian and social).

36. See the papers presented at the International Conference on Financing Human Resource Development of the Asian Development Bank in November 1995, to be published.

37. Formally, this involves relying on partial orderings rather than complete orderings and building on partial social agreements. On this, see Sen (1970, 1985, 1995).

REFERENCES

Agarwal, Bina. 1994. *A Field of One's Own: Gender and Land Rights in South Asia.* Cambridge, U.K.: Cambridge University Press.

Amsden, Alice H. 1989. *Asia's Next Giant: Late Industrialization in South Korea.* Oxford: Clarendon Press.

Anand, Sudhir and Martin Ravallion. 1993. "Human Development in Poor Countries: On the Role of Private Incomes and Public Services." *Journal of Economic Perspectives* 7(Winter):133–50.

Arrow, Kenneth J. 1951. *Social Choice and Individual Values.* New York: Wiley.

Asian Development Bank. 1995. Papers presented at the International Conference on Financing Human Resource Development (to be published).

Atkinson, A.B. 1995. "Capabilities, Exclusion and the Supply of Goods." In Kaushik Basu, Prasanta Pattanaik and Kotaro Suzumura, eds., *Choice, Welfare and Development.* Oxford: Clarendon Press.

____. 1996. "Promise and Performance: Why We Need an Official Poverty Report." In Paul Barker, ed., *Living as Equals: Eva Colorni Memorial Lectures.* Oxford: Clarendon Press.

Baran, Paul. 1957. *The Political Economy of Growth.* New York: Monthly Review Press.

Bardhan, Pranab, ed. 1989. *The Economic Theory of Agrarian Institutions.* Oxford: Clarendon Press.

Barro, Robert J. and Jong-Wha Lee. 1993. "Losers and Winners in Economic Growth." NBER Working Paper 4341. Cambridge, Mass.

Basu, Kaushik. 1990. *Agrarian Structure and Economic Underdevelopment.* Chichester: Harwood.

Bauer, Peter. 1972. *Dissent on Development.* London: Weidenfeld.

____. 1991. *The Development Frontier.* Cambridge, Mass.: Harvard University Press.

Behrman, Jere R. and Anil B. Deolalikar. 1988. "Health and Nutrition." In Hollis Chenery and T. N. Srinivasan, eds., *Handbook of Development Economics.* Volumes I and II. Amsterdam: North-Holland.

Behrman, Jere R. and T.N. Srinivasan, eds. 1994. *Handbook of Development Economics.* Volume III. Amsterdam: North-Holland.

Birdsall, Nancy. 1988. "Economic Approaches to Population Growth." In Hollis Chenery and T. N. Srinivasan, eds., *Handbook of Development Economics.* Volumes I and II. Amsterdam: North-Holland.

Birdsall, Nancy and Richard H. Sabot, eds. 1993a. *Opportunity Forgone: Education, Growth and Inequality in Brazil.* Washington, D.C.: World Bank.

____. 1993b. "Virtuous Circles: Human Capital, Growth and Equity in East Asia." World Bank, Washington, D.C.

Bliss, Christopher and Nicholas Stern. 1978. "Productivity, Wages and Nutrition: 1: The Theory," and "2: Some Observations." *Journal of Development Economics* 5(4):339–62.

Bruno, Michael. 1995. "Inflation, Growth and Monetary Control: Non-linear Lessons from Crisis and Recovery." Paolo Baffi Lecture. Bank of Italy, Rome.

Buchanan, James M. 1954. "Social Choice, Democracy, and Free Markets." *Journal of Political Economy* 62(2):114–23.

____. 1986. *Liberty, Market and the State.* Brighton: Wheatsheaf Books.

Caldwell, J. C., R. H. Reddy and P. Caldwell. 1989. *The Causes of Demographic Change.* Madison: University of Wisconsin Press.

Cassen, Robert and contributors: Denis A. Ahlburg, Lisa M. Bates, Nancy Birdsall, Schuyler Frautschi, Lynn Freedman, Kaval Gulhati, Allen C. Kelley, Cynthia B. Lloyd, Deborah Maine, William Paul McGreevey, Thomas W. Merrick, Theodore Panayotou, Farida Shaheed, Sharon Stanton Russell and Michael S. Teitelbaum. 1994. *Population and Development: Old Debates, New Conclusions.* Washington, D.C.: Transaction Books for Overseas Development Council.

Chakravarty, Sukhamoy. 1969. *Capital and Development Planning.* Cambridge, Mass.: MIT Press.

Chenery, Hollis and T.N. Srinivasan, eds. 1988. *Handbook of Development Economics.* Volumes I and II. Amsterdam: North-Holland.

Dasgupta, Partha. 1993. *An Inquiry into Well-being and Destitution.* Oxford: Clarendon Press.

Dasgupta, Partha, Stephen Marglin and Amartya Sen. 1972. *Guidelines for Project Evaluation.* New York: UNIDO.

Dasgupta, Partha and Debraj Ray. 1986. "Inequality as a Determinant of Malnutrition and Unemployment: Theory." *Economic Journal* 96(394): 1011–34.

Drèze, Jean and Amartya Sen. 1989. *Hunger and Public Action.* Oxford: Clarendon Press.
____. 1995. *India: Economic Development and Social Opportunity.* Oxford: Clarendon Press.
Drèze, Jean and Nicholas Stern. 1987. "The Theory of Cost-Benefit Analysis." In A.J. Auerbach and M. Feldstein, eds., *Handbook of Public Economics.* Amsterdam: North-Holland.
Gertler, Paul J. 1995. "On the Road to Social Health Insurance: Lessons from High Performing Asian Economies." Asian Development Bank, Manila.
Hirschman, Albert. 1958. *The Strategy of Economic Development.* New Haven: Yale University Press.
Hammond, R.J. 1951. *History of the Second World War: Food.* London: Her Majesty's Stationery Office.
Helpman, Elhanan and Paul R. Krugman. 1990. *Market Structure and Foreign Trade.* Cambridge, Mass.: MIT Press.
Ishi, Hiromitsu. 1995. "Trends in the Allocation of Public Expenditure in Light of Human Resource Development—Overview in Japan." Asian Development Bank, Manila.
Jorgenson, Dale. 1995. *Productivity.* Cambridge, Mass.: MIT Press.
Kindleberger, Charles. 1958. *Economic Development.* New York: McGraw-Hill.
Knight, Frank. 1947. *Freedom and Reform: Essays in Economic and Social Philosophy.* New York: Harper.
Leibenstein, Harvey. 1957. *Economic Backwardness and Economic Growth.* New York: Wiley.
Lewis, W. Arthur. 1955. *The Theory of Economic Growth.* Homewood, Ill.: Irwin.
Lindahl-Kiessling, K. and H. Landberg, eds. 1994. *Population, Economic Development, and the Environment.* Oxford: Oxford University Press.
Little, Ian and James Mirrlees. 1968. *Manual of Industrial Project Analysis in Developing Countries.* Paris: OECD.
Lucas, Robert E. 1988. "On the Mechanics of Economic Development." *Journal of Monetary Economics* 22(1):3–42.
Maddison, A. 1982. *Phases of Capitalist Development.* New York: Oxford University Press.
McGuire, James W. 1995. "Development Policy and its Determinants in East Asia and Latin America." *Journal of Public Policy* 14(2):205–42.
Mingat, Alain. 1995. "Towards Improving Our Understanding of the Strategy of High Performing Asian Economies in the Education Sector." Asian Development Bank, Manila.
Murthi, Mamta, Anne-Catherine Guio and Jean Drèze. 1995. "Mortality, Fertility and Gender Bias in India: A District-Level Analysis." *Population and Development Review* 21(4):745–82.
Nurkse, Ragnar. 1953. *Problems of Capital Formation in Underdeveloped Countries.* Oxford: Blackwell.
Nussbaum, Martha and Amartya Sen, eds. 1993. *The Quality of Life.* Oxford: Clarendon Press.
Osmani, Siddiq R., ed. 1992. *Nutrition and Poverty.* Oxford: Clarendon Press.
Pasinetti, Luigi and Robert Solow, eds. 1994. *Economic Growth and the Structure of Long-Term Development.* London: Macmillan.

Osmani, Siddiq R., ed. 1992. *Nutrition and Poverty*. Oxford: Clarendon Press.

Pasinetti, Luigi and Robert Solow, eds. 1994. *Economic Growth and the Structure of Long-Term Development*. London: Macmillan.

Preston, S., N. Keylitz and R. Schoen. 1972. *Causes of Death: Life Tables for National Populations*. New York: Seminar Press.

Ramachandran, V.K. 1990. *Wage Labour and Unfreedom in Agriculture: An Indian Case Study*. Oxford: Clarendon Press.

Romer, Paul M. 1987. "Growth Based on Increasing Returns Due to Specialization." *American Economic Review* 77(2):56–62.

Schultz, T.P. 1981. *Economics of Population*. New York: Addison-Wesley.

Sen, Amartya. 1970. *Collective Choice and Social Welfare*. San Francisco: Holden-Day.

____. 1979. "The Welfare Basis of Real Income Comparisons." *Journal of Economic Literature* 17(1):1–45.

____. 1980. "Equality of What?" In S. McMurrin, ed., *Tanner Lectures on Human Values*. Volume I. Cambridge, U.K.: Cambridge University Press.

____. 1985. *Commodities and Capabilities*. Amsterdam: North-Holland.

____. 1986. "Social Choice Theory." In K.J. Arrow and M. Intriligator, eds., *Handbook of Mathematical Economics*. Amsterdam: North-Holland.

____. 1990. "Gender and Cooperative Conflict." In Irene Tinker, ed., *Persistent Inequalities*. New York: Oxford University Press.

____. 1992. "Missing Women." *British Medical Journal* 304(March):587–88.

____. 1993. "The Economics of Life and Death." *Scientific American* 268 (May):40–7.

____. 1995. "Rationality and Social Choice." *American Economic Review* 85(1):1–24.

____. 1996. "Social Commitment and Democracy: The Demands of Equity and Financial Conservatism." In Paul Barker, ed., *Living as Equals: Eva Colorni Memorial Lectures*. Oxford: Clarendon Press.

Sen, Gita, Adrienne Germain and Lincoln Chen, eds. 1994. *Population Policies Reconsidered: Health, Empowerment and Rights*. Cambridge, Mass.: Harvard University Press.

Smith, Adam. 1776. *An Inquiry into the Nature and Causes of the Wealth of Nations*. Republished, R. H. Campbell and A. S. Skinner, eds. 1976. Oxford: Clarendon Press.

____. 1790. *The Theory of Moral Sentiments*. Revised edition. Republished, D.D. Raphael and A.L. Macfie, eds. 1975. Oxford: Clarendon Press.

Solow, Robert M. 1956. "A Contribution to the Theory of Economic Growth." *Quarterly Journal of Economics* 70(1):65–94.

Srinivasan, T. N. 1994. "Human Development: A New Paradigm or Reinvention of the Wheel?" *American Economic Review* 84(2):238–43.

Stern, Nicholas. 1989. "The Economics of Development: A Survey." *Economic Journal* 99(397):597–685.

Stewart, Frances. 1985. *Basic Needs in Developing Countries*. Baltimore: Johns Hopkins University Press.

Stiglitz, Joseph. 1988. "Economic Organization, Information and Development." In Hollis Chenery and T.N. Srinivasan, eds., *Handbook of Development Economics*. Volumes I and II. Amsterdam: North-Holland.

Stiglitz, Joseph and F. Mathewson, eds. 1986. *New Developments in the Analysis of Market Structure*. London: Macmillan.

Streeten, Paul and others. 1981. *First Things First: Meeting Basic Needs in Developing Countries*. New York: Oxford University Press.

Sugden, Robert. 1993. "Welfare, Resources and Capabilities: A Review of *Inequality Reexamined* by Amartya Sen." *Journal of Economic Literature* 31(4):1947–62.

Suzumura, Kotaro. 1983. *Rational Choice, Collective Decisions and Social Welfare*. Cambridge, U.K.: Cambridge University Press.

____. 1995. *Competition, Commitment and Welfare*. Oxford: Clarendon Press.

Tinbergen, Jan. 1958. *The Design of Development*. Baltimore: Johns Hopkins University Press.

UNDP. 1990. *Human Development Report 1990*. New York: UNDP.

Winter, Jay M. 1986. *The Great War and the British People*. London: Macmillan.

World Bank. 1993. *The East Asian Miracle*. New York: Oxford University Press.

____. 1995. *World Development Report 1995*. New York: Oxford University Press.

3

The Role of Government in the Economies of Developing Countries

JOSEPH E. STIGLITZ

The collapse of the Soviet/socialist economies and the economic successes of the countries of east Asia[1] have had a profound effect on thinking about both the development process and the role of government in that process. Several lessons are particularly relevant to this chapter:

- Development is possible. Four decades ago the Republic of Korea had a per capita income less than that of India and today has one that is many times greater than that of India. China has been experiencing growth at a rate that has exceeded 12 per cent for the past 17 years—compounded, this rate implies that GDP has increased by a factor of eight.
- Markets are at the heart of any modern economy. Government simply cannot replace markets—or any significant part of them.
- Government can play a critical role *through markets* in promoting economic growth.

The purpose of this chapter is to elucidate more precisely what that role should be. There is no pat formula that can guarantee success. Rather, we can gather insights both from historical experience—what seemed to work and what did not—and from economic analysis. Neither presents a "clean" picture: historical experience is clouded by a multitude of special factors that are relevant only to particular cases; formal analysis makes use of theorems employing assumptions that often deviate significantly from circumstances in developing countries. Accordingly, on many issues economists are far from unanimous. Yet there are wide areas of consensus. This chapter not only develops the points of consensus, but also attempts to explain sources of disagreement.

I take the view that neither of the extreme positions—neither the communist ideology, which held that government should be responsible for all or most economic activity, nor the laissez faire ideology, which held that government should do nothing—is tenable. Few, if any, economies have succeeded without some role for government—and a fairly important role at that. In the United States, even before the adoption of the Constitution, strong federal support was provided for education (in the Northwest Ordinance of 1785). The Constitution not only provided for the establishment of intellectual property rights, but also gave the federal government powers to reduce impediments to inter-state commerce. The telecommunications industry has benefitted from government support throughout its life: from the construction of the first telegraph line between Baltimore and Washington in 1842 to the establishment of the internet. Roads, railroads and canals all received extensive government support. The Morrill Act of 1863 established the agricultural research stations and extension services that resulted in enormous increases in US agricultural productivity. The role of government in financial markets—from prudential regulation to the extension of mortgages (with a large percentage of US homeowners receiving mortgages through federally established financial institutions)—is important, widely recognized and, again, dates back almost 150 years.[2] These capital markets are at the heart of capitalism: they ensure that funds are allocated in the most efficient way.

What is remarkable about this litany is how closely it parallels the activities undertaken by many of the governments in east Asia, including support for education, technology, infrastructure and financial institutions. To be sure, there are differences as well, corresponding to differences in the stage of development: in the absence of developed capital markets, there was, in most of the east Asian countries, greater scope for government, reflected, for instance, in Japan's postal savings banks and development banks (Industrial Bank of Japan and the Japanese Development Bank).[3]

Thus the perspective advocated here is one of balance: finding for each country, at each stage of development, the appropriate role for government, including how government can most effectively interact with markets. Changing circumstances and changing ideas have helped to change perspectives on the appropriate balance. Changes in technology have allowed for competition in significant segments of the electricity generation and telecommunications industries—industries that previously were thought to be natural monopolies—necessitating a key government role in either production or regulation. Globalization of the world economy—improved communications and reduced transportation costs—have enhanced the potential for competition from abroad, facilitated the transmission of advanced technologies across national boundaries and helped create an international capital market.

The relatively poor performance of the planned economies, including the failures of the Soviet-style economies with central control and of the more limited experiments with market socialism, reinforced convictions that governments could not replace markets. Governments did not have the informational capacity to replace markets in coordinating economic activity, and it was difficult to replace the incentive structures provided by prices, profits and property. Yet it became increasingly clear that markets operating by themselves might not yield efficient outcomes (see the discussion in the second section), let alone an income distribution that was socially acceptable. But while market failures seemed to be more endemic than had previously been thought, the limitations of government became increasingly recognized.

This perspective, calling for balance, has been criticized both from the left and the right—both by those who argue for a larger and a smaller role for government. The latter, for instance, argue that government inhibits growth. Of the success of the high-performing countries of east Asia, they say that growth would have been even higher had governments not intervened. Unfortunately, there is no convincing test of the proposed counterfactual because there have been few if any examples of success without government playing an important role.

The next section begins with the theoretical framework economists have used now for more than a quarter of century to analyze the role of government: the market failures paradigm. It extends this framework in some important ways. It asks not only what the government should do—when it should intervene—but also how it should do it—how it should intervene. It then applies some of these principles to the problems developing countries face.

THE MARKET FAILURES PARADIGM

The market failures paradigm begins with Adam Smith's insight that the self-interested behaviour of profit maximizing firms will result in firms not only producing efficiently, but producing the goods that individuals want. Markets—prices and profits—provide an effective incentive mechanism. That intuition was formalized in the first fundamental theorem of welfare economics,[4] which delineated the conditions that would ensure markets yielded (Pareto-) efficient outcomes (no one could be made better off without making someone else worse off). When those conditions were not satisfied, there was a market failure.[5] In some instances of market failure the market produces too much of some goods and too little of other goods (this is called *product mix inefficiency*). In other cases goods did not reach the individuals who valued them most: some exchange of goods among individuals could make all individuals better off (this is called *exchange inefficiency*). And in still other cases of market failure the economy does not produce as much as it could, given the resources available. It produces inside, rather than on its production possibilities curve (this is called *production inefficiency*).

In circumstances in which markets failed to produce efficient outcomes, there were actions governments could take to correct the market failure. Interventions could take a number of forms, such as "price" (taxes or fines) interventions or regulations. In this section I first discuss some of the "traditional" market failures—those that have concerned economists for at least 50 years. After turning to the "new" market failures—the importance of which economists have only come to recognize in the past 15 years—I discuss briefly two types of situations in which government is often called upon to take actions, *even when markets produce efficient outcomes.*

Traditional market failures: externalities and public goods

Early discussions of market failures focused on externalities and public goods, like national defense. Pure public goods[6] and goods with positive externalities will be undersupplied in the market, while goods with negative externalities—such as those generating pollution—will be oversupplied. The intuition behind these results is simple: efficiency requires that marginal social costs equal marginal social benefits. In the absence of externalities prices reflect the benefits associated with the goods firms produce and the costs of the resources used in producing them. In a competitive economy firms produce until the marginal return they obtain from producing an extra unit—the price they receive—is equal to the marginal cost of producing that unit—the value of the extra resources used in its production. Thus, in an ideal competitive economy, as firms equate the marginal private benefits of producing an extra unit with the marginal social costs, they are simultaneously equating the marginal social benefits with the marginal social costs. But if there are social costs for which firms are not charged—the costs of dirty air and water or the toxic wastes that are left behind—then marginal social costs will exceed marginal private costs, and firms that equate the price with the marginal private cost will accordingly produce too much.[7]

The same logic works in reverse when there are positive externalities. The marginal social benefits of a new innovation, such as a transistor, far exceed the private benefit that the inventor receives. Thus, those engaged in research and development (R&D) have too little incentive to invest in R&D: there is an undersupply, particularly of research with diffuse benefits. Though economists have long recognized the importance of environmental externalities (Pigou, 1932), only recently—when market failures, from life-threatening smog to dying lakes and rivers, became so apparent that they could no longer be ignored—have they become a major responsibility of government.[8, 9]

The domain over which externalities (or benefits of public goods) are felt may vary greatly. The externalities from some public goods are limited to a small geographical area. They are referred to as local public goods, and there is a strong argument for providing these goods at the local level. Competition among communities in their provision helps promote efficiency and helps ensure that the goods match the preferences of individual consumers.[10] While the idealized conditions under which devolution results in efficiency are restrictive—and devolution is particularly unsuited for addressing issues of income distribution—the theory of local public goods provides the theoretical underpinning of fiscal federalism (the benchmark), just as the first fundamental theorem of welfare economics provides the benchmark for the analysis of the role of government in the provision of private goods.

Some externalities and public goods are *international*, their effects extending beyond national boundaries. To date, in only a few cases, such as the Montreal Convention dealing with ozone depleting chemicals, has there been effective international collective action to address these issues.[11] Other important examples of international public goods and externalities include the institutional infrastructure that underlies the liberal trading regime, international security and the provision of basic research.[12]

Competition policies

Another important category of market failure arose from lack of competition. Markets must be competitive to yield efficient outcomes.[13] And markets were often not competitive. Indeed, market participants had an incentive to attempt to forestall and reduce competition, a point that Adam Smith recognized early, and that, with the growth of major trusts and monopolies in the late 1800s, could not be ignored. Competition issues gave two important roles to government: promoting competition, where competition was feasible, through anti-trust and fair trade law, and regulating the exercise of monopoly power, where competition was not feasible, as in the case of natural monopoly.[14]

While today there is consensus that government is required to enforce competition policies, the extent and form of government action remains controversial. At one extreme are those who contend that as long as there is potential competition, markets will provide effective discipline; if any firm attempts to charge a price in excess of average costs, a new firm will enter, stealing away the high-priced firm's customers. This would hold even in the case of a natural monopoly. According to this view (known as the contestability doctrine[15]), then, government needs to ensure only that there is potential competition, that is, that there are not barriers to entry (many of which are created by government itself). This view is now widely rejected, both on theoretical and empirical grounds. It has been shown that even arbitrarily small sunk costs can act as effective entry barriers, ensuring that an incumbent monopolist can maintain his monopoly position (Stiglitz, 1987d). What matters, as firms contemplate entering, is not the degree of competition ex-ante, but the degree of competition ex post. If firms believe that there will be fierce ex-post competition, they will realize that high profits are illusory: should they enter, they will disappear, as prices are driven to marginal costs. If there are any sunk fixed costs, firms will lose money, and hence will not enter.[16] Empirically, the airline industry, long used by advocates of the contestability doctrine to demonstrate the validity of their theory, has shown precisely the contrary: prices vary markedly with the actual level of competition (see Borenstein, 1992).

While contestability doctrines attempted to argue for a smaller role for competition authorities, more recent research has suggested the existence of a variety of subtle practices that can restrict competition and facilitate collusion. In some cases the practices may have some social benefits and be justified in those terms (the public good of providing customers with product information provides a justification for exclusive dealerships). Then, the difficult issue is balancing the welfare losses from reduced competition with the putative efficiency gains. My own experience is that the former typically dominate the latter.[17] Note the contrast between situations in which there is perfect competition and perfect monopoly and those in which there is imperfect competition. In the former two cases vertical restraints (like exclusive territories or exclusive dealings) would only be undertaken if they were welfare enhancing. But in the last case profits can be enhanced by practices that reduce the degree of competition, regardless of their direct efficiency benefits.[18, 19]

There are other cases in which firms engage in practices that reduce efficiency. A firm may increase its profits by raising its rivals' costs rather than by lowering its own costs. This may in fact provide part of the explanation for exclusive dealerships and a number of other observed vertical restraints (see Salop and Scheffman, 1983).

While today most governments employ a "rule of reason" in evaluating the competitive consequences of vertical restraints (with outright price fixing and retail price maintenance typically not allowed), there is also controversy over the extent to which competition authorities should resort to *structural* actions. Most competition authorities will not break up firms that have achieved a dominant position as a result, say, of innovation, though they will continue to monitor practices that exploit that position to construct entry barriers (though not to raise prices). At the same time they do not allow mergers—the effect of which is to reduce substantially the level of competition.

But there are areas in which monopolists can exploit their positions to deter entry, and the range of practices is so great that regulatory authorities cannot hope to effectively control them. Structural policies are the only solution. The most dramatic example of this occurred in telephone services, where it was recognized that through price policies and discriminatory access, AT&T could leverage its monopoly position in the local loop into a monopoly position in long distance. This recognition was one of the more compelling rationales for the divestiture decree in 1984.

The scope for competition depends on the size of the market, and as transportation and telecommunications costs have fallen, the relevant scope of the market has increased. Thus, today, competition is feasible in a far wider range of products than it was 50 or 100 years ago. Technology has also changed the efficient scale of firms, again enhancing the scope for competition in many cases.[20] It may be that in the future the most important barriers to competition will be those imposed by government: not only tariff barriers (which are decreasing rapidly), but non-tariff barriers, including regulations ostensibly imposed for other reasons (such as safety or the environment) as well. Such regulations fragment the market and thus reduce the effectiveness of competition.[21]

Recent advances in analysis of market failures

The intuition behind Adam Smith's (1776) invisible hand theorem, which argues that in competitive markets individuals pursuing their own self interest maximize the public interest, is a compelling one: by producing goods that people want and by producing them at lower prices, profits are increased.

Man has almost constant occasion for the help of his brethren, and it is in vain for him to expect it from their benevolence only. He will be more likely to prevail if he can interest their self-love in his favour, and show them that it is for their own advantage to do for him what he requires of them....It is not from the benevolence of the butcher, the brewer, or the baker, that we expect our dinner, but from their regard to their own interest. We address ourselves, not to their humanity but to their self-love, and never talk to them of our necessities but of their advantages. (book 1, chapter 2)

The externalities that we discussed in the previous section are instances in which this logic does not apply or, more accurately, in which the pursuit of self interest works against the public interest. More recently, economists have become aware of a much wider range of circumstances in which markets fail to produce efficient outcomes. These market failures hinge on a set of assumptions that were hidden in the framework of the Arrow-Debreu model, which established the efficiency of competitive markets. The import of these assumptions has only slowly been fully realized.[22]

Innovation

Innovators typically appropriate only a fraction of the social benefits that accrue from their innovations (that is, there is a positive externality associated with innovative activity). This is true of basic research, as of much applied research. There is a continuum: the degree of spillover is obviously smaller the more applied is the research.[23] As a result social returns typically exceed private returns—and the evidence is that such returns are indeed very high.[24]

Without government support in both basic research and applied research with large spillovers, there will be underinvestment in these activities.

Similar issues arise in developing countries with respect to the adoption and adaptation of technologies. Typically, developing countries employ technologies that are far below state of the art. But the ability of innovators—who may risk considerable capital ascertaining whether a particular technology will work in their country— to appropriate fully the returns to their entrepreneurship is limited. If they fail, they bear the losses themselves. If they succeed, other firms will observe their success and will quickly enter. Facing a "heads you win, tails I lose" situation, firms are loathe to undertake the risks of innovation. Stagnation can result.[25] Government assistance toward the development and transfer of technology can take a variety of forms, including support of institutional infrastructure (education and research institutions). Individual producer risk provides the rationale for agricultural research and extension services, which have been so successful in increasing productivity in the United States and many other countries. One of the arguments for government encouragement of exports is that active involvement in international markets facilitates the transfer of best practice technology. (For a discussion of the market failure rationale for these policies in the context of east Asia, see Stiglitz, 1996.)

Information imperfections

Information imperfections arise in all economies, though especially in developing countries. Information is costly, and hence one would not expect perfect information. But information has many of the properties of a public good. If I know something, and tell you, it does not detract from what I know (though it may detract from what I can do with that information). It thus possesses the property of non-rivalrous consumption. Moreover, it is often difficult to exclude others from reaping some of the benefits of knowledge that we purchase; if I purchase information telling me where some commodity can be obtained cheaply, anyone watching where I made my purchase can infer the information from my behaviour. It thus possesses the property of non-excludability.

A major theme in the modern literature on the economics of information is that markets with imperfect information are fundamentally different from markets with perfect information.[26]

- *Markets may not exist* (Akerlof, 1970 and see below).[27] Akerlof described the market for used cars: the seller knows whether or not his car is a lemon, and buyers suspect that the only reason the seller is willing to sell the car is that the price exceeds its worth.[28] Similar arguments apply to "used" labour markets and capital markets. An employer trying to steal a worker away from another employer worries: the current employer knows more about the worker's abilities; he will match my offer as long as the worker's productivity exceeds the wage, but will refuse to match it if I bid too high. Only if there are sufficiently large gains to "matching" will there be a "secondary" market for workers (see Greenwald, 1986). Similarly, if investors believe that issuers of equity are more informed about the firm's prospects, they will worry: only if they offer a price for a share that exceeds the value will the owner of the shares be willing to sell them. Thus only if there are sufficiently large gains from risk diversification will there be a market for equities (see Greenwald, Stiglitz and Weiss, 1984). The greater information imperfections in developing economies may account for the greater prevalence of situations in which markets do not exist. The informational infrastructure required for well-functioning equity markets, for instance, is likely to be missing. The absence of labour market institutions (such as well-functioning employment agencies)[29] may enhance segmentation and rigidities within labour markets.

- *When markets exist, they may not be competitive* (Diamond, 1971; Stiglitz, 1988b). Because of information imperfections, firms know that if they lower their price slightly, they will not garner all customers from the market: each firm faces a downward sloping demand curve. If search costs are larger in developing countries, then demand curves will be more steeply downward sloping and the inefficiencies associated with monopolistic markets will be more prevalent.

- *Markets may be characterized by price dispersion* (Salop and Stiglitz, 1977, 1982).[30] Again, given the higher costs of search (associated, for instance, with less effective telecommunications infrastructure),[31] price dispersion may be larger.

- *Market equilibrium may be characterized by demand not equalling supply* (unemployment in the labour market or credit rationing in the capital market.)[32] Firms recognize that lowering wages may lead to a less productive labour force. Thus even when labour is in excess supply, firms may not be willing to lower wages.[33] The theory that holds that productivity may increase with wages and that, as a result, equilibrium wages may exceed the market clearing level, is referred to as the "efficiency wage theory". In developing economies, in which nutritional deprivation is greater or in which information problems are larger, these considerations may play a more important role, and may help explain the greater prevalence of persistent unemployment.

- Most importantly from our current perspective, *whenever information is imperfect, markets are essentially never even constrained Pareto efficient.*[34] That is, there exist interventions in the market that, while respecting the imperfections and costs of information, make some individuals better off without making anyone worse off (Greenwald and Stiglitz, 1986, 1988; Arnott, Greenwald and Stiglitz, 1994). Although there is no simple intuition behind this result, the examples that follow may help elucidate what is at issue.

There are two important categories of information failures: moral hazard and adverse selection. The typical moral hazard problem arises in insurance markets. Insured individuals have insufficient incentive to avoid the event that they are insured against. Consequently, some of the costs are borne by the insurance firm. Thus an externality arises: as individuals become more careless, the required premium increases. But in deciding on the level of care, each individual fails to take this into account. Government interventions may be able to ameliorate the effects of this externality, even if they cannot directly monitor individuals, and thus directly ensure that individuals take appropriate actions. Consider the hazard of smoking in bed. The government may not be able to monitor smoking in bed, but by imposing a tax on cigarettes, it can discourage smoking in general, and thus reduce somewhat the likelihood of a fire resulting from smoking in bed.[35]

Or, consider the following selection problem. Employers do not know the ability of the workers they hire, say, at a hiring hall. They pay the workers the mean marginal product. Thus when a low-productivity worker enters the labour market, he creates an externality: he lowers the mean marginal productivity and thus the wage of all other workers. Again, even if the government cannot directly observe the ability of individuals (and thus cannot directly redress this externality problem), it can impose taxes and subsidies that ameliorate its effects by encouraging the labour force participation of high-productivity workers.

Information imperfections are particularly rife in developing economies because the institutions (markets) for the production and dissemination of information are weak and because rapid growth will be accompanied by marked changes—and change imposes a greater burden on the information gathering and dissemination abilities of any economy.

The information market failure can also be related to some of the hidden assumptions in the Arrow-Debreu framework. Just as the standard competitive model assumed that technology was exogenous, so too did it assume that changes in information were exogenous. Not only did individuals not spend money to acquire further information, nothing that occurred in the economy changed their beliefs.

There is a certain irony here. Traditionally, the market economy is touted for its informational efficiency: producers do not have to know the preferences of each consumer, and consumers do not have to know the technologies firms used to produce each commodity or the overall scarcity of each resource. Prices convey all the relevant information. We now recognize that the information needed to run an economy is far richer: we must know, for instance, the attributes of different commodities, different workers and different investment projects. Individuals must know where to find the products they want and at what prices the products are available. The traditional theory had nothing to say about these dimensions of information.[36]

Missing markets

The standard competitive model assumed that a complete set of markets existed. Yet even in industrial economies, risk and capital markets are imperfect. And in developing economies market imperfections are even greater. We now have a better understanding of some of the causes of these market imperfections (often related to moral hazard and adverse selection problems)[37]—but with this understanding has come an appreciation of how widespread and pervasive they are.

In the absence of a complete set of markets Greenwald and Stiglitz have shown generically that competitive markets are not constrained Pareto efficient (see also Newbery and Stiglitz, 1982; Stiglitz, 1982).[38] A large number of government actions can be seen as attempting to remedy this kind of market failure—the provision of student loans, the creation of development banks and the establishment of a wide range of social insurance programs covering risks that the market failed to insure, at least at the time these programs were established.[39]

Others have emphasized that in the absence of markets, prices cannot perform their role in coordination. As a result, coordination failures can arise easily. Though Rosenstein-Rodan's "big push" theory is perhaps the most well known example of such coordination failures, perhaps the most convincing model is that of Rodríguez-Clare (1992). He argues that firms often must choose among technologies. If they all choose advanced technologies, there will be a demand for non-traded complex inputs. Given returns to scale in these industries, such goods can be produced at low costs, making the advanced technologies economically desirable. But if all choose the simple (primitive) technology, there will be little demand for the non-traded, complex inputs. These will thus have a high price, making the choice of the simple technology optimal.[40]

Perhaps the most important and often cited gap is associated with futures (and risk) markets. Without such markets the standard market mechanisms for the allocation of investment will not work. Firms do not know what prices they will be able to get for their products. They must form expectations, and those expectations may or may not be fulfilled. Thus even advocates of market socialism argued that the government had to have a central role in allocating investment.

Planning was supposed to fill this gap. But governments seldom had the information required to ascertain accurately what prices on futures markets would be, if there were futures markets at all. Indicative planning did little better: firms seldom had the incentive to truthfully reveal their plans. Moreover, plans were typically contingent on a large number of variables. The central planning process could not integrate effectively even just the major relevant contingencies. For many countries, the opening up of trade has reduced the need for planning: gaps in material balances can easily be filled by imports and exports.

Thus, today, most economists recognize that the advantages of planning at the level of the firm (and all major firms do engage in planning), which incorporates more of the detailed analysis relevant for most project decision-making, far outweigh the advantages of central planning, in spite of the "danger" that firms must rely on expectations that may not be fully consistent (in the sense that each firm does not take into account simultaneously all of the decisions being made by all other firms). To be sure, planning at the national level and planning at the firm level are not mutually inconsistent. The question is, what is the *valued added* of planning at the national level?

Today, planning has a more limited role: it guides the government in making its investment decisions; possibly plays an entrepreneurial role, in suggesting to the private sector areas in which returns appear to be high; and identifies areas in which there are large spillovers, where, absent government intervention, there will be underinvestment. (Given the prevalence of credit rationing, there is often scope for the allocation of investment among those who are willing to pay the going interest rate. It makes sense for government to prioritize those investments and to try to direct investment towards those areas with the highest social returns.)

Unemployment

In a sense the most important instances of market failure are the episodes of underutilization of resources—particularly the massive underutilization associated with depressions. While an extensive literature attempts to explain this market failure (some of which relates to other market failures, such as information imperfections), the fact is that recessions and depressions, more than any other phenomena, have eroded confidence in market mechanisms that are left to themselves. Today, governments throughout the industrial world have assumed a responsibility for macroeconomic stabilization. And a feature shared by most of the high performing countries of east Asia is that they not only assumed this responsibility, but were fairly successful in carrying it out.[41]

Today, we recognize that the instances in which markets fail to produce efficient outcomes are far more pervasive than the limited failures upon which traditional discussions focused. But the pervasiveness of these failures is as much a critique of the market failures paradigm as it is a guide to action: the failures of the market (defined in terms of constrained Pareto optimality) are so pervasive that there is potential for government action in almost every sphere. A pragmatic approach requires identifying areas in which market failures are most significant and government interventions are most likely to make a difference.

Beyond market failures

Admittedly, there may be a limited role for government, even when there are no market failures, if the resulting distribution of income is not desirable.[42] The market failures approach only assured the efficiency of the market; no one can be made better off without making someone else worse off.

Redistribution

The central policy question is how much and what form of intervention is required to correct for these inequalities. Political rhetoric condemns the development and perpetuation of a society of haves and have nots. There are fears that letting market forces reign will widen already existing disparities. Such arguments have, for instance, been raised in discussions of telecommunications policy as a justification for the maintenance of state monopolies.

Traditional economic theory provides a simple, unambiguous answer: only limited government intervention is required. Government needs only to change the initial distribution of income, leaving the rest to the market. This result is known as the second fundamental theorem of welfare economics. The theorem states that any Pareto optimal resource allocation can be attained through competitive mechanisms, provided the government engages in the appropriate redistribution of initial endowments. But the conditions of that theorem are highly restricted. In particular, governments cannot costlessly change the initial distribution of income (endowments). In practice, governments have used a portfolio of policies aimed at redistribution. This portfolio consists of two sets of policies:

- *Policies aimed at making the after-tax/subsidy distribution of income more egalitarian than that yielded by the market.* Such policies include progressive income taxes, income and wage subsidies to low-income families and provision of, or subsidies for, particular goods and services, such as housing, health and food. There has been increasing concern about the incentive effects of such redistributive programs, particularly when their combined interactive effects are taken into account. Thus the impact of reduced housing, health and food benefits as incomes rise may result in an effective tax rate of close to (and in some cases higher than) 100 percent. While the effective marginal tax rate may be reduced by expanding the income range over which benefits are phased out, this has severe budgetary impacts. In designing redistributive programs, governments must balance incentive and budgetary impacts with redistributive benefits. In recent years these concerns have led to a lessening role of these broad-based redistributive programs in favour of other programs (described below).[43]

One way in which redistributive benefits can be enhanced is by improving targeting—ensuring that benefits go to those who really need them or to those for whom incentive effects are smaller. This is one reason to provide more redistributive benefits to the poor elderly, since their labour supply elasticities are likely to be low. However, the provision of such benefits may have adverse effects on savings.

Economists have long argued that it is more efficient to provide cash benefits than benefits in-kind (such as for food or housing). But countering this presumption is the view that what society cares about is not inequality per se, but certain manifestations of inequality, such as lack of access to food, shelter and medicine. Tobin (1970) refers to this as "specific egalitarianism". Moreover, in some circumstances providing non-cash benefits may enhance the effectiveness of targeting. Health benefits, in particular, are more likely to be taken up by those who actually need the services. There is another reason for the provision of these in-kind benefits: political pressure from the housing construction industry provides much of the support for housing programs and pressure from the agricultural sector for food stamp programs.

In practice, in-kind benefits have not been very effective in accomplishing their objectives. Government food subsidies may not lead to significant increases in the level of food consumption.[44] Direct provision of housing has often been inefficient (with significantly higher costs per square foot) and has interfered with the functioning of labour markets.[45] (Long and separate queues in different areas have meant that once an individual receives subsidized housing, there is a large disincentive against moving to another locale.)

• *Policies aimed at improving the before-tax/subsidy distribution.* For a variety of reasons, including the costs associated with redistributive taxes, there has been increased emphasis on attempts to improve the before-tax/subsidy distribution of income (leaving a smaller burden on after-tax/subsidy redistribution).

The most important of such activities are education and training programs aimed at enhancing productivity, particularly of low-skilled individuals. Since lack of nutrition and adequate health care, including prenatal care, also contribute to low productivity, programs in those areas also enhance the before-tax distribution of income.[46]

Changed perspectives on concepts of social justice

The commonly accepted philosophical premises underlying government interventions to redistribute income have changed over time. While economists traditionally approached these questions using a social welfare function, development economists have often taken a different tack, emphasizing "basic needs". But more recently, the focus has turned to "opportunities". Social justice should not be evaluated as much in terms of equality of outcomes as in terms of equality of opportunities. If society provides educational opportunities to all children, it has fulfilled its responsibility, even if some individuals fail to avail themselves of those opportunities.[47]

Merit goods

In some instances governments have consistently rejected the premise of consumer sovereignty, even when there are no externalities associated with that behaviour. Thus consumption of drugs and alcohol may be proscribed, not just on instrumental grounds (because they have deleterious effects on society), but on moral grounds. By the same token, government may require individuals to undertake some actions because they are believed to be good, quite apart from individuals' own evaluation of the personal benefits.

The strongest cases against consumer sovereignty arise with children, who typically do not make choices for themselves. The question then is, should parents or the state make decisions, such as how long the child should stay in school? Most of the activities that government mandates or proscribes are associated with significant external effects: an uneducated child or an individual who fails to put aside sufficient funds for his retirement[48] is more likely to be a burden on society in the future; a drunk driver is more likely to cause an automobile accident.

The role of government in establishing institutional infrastructure

Market failure theory begins by identifying these market failures, and then describing how government might correct them. This defines the economic role of government.

It has become apparent—particularly in the aftermath of the collapse of the eastern bloc economies—that there is a prior set of roles: government must set up an institutional framework within which markets can function. Markets require effective contract enforcement: a legal system with well defined rules that reaches decisions quickly. The Arrow-Debreu model simply assumed that individuals would perform in the way contracted for; presumably, there was a legal system that enforced all such contracts. It failed to discuss either the role of government in establishing and implementing the legal structure or the problems with the legal structure, including costs and imperfections in enforcement.

Even prior to contract enforcement is the responsibility of government to establish and enforce a set of property rights. Today, economists recognize the complexity of the concept of property rights—the imposition of rent control, for instance, is a transfer of certain property rights from the owner of the property to the renter; tenure provides workers with a kind of restricted property right in their jobs—and the distortions associated with both ill-defined and misassigned property rights.

Other important aspects of the institutional infrastructure include regulations affecting infrastructure, the financial sector and telecommunications. Almost every government has provided a set of regulations affecting these sectors, and the structure of those regulations have a major impact on the efficiency and efficacy of these sectors. Economists' rationale for a government role in each of these areas is related to market failure. In telecommunications, for instance, it was widely believed that there was a natural monopoly in telephony.[49] Changes in technology affect which regulatory structure is appropriate. For instance, it is now recognized that the telecommunications sector can be subdivided into a large number of subsectors and that in many of these sectors competition is viable, while in a few bottleneck areas, competition is not viable. There can be competition in long distance, but at least for a while, there is little effective competition in the "last mile" connecting the switchboard to the final user. The challenge of regulators is how to devise regulatory structures that encourage competition in viable subsectors, while retaining safeguards in the non-competitive portions. That was the objective of the recently passed telecommunications legislation in the United States.

The institutional infrastructure defines the "rules of the game". The rules of the game, in turn, have a major impact not only on efficiency, but also on equity. There is a concern, for instance, that inappropriately designed contract and tort laws may work to the disadvantage of the poor.

The interaction between equity and efficiency concerns in establishing the institutional infrastructure is often complex. For instance, many countries have imposed universal service requirements on their telecommunications sector (and have used a fear of lack of universal service as a justification for maintaining state monopolies). But the fact of the matter is that competition, by lowering prices and increasing the range of services provided, has done more to extend the range of services provided, especially in developing countries, than either government monopolies or mandates. Indeed, government monopolies have typically been faced with severe budgetary restrictions, which have resulted in limitations on services, with waiting lines for connection often exceeding two years.[50]

GOVERNMENT FAILURES

Absent market failures, no government, no matter how efficient and effective, can improve upon the allocation of resources. With market failures, there is a potential role for government. But traditional market failure analysis argued only that there were actions that government might undertake to improve economic efficiency. The early discussions may have underestimated the scope of market failures, but also may have overestimated the ability of government to correct these failures. Critics of government intervention make three assertions:

- Government intervention is unnecessary.
- Government intervention is ineffective.
- Government intervention is counterproductive.

The first contention is partially refuted by the market failures described above. But advocates of non-intervention argue that anything the government can do, the private sector can do better and that non-market (voluntary) arrangements can always substitute for government action when markets fail (as in the case of externalities). Both of these propositions are false. Government, through its powers of taxation, proscription and compulsion, can do things that voluntary arrangements cannot. These powers are associated with constraints—constraints like restrictions on hiring and firing (civil service) and procurement—to reduce the likelihood that these powers are abused.[51] And there are other constraints, such as on the ability to make binding commitments (the government enforces private sector contracts, but there is no outside party to enforce government commitments; they have to be self-enforcing)[52] that imply that government may not be able to do things that the private sector can.

Similarly, there are situations in which, as Coase (1960) suggested, bargaining among individuals can adequately address problems of externalities *provided adequate property rights are established.* However, those situations are highly restricted, typically involving few individuals and perfect information (see Farrell, 1987).[53]

Indeed, it is not the case that non-market (voluntary) actions that are motivated by a desire to remedy a market failure always lead to a welfare improvement. For instance, as a result of moral hazard (incentive) problems, markets typically offer incomplete insurance for risks. This provides an incentive for non-market institutions to fill in the gap. But non-market insurance may attenuate incentives no less than market insurance; non-market insurance may thus crowd out market insurance. But since non-market institutions typically cannot spread risks as effectively as can market institutions, overall welfare will fall.[54]

The second contention—that government intervention is ineffective—is based on the premise that any government action can be undone by the private sector. While there are some limited circumstances and forms of intervention for which this is true, the private sector cannot generally undo government actions.[55] This is obvious for interventions in which the government changes relative prices, but is also true for other forms of intervention.

The third charge, that government interventions are counterproductive, is partially motivated by some historical experiences. In practice, governments, even when they attempted to remedy market failures, often failed to do so. And in many cases they actually instituted policies that worsened the allocation of resources. In many of the eastern bloc countries governments themselves were major contributors to pollution. In many other countries agricultural policies contributed to environmental degradation.

Economists have attempted to delineate the systematic factors that contribute to government failure, just as they have analyzed the factors that systematically lead to market failure. Only by assessing these factors can one make an informed judgment about circumstances in which government intervention is likely to improve the market allocation of resources.

Many of the problems that contribute to market failure—such as imperfect information and principal-agent problems—contribute to government failure. In addition, the nature of collective decision-making in political processes may also contribute. Many economists have emphasized in particular the role of rent-seeking activities. The resources wasted are not only those associated with resource diversion, but also the resources that are dissipated by the activities themselves. The assumption that the rent rectangle will be fully dissipated in turn rests on the assumption of perfect competition in rent seeking. Just as imperfect competition may result in the persistence of monopoly profits, so too can imperfect competition in rent seeking result in little, if any, of the rent rectangle being dissipated (Stiglitz, 1988a).

Moreover, we have increasingly recognized that many of the problems of government failure are similar to those that arise in any large organization. In both there are significant principal-agent problems. Rent seeking can occur in private organizations just as it can in public organizations. Indeed, studies (such as Boycko, Shleifer and Vishny, 1996; Edlin and Stiglitz, 1995) have shown how managers in private organizations may distort their decisions to increase their ability to obtain rents and to limit competition from outside entrants.

THE PERFORMANCE AND ROLE OF THE PUBLIC SECTOR

Any attempt to assess the appropriate role of government in development must come to terms with the limitations of government, as well as the limitations of markets. In countries where governments remain ineffective, obviously, the scope for their actions should be correspondingly limited.

Using market mechanisms

There are ways in which governments can improve their efficiency and efficacy and can mitigate the government failures discussed in the previous section by appropriately designing employment (civil service) and procurement rules. To a large extent these entail trying to use market mechanisms within the public sector, for example, designing and using performance standards,[56] establishing incentive systems based on performance standards,[57] employing auctions for procurement and granting spectrum licenses, and using performance standards for establishing regulations. Open and transparent systems both enhance efficiency and reduce corruption.

In many cases government can use information extracted from the private sector to enhance its own efficiency. Thus, information about productivity in a similar private sector activity can be used as a norm in establishing performance standards in the public sector. In some cases, programs can be designed to elicit the desired information. For instance, by requiring a tranche of uninsured capital in banks, the government may be able to elicit information about the market's perception of the riskiness of a bank's portfolio from the way the market prices that tranche, and use that information to determine rates for deposit insurance.

Market mechanisms can also reduce the scope for rent-seeking activities: auctioning off natural resources, spectrum, quotas and so on has advantages both in collecting revenues for the public and in reducing incentives for the artificial creation of scarcity (for example, through trade barriers). Similarly, the use of fines and tradeable permits in environmental regulation not only ensures that environmental benefits are achieved at the lowest cost, but reduces the temptation to use regulatory mechanisms as a competitive device (such as imposing the use of scrubbers on low-sulfur coal).

Corporatization, privatization and competition

In much of the world confidence in the ability of government to produce efficiently has been so eroded that there is a mass movement towards privatization. Privatization by itself does not ensure efficiency, nor does it necessarily resolve the other problems of market failure. A private, unregulated monopoly may be even less likely to offer low prices to consumers than a government monopoly. And there is some evidence that, insulated from competition, private monopolies may suffer from several forms of inefficiency and may not be highly innovative.

Privatization, in turn, may raise a host of difficulties. While some (such as those associated with charging monopoly prices) may be addressed by regulation (though that too has its cost), others may not be so easily addressed. For instance, most governments have been reluctant to privatize their uranium enrichment corporations, partially out of security concerns. Though, in principle, these security concerns might be addressed by close monitoring of the sale and transfer of enriched uranium and uranium enrichment technology, the issue is whether the gains in efficiency outweigh the costs of regulation and the risks associated with imperfect regulation.

Similarly, some have worried that safety concerns might not be adequately addressed if the air traffic control system was privatized. Some have argued, to the contrary, that separating the agency responsible for managing the air traffic control system and the agency responsible for enforcing air traffic safety might actually enhance overall safety.

An important issue in privatization is ensuring that government receive full value for the assets sold. While auctions may maximize revenues, even with auctions, if there are few bidders or if there are asymmetries of information among bidders, government will obtain a small fraction of the full value. In practice, especially when governments try to dispose of assets very rapidly, the number of bidders may be small. Moreover, private bidders typically employ higher risk and time discounts than does the public sector.[58, 59]

If these public interest issues cannot be fully resolved by regulation, government still has another alternative: corporatization. Corporatization involves establishing a structure very similar to that of a private enterprise. There is typically a hard budget constraint— the corporation must rely on a specified source of revenues (sales, a ticket-user fee) to pay its costs. The corporation may borrow, much like a private firm. The fundamental difference arises in ownership and governance: ownership is vested in the government, and in governance public officials typically have a large role, though affected private parties (such as airline companies) may also play an important role.

Between formal corporatization and conventional public sector agencies lie performance-based organizations (PBOs). These may be particularly appropriate if there are many conventional production-like activities inter-mixed with public policy concerns. Thus the United States and the United Kingdom are converting their patent and trademark offices into PBOs, hoping that the policy issues associated with the granting of patents (breadth and scope, novelty) can be effectively separated from the standard processing aspects.

The important point to stress is that there is a continuum of institutional arrangements, running from government enterprises to private enterprises. The evidence is that much of the gains from privatization occur prior to privatization—they arise from the process of corporatization, from putting into place effective individual and organizational incentives.

Perhaps more important than the issue of ownership is that of competition. A government enterprise subject to a hard budget constraint and competition may operate just as efficiently as a private enterprise.[60] While in many areas in which government takes an active role the scope for competition may be limited, in parts of those sectors some competition is viable.[61]

Forms of intervention

The issue of corporatization versus privatization is only one part of the choice of form of intervention when there is a market failure. In many cases government needs to intervene only financially, for example, by subsidizing the production of some good with a positive externality. In other cases it intervenes through regulations, though, as noted above, there are strong arguments to make such regulations as market oriented as possible. In still other cases government production (directly, or increasingly, through corporatization) may be appropriate. Finally, government can play a catalytic role; it can help create markets and institutions, withdrawing from active intervention after this initiating role. For example, in the United States, after creating a national market for securitization of mortgages through the Federal National Mortgage Association (a government-sponsored enterprise), the government has played a very limited role in this market.

There is a simple method for choosing the appropriate form of intervention, especially in developing economies. If we begin by recognizing that competitive markets provide strong incentives for efficiency and that the constraints described earlier inhibit the range of actions that governments can undertake, then the question is, what is the minimal role government can assume that will assure that public objectives are met?[62] Can parts of the activity (for example, procurement of particular services) be subjected to the discipline of a competitive market? In many developing countries markets are sufficiently thin that competitive processes may not be very effective or efficient; privatization could actually raise costs. Government might, in such circumstances, actively try to *create* a competitive market by encouraging, for instance, the formation of new enterprises.

As always in economics, there are trade-offs. Public objectives and private incentives may not coincide perfectly, but if they coincide sufficiently, greater reliance can be placed on private incentives. Consider privatizing the air traffic control system. The public has a strong interest in safety. But if there are well capitalized airlines that have a great deal to lose from a loss of reputation, then there is likely to be little difference in concerns about safety.[63] On the other hand, countries may want their educational institutions to play an important role in nation building. But these socialization objectives may conflict with private incentives (human capital formation, signalling) and may be hard to specify within a contract. In these circumstances private provision of education may be more problematic.

CASE STUDIES

Here, I review briefly several of the important areas in which government has traditionally taken an active role, in light of the principles outlined earlier. There are some similarities among the areas that have received widespread government support in countries that have had successful development experiences—including the currently industrialized countries and the newly industrialized countries (NICs). Governments have provided what I have referred to as the institutional and economic infrastructure: they have provided the legal framework within which firms can interact (contract enforcement) and that promotes competition (anti-trust policy); universal education and the development of research and technology (intellectual infrastructure); they have ensured (either through regulation or direct government provision) that there is a physical infrastructure that provides efficient transportation and communication; and they have ensured that there is a sound financial system. Today, most governments have gone beyond these measures, recognizing that there are other important dimensions to standards of living that may not be well captured in GDP statistics. They have taken actions to protect the environment and the health and safety of consumers and workers, and they have made some provisions for basic social services, particularly those that affect the life prospects of children.

Provision of infrastructure

One of the responsibilities that traditionally fell to government was the provision of infrastructure. But there is increasing recognition that much infrastructure can be provided (financed and run) privately, assuming the appropriate regulatory structure is in place. The example just given of the telecommunications sector is perhaps the most dramatic instance—country after country has replaced a government enterprise with a private monopoly and attempted to create competitive markets within large parts of that sector.

In March 1995 the advanced industrialized countries (the G–7 countries) adopted a set of principles guiding the development of this increasingly important component of infrastructure. These principles emphasized private investment and competition, but recognized that some regulation would be required because, at least in the near future, elements of monopoly power would remain, especially in the local loop, and it was important that these elements not be leveraged further. Thus the principles explicitly recognized the importance of open access. They also recognized the importance of equity and broader social goals by noting the importance of universal service and diversity of content.[64]

In April 1996 a large group of developing countries, meeting with the G–7 countries in South Africa, discussed the applicability of those principles to their situations. The examples of price reductions and expansion of services in those countries that had in fact opened up their telecommunications sector made it clear that a competitive, privately provided telecommunications sector was viable within developing countries. Indeed, the argument was made that given the greater scarcity of public resources, the more limited technological capacities of government and the greater gaps in the current infra-structure, the imperatives for a competitive private sector were even greater. Competition would lower prices and extend services more effectively than governments would be able to, even with universal service objectives. Thus, at least in the immediate future, there may be no real trade off between equity and efficiency. And the development of strong competition among the companies in industrial countries willing to provide these services make it less likely that the developing countries will be exploited. Provided there is an open system of, for example, selling off the spectrum through transparent auctions, the customers in developing countries would benefit from this competition.

It is also apparent that even in those countries in which ingrained public monopolies in the telecommunications sector effectively resist privatization and competition, there are large areas (like cellular) in which they do not provide services. Countries can open up competition in these "value added" services. While countries that do so would not reap the full benefits from opening up the whole sector, substantial benefits can be gained from this incremental approach.

A similar pattern of increasing viability of competition is emerging in electricity, in which transmission is recognized as a natural monopoly (that will have to be regulated), but in which generation can be competitive, provided the appropriate regulatory structure is created.

The scope for private road construction is just beginning to be realized. Although the tolls imposed on users of these roads can be viewed as a form of benefit taxes, there are strong arguments for the use of benefit taxes, particularly in countries facing budget stringency—typical in developing economies. The requirement that tolls pay for the cost of the road provides a rigorous benefit-cost test that, while it may prevent some roads with high associated consumer surplus from being constructed, ensures that roads with costs exceeding benefits are not constructed (or if they are, the losses are not borne by taxpayers). These gains (as well as the enhanced equity from making those who benefit from a public service pay for it) may far outweigh the social costs arising from the underutilization derived from charging tolls.

The financial sector

The financial sector of the economy is sometimes likened to the brain: a well-functioning financial sector ensures that scarce capital resources are efficiently allocated. One of the remarkable aspects of the east Asian miracle was that those countries were able to allocate vast amounts of capital efficiently. In other instances of rapid accumulation, incremental capital-output ratios soared. The financial sector is concerned with information: finding out what projects are good and monitoring how funds are used. As we noted, while standard market mechanisms (the price system) work well in many instances, they encounter problems if information problems loom large. But conventional markets, even in more developed economies, do not simply rely on the price system for the allocation of capital. Loans are not provided to those who are willing to pay the highest interest rate, nor is equity provided to the investor who claims the highest expected return. (Indeed, one of the main insights of the Stiglitz-Weiss, 1981 analysis of credit rationing is that expected returns may actually fall as lenders charge higher interest rates, both because of the adverse effect on the mix of loan applicants—the applicants with the highest probability of repaying decide it is not worth borrowing at high interest rates—and because of adverse incentive effects—at high interest rates borrowers are encouraged to undertake greater risks, increasing the likelihood of default.)

Banks allocate funds, forming judgments of the likelihood of success of the project, not unlike a process that might occur within a government bureaucracy evaluating proposals. There are two differences: banks that make poor decisions will go bankrupt, while government agencies simply wind up drawing on the public purse. And banks look only at private returns, while government agencies look at social returns, and in the context of development the two may differ markedly. Thus there is some evidence that the social returns to investment in plant and equipment may exceed the private returns (see De Long and Summers, 1991), while investments in speculative real estate may have particularly low social returns (especially when account is taken of the destabilizing effect that real estate speculation often seems to have on the overall financial system, and the effect that it often seems to have on housing costs). Loans to promote exports may have high social returns (especially when, because of government intervention, there is a scarcity of foreign exchange, but even in the absence of foreign exchange controls, as they may facilitate the establishment of high standards and the transfer of technology), but may be viewed as highly risky by domestic banks that are ill-informed about market conditions abroad. Meanwhile, loans to domestic monopolists may have high private returns (since banks can be assured of repayment).

Many of the successful NICs bridged the gap by trying to impose commercial standards on individual loans at the same time as they prioritized sectors for lending (and limited lending in some areas, such as for consumer durables and speculative real estate investments). They created institutions and markets, noting the lacunae in the services provided by the private sector, for example, the absence of bond and equity markets and the lack of availability of long-term credit from banks. But the development banks they established operated largely on commercial principles (though, as noted, recognizing the importance of disparities between social and private returns). It is worth observing that even in more developed economies, governments have played a large role in extending financial markets, for example, in securitizing mortgages and providing student loans. In some cases, government intervention was largely entrepreneurial: securitized mortgage markets survive, at this juncture, without any government assistance.

Finally, in all economies governments have provided the institutional infrastructure required for financial markets to function effectively. Equity markets must have strong fraud laws and high auditing standards—both have enhanced confidence that there is a level playing field and thereby strengthened these markets. There is general agreement today that government has a responsibility to maintain the safety and soundness of the banking system; deposit insurance and the establishment of a lender of last resort have served to reduce the incidence of runs, which contribute to financial fragility. These actions can be justified in terms of standard market failures (see Stiglitz, 1993a), but it was experience, not theory, that drove governments towards the kinds of policies currently in place in the more advanced economies.[65, 66]

CONCLUDING REMARKS

The market is the engine of economic growth. The standard market model only partially captures its strengths, including its incentives to innovate. Yet in spite of its strengths, there are important instances in which private incentives are not well aligned with the public interest: firms may, for instance, produce too much pollution and invest too little in basic research. These market failures are significant enough that there is a role for government—in preserving and enriching the environment, ensuring educational opportunity, and promoting technology and basic research. In arriving at a balanced perspective on the scope of government, one must juxtapose the strengths and limitations of the private sector with the strengths and limitations of government. And whatever tasks are assigned to government, one must ensure that they are undertaken in the most efficient way, and in ways that are most conducive to the efficiency of the private sector. In recent years there have been marked advances in our understanding of how this can be done, and in the range of alternatives that are available within the public sector.

The challenge facing many developing countries is that while market failures may be more pervasive, governments' ability to correct those failures may be more limited. Given these limitations, governments will need to prioritize what they do. And among the areas with the highest priority are establishing an institutional framework and economic environment—including a sound macroeconomic policy—that allows the market to do what it does best and focusing on those activities, like investments in people, that simultaneously promote economic growth and increase equity.

NOTES

The views expressed are solely those of the author, and do not represent the views of any organization with which he is or has been affiliated.

1. A large literature offers varying interpretations of the east Asian experience. See, for instance, World Bank (1993), Amsden (1989), Alam (1989), Wade (1990), Stiglitz (1996) and Stiglitz and Uy (1996).

2. The National Banking Act was adopted 1863, when, in the midst of the US Civil War, the imperatives of creating a national economy—and with it, a sound national banking system—became clear. This was the first governmental regulatory body assigned the task of assuring the safety and soundness of financial institutions. The fragility of those institutions had contributed on numerous occasions to the sharp economic downturns that marked the early decades of the industrial revolution. The oversight provided by the Office of the Comptroller did not fully resolve the issues associated with financial fragility (it did not, for instance, provide either for a lender of last resort or for deposit insurance, and so, until these were established, runs could still destroy an essentially solvent financial institution), but it did represent a marked improvement over what had existed previously.

3. The enhanced role of government in financial markets may also have been a consequence of greater expectations: as expectations rose Japan not only recognized that markets failed to provide adequate long-term credit, but also that there were instances where government actions had helped fill this lacuna.

4. See Arrow (1951) and Debreu (1952).

5. For an early discussion of the market failure approach, see Bator (1958). Today, this approach is at the center of most textbook discussions of the economics of the public sector. See, for instance, Stiglitz (1988b, 1993c) and Atkinson and Stiglitz (1980). For a more thorough treatment, see Stiglitz (1989c).

6. Pure public goods are those with non-rivalrous consumption (the enjoyment of the good by one individual does not detract from that of another) and non-excludability (it is difficult if not impossible to exclude others from enjoying the good). See Samuelson (1954, 1955) or any standard text.

7. Public goods represent an extreme case. The marginal cost for an extra individual to enjoy the public good is zero. Hence, efficiency requires that there be no charge associated with his receiving those benefits. But if there are no charges, it cannot be profitable to provide the good. With non-exclusivity, it is in effect impossible to charge for the use, and underproduction is apparent. In

some cases it is possible to charge (while the marginal cost of an additional individual enjoying a TV program may be zero, it is possible to use scramblers to force those who wish to enjoy the program to pay). But then there will be underutilization.

Note that many publicly provided goods are not *pure* public goods in the sense that we have defined them. They are *publicly provided private goods* (see Stiglitz, 1974a). Many goods partially possess properties of pure public goods. See Atkinson and Stiglitz (1980).

8. Coase (1960) argued that private parties could effectively deal with problems of externalities, provided that an appropriate system of property rights was established. See below for a critique of this assertion.

9. Though I will say little about environmental policy in the remainder of this essay, the following point should be emphasized: sometimes developing countries treat the protection of the environment as a luxury—something that advanced economies can afford, but they cannot. The evidence, however, is that the costs of inadequate environmental protection are enormous—the health costs of contaminated water, for instance, may be very large—and it is often extremely expensive to reverse environmental damage. At the same time, the incremental costs of protecting the environment may be relatively low.

10. This idea was originally put forward by Tiebout (1956). He suggested that since individuals could choose the community in which they lived, they could vote with their feet, just as they vote with dollars in conventional markets. The pure theory of local public goods is set forth in Stiglitz (1977, 1983a, 1983b) and Milleron (1972). These papers make clear that the conditions under which decentralized provision of local public goods (with free migration) results in efficiency are even more restrictive than the conditions underlying the corresponding theorem for the provision of private goods (the fundamental theorem of welfare economics referred to earlier).

11. For further discussion of the concept and implications of international public goods and externalities, see Stiglitz (1995). There is increasing evidence of the importance of other international environmental externalities. There is today little doubt about the increase in the atmospheric concentration of carbon dioxide and other gases that contribute to global warming (see IPCC, 1995), and there is a growing consensus that such increases will have some effect on climate. Though the magnitude of the economic impacts of those effects remain controversial, it is clear that *some* countries will be adversely affected—and significantly so. It is also clear that the atmospherical concentration is a result of the actions of *all* countries. Thus pollution that contributes to increases in the atmospheric concentration is a true international externality. The Rio Convention of 1992 recognized this, and set forth a framework for addressing this concern.

12. In addition, just as markets do not deal effectively with redistribution *within* a country, so too do markets fail to address issues of redistribution among countries. The importance of the role of government in establishing the appropriate "rules of the game", or what I refer to later as the "institutional infrastructure" is stressed below.

13. For economies to be efficient, competition must be perfect, that is, there must be so many firms that each firm believes that it faces a horizontal demand curve for its product: it is a price taker. If it raises its price ever so little, it would lose

all of its market. In general, if competition is very keen, that is, firms face very elastic demand curves, then the market will be close to efficient. But markets can be "very competitive" in the ordinary sense of the term—a few large firms competing fiercely with each other—and the market can be far from efficient, as each firm directs much of its energies to reducing the degree of competition between them.

14. Many countries took the view that when competition was not viable, government should take responsibility for production. The widespread perception that government-run enterprises are less efficient than their private counterparts (such as in telephone service) led to large-scale privatizations in the 1980s. Interestingly, the theoretical rationale for privatizations in these cases was, at best, limited (see Sappington and Stiglitz, 1987).

15. See, for example, Baumol, Panzar and Willig (1982), Baumol (1982) or Grossman (1981). For an earlier discussion in the same vein, see Demsetz (1970).

16. This literature has also demonstrated that in the attempt to discourage entry, firms may engage in socially wasteful expenditures. Accordingly, potential competition does not ensure economic efficiency in general. See Stiglitz (1981, 1987c).

17. An example of the kind of specious argument that industries put forward was provided in a recent case involving exclusive dealerships for canned beer. The company argued that there was a problem with stale beer, that customers would blame the producer and not the retailer if the beer was stale. But dating the product—as is conventionally done with other goods that have a limited shelf life—would only "confuse the customer".

18. Restrictive practices may, for instance, reduce the perceived demand curve facing each firm, thus inducing it to raise its prices relative to its marginal costs. When all producers in the industry do this, their profits increase—enough to offset any losses from the inefficiencies associated with the vertical restraints (such as "double marginalization", which may arise with exclusive territories). For a more extensive discussion of this point, see Rey and Stiglitz (1988, 1995).

19. The difficulty of ascertaining whether a particular practice is anti-competitive needs to be emphasized, and puts a limit on the scope of actions that the competition authorities can undertake. Practices like "meeting the competition clauses", which seemingly promote competition may actually be anti-competitive—or if rivals enact such clauses, it removes any incentive for a firm to lower its price.

20. See below for the important implications in traditionally regulated industries like electricity and telecommunications.

21. The advantages of enhanced competition must be set against infant-industry or strategic-trade arguments for trade restrictions. While capital market imperfections provide a convincing rationale for government subsidies to infant industries (see Dasgupta and Stiglitz, 1988), there is a strong case for making such subsidies transparent (that is, avoiding protection), short-lived and in forms that maintain competitive pressures.

22. The implications of many of these new market failures to developing countries have been explored in a series of papers and books, and form the basis of the emerging theory of rural organization. For two collections of essays, see

Bardhan (1989) and Hoff, Braverman and Stiglitz (1993). See also Stiglitz (1985a, 1988a, 1989c).

23. Indeed, the fruit of much basic research is not even patentable (for example, mathematical constructs). Even when advances can be patented, there is a conflict between short-run efficiency (since the marginal cost of an additional individual or firm using an idea is zero, and, with a patent, firms have monopoly power, and so charge prices in excess of marginal costs) and dynamic efficiency—a conflict not addressed in the standard Arrow-Debreu framework.

For an early discussion of underinvestment in research in market economies, see Arrow (1962) and the essays in Shell (1967). For more recent discussions, including those emphasizing the public goods nature of R&D, see Stiglitz (1986b, 1987b, 1994b).

Schumpeter (1942) emphasized that in markets in which innovation was important, competition centered not around prices but around innovation. "Schumpeterian competition", as this form of competition has come to be called, is markedly different from the kind of competition envisaged in standard competitive models. While Schumpeter praised the incentives for innovation that such competition provided to markets, more recent analyses have questioned several of Schumpeter's conclusions. Firms may engage in just enough research to pre-empt rivals, and the amount of research required to do so may be very limited. More generally, competition tends to be limited in markets where innovation is important. See, for example, Stiglitz (1994b) and the literature cited there.

24. For a survey see Council of Economic Advisers (1995). The evidence cited there not only supports the view that social returns are much higher than private returns, but also that private returns are higher than private returns in other forms of investment. This can be attributed at least in part to imperfections of capital markets, such as the difficulty of raising equity capital (since innovators would have to disclose valuable information that could be misappropriated to persuade potential investors to provide capital) and the inability to collateralize investment in research.

25. While the market economy's ability to promote innovation has long been heralded as one of its main strengths, the Arrow-Debreu model assumed that technology was unaffected by the action of a single firm. Technology was assumed to be exogenous. This assumption clearly limits the usefulness of the Arrow-Debreu model in appraising the effectiveness of market economies.

26. See Stiglitz (1985b, 1989b, 1994b). A major insight of this literature is that economies with a small amount of information imperfection may look markedly different from economies with perfect information. The standard presumption of continuity does not seem to hold.

27. A quite different set of explanations for why markets may not exist is provided by Rothschild and Stiglitz (1976). They argued that in markets with adverse selection (that is, where individuals differ in their characteristics), there are incentives to "cream skim", that is, for insurance firms to try to obtain the best risks, or employers to hire the workers who are most undervalued. In insurance markets discrimination occurs, for instance, by offering policies with large deductibles, which will be purchased disproportionately by low-risk individuals. Since low-deductible policies will be purchased only by high-risk individuals, the premium will be high. Rothschild and Stiglitz show that this "separating

equilibrium" may itself not be an equilibrium, since low-risk individuals may then not be willing to pay the high cost—in terms of limited insurance—to set themselves apart.

28. Typically, markets will exist, but will be thin. Assume that lemons break down more often. Those for whom time is less valuable may find such cars worth more than would someone whose time is extremely valuable.

29. It is worth noting that even in more advanced economies, governments often take an active role in promoting re-employment of workers. (These are referred to as "active labour market policies".)

30. A basic property of the standard model is the "law of the single price": the same commodity sells at the same price everywhere in the market. Obviously, if it is costly to ascertain the price charged at different places in the market, prices may differ. The cited results are more interesting: they argue that the *only* equilibria may entail price dispersion. The market creates noise, even if it does not originate from other sources. If all firms charged the same price, which was lower than the monopoly price, it would pay any firm to raise its price (since if there are slight search costs, it would not pay any customer who arrived at the store to continue searching). But if all firms charged the monopoly price, it might pay a large firm to lower its price to induce individuals to continue to search and thus garner for itself a larger share of the market.

31. There is evidence that in developing countries improved telecommunications allows poor farmers in effect to arbitrage markets, obtaining on average higher prices for their products.

32. See, for example, the large literature on efficiency wages (Shapiro and Stiglitz, 1984) or on credit rationing (Stiglitz and Weiss, 1981). For a survey, see Stiglitz (1986a or 1987a) or Akerlof and Yellen (1986). The principle underlying credit rationing is the same as that underlying unemployment: when there is excess demand, lenders worry that if they raise interest rates, the borrowers with the highest probability of success (of repaying the loan) will decide that it is not worth borrowing (the adverse selection effect), and all borrowers may decide to undertake riskier projects, increasing the probability of default (the moral hazard effect).

33. Note how this result is related to information imperfections: with perfect information, output is observable and measurable, and hence compensation can be directly related to productivity. If information imperfections are more prevalent, then it is more likely that markets may not clear. In some cases there may be dual markets—that is, there may be an excess supply of labour in the more advanced sector, while the market clears in the more primitive sector, where information problems do not arise.

34. The standard theory, in establishing the Pareto efficiency of the market, required that there be no price dispersion, all firms face horizontal demand curves and all markets exist and clear. Thus each of the problems noted earlier give rise to a potential source of inefficiency. But more striking is the result that even when there is no price dispersion, all firms face horizontal demand curves and markets exist and clear, the market equilibrium is not in general Pareto efficient.

35. The optimal tax will balance the dead-weight loss from the tax with the externality benefit from reduced fire losses. See Arnott and Stiglitz (1986).

36. Some naive economists suggested that information was like any other commodity, with competitive markets ensuring its efficient supply. A little thought reveals the many ways in which information differs from standard commodities. It has, for instance, attributes of public goods (non-rivalrous consumption, non-excludability). No two pieces of information are the same (I cannot sell you the same piece of information twice). With standard commodities, one knows what one is buying before one purchases it. With information, by definition, one cannot know what one is getting beforehand. If one were told, for instance, "Pay me a certain amount and I will give you information that you value", the buyer clearly has an incentive to say, "I already knew that", or "That information isn't of any value to me". Although in certain idealized situations one can resolve these problems with incentive-compatible contracts (for example, if there is common knowledge with respect to what income would have been in the absence of the information, the buyer of the information could offer to pay the seller a fraction of the increment in income), more generally, one cannot.

37. For a discussion of how these problems lead to equity rationing see, for example, Myers and Maljuf (1984) or Greenwald, Stiglitz and Weiss (1984). For a discussion of how they lead to credit rationing, see Stiglitz and Weiss (1981, 1986, 1992). For a discussion of some of the macroeconomic consequences of equity and credit rationing, see Greenwald and Stiglitz (1993a) and Stiglitz and Weiss (1992).

38. At one level the result should seem almost obvious: market economies result in efficient outcomes by equating price (the marginal social benefit) with marginal cost. If there is no market, how are marginal social costs and benefits to be equated?

    The market failure to which Greenwald and Stiglitz and Newbery and Stiglitz call attention is more subtle: the issue is that production at *existing* markets may not be set at the optimal level. The simplest examples entail production decisions in one sector that have risk spillovers on others.

39. In some cases, such as annuities, the market provided some insurance, but at very high transaction costs (so high that most elderly individuals would be better off buying long-term bonds). While in many cases today's social insurance problems embody an element of redistribution, the fact is that private markets for disability insurance, unemployment insurance, health insurance for the aged or retirement insurance were very underdeveloped when these programs were established. Even today in the United States, social security provides the only fully indexed annuity. The fact that there are important moral hazard and adverse selection problems impeding the private establishment of such markets does not necessarily imply that welfare would not be enhanced by government provision, though, to be sure, in establishing a program, government must be cognizant of the moral hazard and adverse selection problems.

    There is another rationale for government action in this area: as long as governments are sufficiently compassionate to not allow individuals who fail to provide for their old age or buy health insurance to bear the full consequences of their actions, a moral hazard problem will arise, leading to the underprovision of insurance privately. The resolution of this problem does not, however, require government insurance, but rather government mandates. See Stiglitz (1993b).

40. There have also been several recent attempts to formalize the Rosenstein-Rodan story (see, for example, Murphy, Shleifer and Vishny, 1989; for an intuitive interpretation, see Krugman, 1993). But these models typically assume that the economy does not produce tradeable goods, that is, firms must rely on domestic demand for the purchase of their products. Thus in the standard big push theories, the steel industry does not develop because the steel-using industries do not develop, and the steel-using industries cannot develop because of the lack of steel. More recent theories focus on aggregate demand. With increasing returns in the advanced sector, high levels of income generate high demands for the products of the advanced sector. And the high levels of output of the advanced sector generate the incomes required to sustain demand. The east Asian countries, by contrast, relied heavily on exports, suggesting that closed economy models may provide limited insights into development strategies. For a fuller critique of these models, see Stiglitz (1993a).

41. The neoclassical synthesis was an attempt to reconcile microeconomic views that markets efficiently allocated resources with macroeconomic analyses, which suggested that resources might be underemployed for extensive periods of time. It argued that once the government succeeded in restoring the economy to full employment, the standard microeconomic analysis became operative. Despite widespread acceptance of the idea, the neoclassical synthesis was simply an assertion, unsupported by analysis or evidence. The more plausible hypothesis is that there are underlying reasons that markets fail to assure full employment, and that whatever those reasons, they manifest themselves in many ways, adversely affecting the economy's overall efficiency. Periods of massive unemployment are only the tip of the iceberg—the most dramatic manifestation of these inefficiencies. See Greenwald and Stiglitz (1987).

42. The question of what is desirable may be approached from either a normative or a descriptive perspective. Analytic approaches to the former attempt to define evaluation criteria, that would presumably receive widespread accord. Economists traditionally summarize these judgments in a "social welfare function", examples of which include the utilitarian social welfare function (maximizing the sum of utilities) and the Rawlsian social welfare function (maximizing the utility of the worst off individual). There is a large literature discussing the properties of these normative criteria. See, for example, Sen (1973); Rothschild and Stiglitz (1973).

The descriptive perspective attempts to elucidate the views that would be expressed through a political process, such as majority voting. Unfortunately, unless severe restrictions are imposed (for example, on the underlying population or the set of available choices—such as those generated by a linear income tax system), a majority voting equilibrium will not exist. See Foley (1967); Romer (1975).

Still a third perspective emphasizes that the degree of inequality in a society can affect macroeconomic behaviour (the rate of growth); there may be externalities associated with excessive inequality. This provides a rationale for government intervention on efficiency grounds. See, for example, the discussion of the role of egalitarian policies in east Asia (World Bank, 1993; Birdsall and Sabot 1993; Stiglitz, 1996).

43. In the United States the earned income tax credit raises the after-tax income of low-income wage earners (by an amount that depends on family size). The maximum supplement may raise a family's after-tax income by as much as 40 per cent. For those below the maximum transfer payment, there is an incentive to overreport. In practice, this problem does not seem to have been particularly important.

44. The price elasticity of food is relatively low, so even when the food subsidy takes the form of lowering prices, it may not lead to much increased consumption. If the price subsidy applies to only limited quantities, then for all those who consume more than that quantity, the effect is equivalent to an income transfer. The same is true in countries like the United States, which provides food stamps. In the United States the evidence is that each dollar of food subsidy increases food consumption by around 10 to 15 cents. Moreover, it is often difficult to prevent resale. Thus if individuals wish to consume less food than provided by their food coupons, they resell the coupon, often at a fraction of its original value.

45. Portable housing vouchers can help address these problems, as well as the other major objection to public housing: by housing the poor in the same area, it may contribute to social dysfunction.

46. Minimum wages have also been used to improve the before-tax/subsidy distribution of income. The economic consequences of minimum wages have recently been the subject of extensive controversy. See Card and Krueger (1995).

47. There are deep questions, into which we cannot delve in this chapter, concerning whether a proclivity to avail oneself of opportunities should be a concern of government.

48. Society has a difficult time making a commitment not to assist those who do not make adequate provision for their old age. Given this, individuals have an incentive not to make adequate provision. For a fuller discussion of this rationale for mandatory savings programs (or other mandated insurance programs) see Stiglitz (1993c).

49. The rationale for government action in the financial sector is far more complex and is related to a series of market failures, mostly arising from information imperfections. See Stiglitz (1994a).

50. Critics of universal service question whether telephone service should be included within the range of commodities to be covered by specific egalitarianism. Consumption of telephone services typically represents a sufficiently small fraction of an individual's budget that the overall impact on equality of subsidies associated with universal service is small. As countries proceed to privatize the telecommunications sector and introduce competition, and as the range of services within the sector expands, it is increasingly difficult to define universal service and to devise ways of implementation that do not have significant adverse efficiency consequences. Economists typically prefer open systems of subsidies (directed at consumers, who can make choices reflecting their preferences, rather than at producers) to hidden subsidies through cross-subsidization. South Africa has recently proposed such a universal service fund.

51. Other restrictions entail due process—restrictions on how government conducts its business and on equity—to make it less likely that government uses its powers to advantage one group over others.

52. In structuring its actions at one date, the government can attempt to increase the likelihood that it will live up to its commitments at a subsequent date.

53. Coase's argument was simple. Consider a room that must be shared by smokers and non-smokers. If property rights are appropriately assigned, for example, to one individual, then the "owner" of the air rights will ascertain whether the smokers or non-smokers are willing to pay the most. If the value of the clean air to non-smokers exceeds the value of smoking to smokers, the owners will not allow smoking. Apart from income effects, the decision of whether to allow smoking does not depend on how property rights are assigned, only that they be assigned. But the problem is that the difference between smoke and no smoke in the air is a public good, and each smoker would prefer to have others pay to establish the right to smoke, claiming that he himself obtains little consumer surplus from smoking. When there are many individuals and imperfections of information concerning individuals' valuations of smoking versus non-smoking, bargaining costs can be high and the outcomes inefficient.

54. See Arnott and Stiglitz (1991). Whether non-market insurance increases or decreases welfare depends on whether the providers of non-market insurance can monitor moral hazard more effectively.

55. For instance, if there are no asymmetries of information and households are risk-neutral, then changes in monetary policy can be offset by changes in price level, with no effect on the real economy. The empirical evidence strongly suggests that monetary policy does matter. Similarly, there are circumstances in which government deficits are fully offset by increases in private savings (Barro, 1974), but these circumstances are highly restricted (Stiglitz, 1988c). And, again, the empirical evidence suggests that in practice the private sector does not fully offset government deficits.

56. Governments are also being encouraged to behave more like market institutions in other ways, for instance, by being more consumer oriented, referring to those that they serve as "clients", and developing metrics for customer satisfaction.

57. There is an important caveat though: activities within the public sector often differ from those within the private sector, and in many cases it is difficult to develop metrics.

    Private firms have simple, bottom-line performance measures: profits and market value. While government as a whole has no comparable summary statistic for performance, performance at particular activities (typing letters, issuing airline tickets, processing drivers' licenses) can be identified and measured. It is important that output and not process or input measures be used—too often, rewards are based on how well a worker complied with the standard operating procedures.

    In many cases there are sufficient similarities between activities performed in the public and private sector, so that private sector performance can provide a yardstick of comparison. For instance, while every firm has slightly different travel needs, it is possible to obtain a range of estimates of the administrative costs associated with travel, to see where government agencies fall within that range and to use performance relative to those norms as a basis for rewards.

    But many of the activities conducted within the public sector are different from those conducted in the private sector. Public sector activities are disproportionately administrative, and measuring individual performance in this arena is particularly difficult. We do not know how to measure the quality of the decisions being made collectively, let alone the contribution of any single individual.

In many of these activities there is no single metric of performance. Consider, for instance, education. We can measure with some accuracy student performance in certain basic skills, but we have far greater difficulty measuring higher order cognitive skills, let alone creativity. A good education system must teach basic skills, but it should also go beyond that to enhance cognitive skills and creativity. Were we to reward teachers on the basis of performance, we would want to measure all of these, and we would want in particular to measure the teacher's value added, that is, taking into account the skills and abilities of the student at the time the student entered the class. The fact is that at the current time, our measures are at best imperfect. For an early discussion of these limitations of piece-rate/performance systems, see Stiglitz (1975). For a more recent discussion, see Holmstrom and Milgrom (1991).

What is of particular concern is that rewarding measurable aspects of performance will inevitably distort resource allocations towards producing more of those things that are measured and rewarded. In the case of education, rewarding only performance in terms of basic skills will divert resources away from developing higher order and cognitive skills. It may be possible, however, to mitigate these effects by appropriately designing the production process, for example, by assigning different teachers different tasks (see Hannaway, 1992).

It may be difficult to ascertain with precision the magnitude of these problems. Consider the issuance of patents. One can easily measure the speed with which patents are issued, as well as the cost (person-hours used to evaluate and process). One can measure the appeals. With a long lag one can measure the error rate—the fraction of those rejected that upon appeal are granted, and the fraction of those accepted that are challenged, and in which the challenge is upheld. One cannot measure with much accuracy the frequency of instances in which the applicant was turned down, but does not think the cost of an appeal is worth the expected benefit nor the instances in which parties pay royalties rather than attacking the patent in court.

58. This clearly would not be the case if capital markets were perfect. But they are not. These considerations must be balanced against gains from greater efficiency resulting from privatization. In some cases the efficiency gains may be relatively small, while in other cases, they may be quite large.

59. The Sappington-Stiglitz (1987) fundamental theorem of privatization referred to earlier identifies conditions under which government can obtain full value for its assets and fully implement other public objectives. But those conditions are highly restrictive, remarkably similar to the conditions under which markets themselves yield efficient outcomes (the conditions of the first fundamental theorem of welfare economics).

60. See the comparison between the Canadian National Railway and Canadian Pacific, cited in Caves and Christensen (1980).

61. On the other hand, one must be careful to recognize that many of the goods produced within the public sector are fundamentally different from those provided privately. The issue, for instance, of private versus public education has many dimensions to it that extend beyond the efficiency of provision.

62. This question puts the matter too starkly. In many cases what is at issue is transaction costs. Government could, for instance, obtain secretarial services

in the private market, but the transaction costs (including the bidding process, the establishment of the conditions for work, and changing those conditions in response to changes in circumstances) might be much higher than hiring secretaries directly. The issue here is parallel to that posed by Coase in his analysis of the boundaries of the firm. See Coase (1937) and Williamson (1975).

63. Government may have a role in ensuring that airlines are well capitalized so that they have appropriate incentives, or ensuring that they have adequate insurance (or bonds) so that the insurance company (bonding agency) has incentives to monitor safety. Because of spillover reputation effects to the industry as a whole, these private incentives may still be inadequate: the social cost of an accident may exceed the private cost by a considerable amount.

64. Improved telecommunications systems allow for greater diversity; it is possible to have many more television and radio channels, allowing a wider range of expressions of views, more languages and a diversity of cultural content. There are some who worry that these new technologies will generate a more competitive market place for ideas and cultures, and in that more competitive market place some may tend to dominate. The proponents of this view do not believe in consumer sovereignty (see the discussion of merit goods above) or worry that there is a "network externality" in which the market solution may not be socially efficient. On the other hand, these arguments for cultural diversity may simply be an attempt by domestic industries to find an acceptable rationale for protection.

65. For instance, monitoring and information about the financial status of a financial institution are public goods. There are large externalities associated with systemic financial failures, implying that individual institutions may take insufficient care.

66. There are often trade-offs between different objectives: restrictions on entry may increase the franchise value of a bank, and thus enhance directly, and through incentive effects, the safety and soundness of the banking system. But such restrictions also reduce the extent of competition. Countries in different circumstances will weigh these considerations differently. In doing so, it is important to note that banks provide a range of services, in some of which competition may be very limited, while in others it may be quite keen. Thus, typically, competition for depository services is intense, but for loans to small businesses (because of the information-intensive nature of the process) competition may be very limited.

REFERENCES

Akerlof, G. 1970. "The Market for 'Lemons': Qualitative Uncertainty and the Market Mechanism." *Quarterly Journal of Economics* 86:488–500.

Akerlof, G. and J. Yellen, eds.1986. *Efficiency Wage Models of the Labor Market.* Cambridge, U.K.: Cambridge University Press.

Alam, M.S. 1989. *Governments and Markets in Economic Development Strategies.* New York: Praeger Publishing.

Amsden, Alice H. 1989. *Asia's Next Giant: South Korea and Late Industrialization.* Oxford: Oxford University Press.

Arnott, R., B. Greenwald and J.E. Stiglitz. 1994. "Information and Economic Efficiency." *Information Economics and Policy* 6(1):77–88.

Arnott, R. and J.E. Stiglitz. 1986. "Moral Hazard and Optimal Commodity Taxation." *Journal of Public Economics* 29(1):1–24.

____. 1991. "Moral Hazard and Non-market Institutions: Dysfunctional Crowding Out or Peer Monitoring." *American Economic Review* 81(1):179–90.

Arrow, K.J. 1951. "An Extension of the Theorem of Classical Welfare Economics." In J. Newman, ed., *Proceedings of the Second Berkeley Symposium on Mathematical Studies and Probability.* Berkeley: University of California Press.

____. 1962. "Economic Welfare and the Allocation of Resources for Invention." In National Bureau for Economic Research, *The Rate and Direction of Inventive Activity.* New York: Arno Press.

Atkinson, A.B. and J.E. Stiglitz. 1980. *Lectures on Public Economics.* New York: McGraw-Hill.

Bardhan, P., ed. 1989. *The Economic Theory of Agrarian Institutions.* Oxford: Clarendon Press.

Barro, R.J. 1974. "Are Government Bonds Net Wealth?" *Journal of Political Economy* 82(6):1095–117.

Bator, Francis M. 1958. "The Anatomy of Market Failure." *Quarterly Journal of Economics* 72(August):351–79.

Baumol, William J. 1982. "Contestable Markets: An Uprising in the Theory of Industry Structure." *American Economic Review* 72(1):1–15.

Baumol, William J., John C. Panzar and Robert D. Willig. 1982. *Contestable Markets and the Theory of Industry Structure.* New York: Harcourt Brace Jovanovich.

Birdsall, Nancy and Richard H. Sabot. 1993. *Virtuous Circles: Human Capital Growth and Equity in East Asia.* Washington, D.C.: World Bank.

Borenstein, Severin. 1992. "The Evolution of U. S. Airline Competition." *Journal of Economic Perspectives* 6(2):45–73.

Boycko, Maxim, Andrei Schleifer and Robert W. Vishny. 1996. "A Theory of Privatization." *Economic Journal* 106(435):309–19.

Buchanan, James M. 1965. "An Economic Theory of Clubs." *Economica* 32(February):1–14.

Buchanan, James M. and Charles Goetz. 1972. "Efficiency Limits of Fiscal Mobility: An Assessment of the Tiebout Model." *Journal of Public Economics* 1(April):25–43.

Card, D. and A.B. Krueger. 1995. "Time-Series Minimum-Wage Studies: A Meta-Analysis." *American Economic Review* 85(2):238–43.

Caves, D.W. and L.R. Christensen. 1980. "The Relative Efficiency of Public and Private Firms in a Competitive Environment: The Case of Canadian Railroads." *Journal of Political Economy* 88(5):958–76.

Coase, Ronald H. 1937. "The Nature of the Firm." *Economica* 4(16):386–405.

____. 1960. "The Problem of Social Cost." *Journal of Law and Economics* 3(October):1–44.

Council of Economic Advisers. 1995. "Supporting Research and Development to Promote Economic Growth: The Federal Government's Role." October.

Dasgupta, P. and J.E. Stiglitz. 1988. "Learning by Doing, Market Structure and Industrial and Trade Policies." *Oxford Economic Papers* 40(2):246–68.

Debreu, G. 1952. *The Theory of Value.* Wiley: New York.

De Long, J. Bradford and Lawrence H. Summers. 1991. "Equipment Investment and Economic Growth." *Quarterly Journal of Economics* 106(2):445–502.

Demsetz, Harold. 1970. "The Private Production of Public Goods." *Journal of Law and Economics* 13(October):293–306.

Diamond, P. 1971. "A Model of Price Adjustment." *Journal of Economic Theory* 3(2):156–68.

Diamond, P. and J. Mirrlees. 1971. "Optimal Taxation and Public Production, II: Tax Rules." *American Economic Review* 61(3):261–78.

Edlin, Aaron S. and J.E. Stiglitz. 1995. "Discouraging Rivals: Managerial Rent-seeking and Economic Inefficiencies." *American Economic Review* 85(5): 1301–12.

Farrell, M.J. 1987. "Information and the Coase Theorem." *Journal of Economic Perspectives* 1(2):113–29.

Foley, D.K. 1967. "Resource Allocation and the Public Sector." *Yale Economic Essays* 7(1):45–98.

Greenwald, B. 1986. "Adverse Selection in the Labor Market." *Review of Economic Studies* 53(3):325–47.

Greenwald, B. and J.E. Stiglitz. 1986. "Externalities in Economies with Imperfect Information and Incomplete Markets." *Quarterly Journal of Economics* 101(May):229–64.

____. 1987. "Keynesian, New Keynesian and New Classical Economics." *Oxford Economic Papers* 39(March):119–33.

____. 1988. "Pareto Inefficiency of Market Economies: Search and Efficiency Wage Models." *American Economic Review* 78(2):351–55.

____. 1992. "Information, Finance and Markets: The Architecture of Allocative Mechanisms." *Journal of Industrial and Corporate Change* 1(1):37–63.

____. 1993a. "Financial Market Imperfections and Business Cycles." *Quarterly Journal of Economics* 108(1):77–114.

____. 1993b. "New and Old Keynesians." *Journal of Economic Perspectives* 7(1):23–44.

Greenwald, B., J.E. Stiglitz and A. Weiss. 1984. "Informational Imperfections in the Capital Markets and Macro-economic Fluctuations." *American Economic Review* 74(1):194–9.

Grossman, S.J. 1981. "Nash Equilibrium and the Industrial Organization of Markets with Large Fixed Costs." *Econometrica* 49:1149–72.

Hannaway, Jane. 1992. "Higher Order Skills, Job Design, and Incentives: An Analysis and Proposal." *American Educational Research Journal* 29(1):3–21.

Hoff, K., A. Braverman and J.E. Stiglitz. 1993. *The Theory of Rural Economic Organizations*. Oxford: Oxford University Press.

Holmstrom, B. and Paul Milgrom. 1991. "Multitask Principal-Agent Analyses: Incentive Contracts, Asset Ownership, and Job Design." *Journal of Law, Economics and Organization* 7(1):24–52.

IPCC (Intergovernmental Panel on Climate Change). 1995. *Climate Change 1994: Radiative Forcing of Climate Change and an Evaluation of the IPCC IS92 Emission Scenarios*. J.T. Houghton and L.G. Mesra Filko, J. Bruce, Hoesung Lee, B.A. Callander, E. Haites, N. Harris, K. Maskell, eds. Cambridge, U.K.: Cambridge University Press.

Krugman, P. 1993. "Towards a Counter-Counter Revolution in Development Theory." *Proceedings of the Annual World Bank Conference on Development Economics 1992*. Washington, D.C.: World Bank.

Leibenstein, H. 1966. "Allocative Efficiency and X-efficiency." *American Economic Review* 56(3):392–415.

Lerner, A.P. 1944. *The Economics of Control*. New York: Macmillan.

Majluf, N. and S. Myers. 1984. "Corporate Financing and Investment Decisions when Firms Have Information that Investors Do Not Have." *Journal of Financial Economics* 13(2):187–221.

Mankiw, N. Gregory. 1993. "Symposium on Keynesian Economics Today." *Journal of Economic Perspectives* 7(1):3–4.

Milleron, J.C. 1972. "Theory of Value with Public Goods: A Survey Article." *Journal of Economic Theory* 5(3):419–77.

Mirrlees, J. 1971. An Exploration in the Theory of Optimum Income Taxation. *Review of Economic Studies* 38(2):175–208.

Murphy, K.M., A. Shleifer and R.W. Vishny. 1989. "Industrialization and the Big-Push." *Journal of Political Economy* 97(5):1003–26.

Musgrave, R.A. and P.B. Musgrave. 1976. *Public Finance in Theory and Practice*. Second edition. New York: McGraw-Hill.

Nalebuff, B. and J.E. Stiglitz. 1983. "Prizes and Incentives: Towards a General Theory of Compensation and Competition." *Bell Journal of Economics* 14(1):21–43.

Newbery, D. and J.E. Stiglitz. 1982. "The Choice of Techniques and the Optimality of Market Equilibrium with Rational Expectations." *Journal of Political Economy* 90(2):223–46.

____. 1984. "Pareto Inferior Trade." *Review of Economic Studies* 51(January):1–12.

Oakland, William. 1987. "Theory of Public Goods." In A.Auerbach and M. Feldstein, eds., *Handbook of Public Economics* 2. New York: North Holland.

Pigou, A.C. 1932. *The Economics of Welfare*. Fourth edition. London: Macmillan.

____. 1947. *A Study in Public Finance*. Thirty-fourth edition. London: Macmillan.

Rawls, J. 1971. *A Theory of Justice*. Cambridge, Mass.: Harvard Univesity Press.

Rey, P. and J.E. Stiglitz. 1988. "Vertical Restraints and Producers' Competition." *European Economic Review* 32(2/3):561–68.

____. 1995. "The Role of Exclusive Territories in Producers' Competition." *Rand Journal of Economics* 26(3):431–51.

Rodríguez-Clare, A. 1992. "The Big-Push in a Small Open Economy." Department of Economics, Stanford University.

Romer, P. 1986. "Increasing Returns and Long-Run Growth." *Journal of Political Economy* 94(5):1002–37.

Romer, T. 1975. "Individual Welfare, Majority Voting, and the Properties of a Linear Income Tax." *Journal of Public Economics* 4(2):163–95.

Rosenstein-Rodan, P.N. 1943. "Problems of Industrialization in Eastern and Southeastern Europe." *Economic Journal* 53(June-September):202–11.

Ross, S. 1973. "The Economic Theory of Agency: The Principal's Problem." *American Economic Review* 63(1):134–9.

Rothschild, M. and J.E. Stiglitz. 1973. "Some Further Results on the Measurement of Inequality." *Journal of Economic Theory* 6(2):188–204.

____. 1976. "Equilibrium in Competitive Insurance Markets: An Essay on the Economics of Imperfect Information." *Quarterly Journal of Economics* 90(4):629–49.

Salop, S. and D. Scheffman. 1983. "Raising Rivals' Costs." *American Economic Review* 73(2):267–71.

Salop, S. and J.E. Stiglitz. 1977. "Bargains and Ripoffs: A Model of Monopolistically Competitive Price Dispersions." *Review of Economic Studies* 44(October):493–510.

____. 1982. "The Theory of Sales: A Simple Model of Equilibrium Price Dispersion with Identical Agents." *American Economic Review* 72(5):1121–30.

Samuelson, P.A. 1954. "The Pure Theory of Public Expenditure." *Review of Economics and Statistics* 36(4):387–9.

____. 1955. "Diagramatic Exposition of a Theory of Public Expenditure." *Review of Economics and Statistics* 37(4):350–6.

____. 1958. "Aspects of Public Expenditure Theories." *Review of Economics and Statistics* 40(4):332–8.

Sappington, D. and J.E. Stiglitz. 1987. "Privatization, Information and Incentives." *Journal of Policy Analysis and Management* 6(4):567–82.

Schumpeter, J. 1942. *Socialism, Capitalism, and Democracy.* New York: Harper.

Sen, A.K. 1973. *On Economic Inequality.* Oxford: Oxford University Press.

Shapiro, C. and J.E. Stiglitz. 1984. "Equilibrium Unemployment as a Worker Discipline Device." *American Economic Review* 74(3):433–4.

Shell, K., ed. 1967. *Essays on the Theory of Optimal Economic Growth.* Cambridge, Mass.: MIT Press.

Smith, Adam. 1776. *The Wealth of Nations 1776.* Book 1, chapter 2.

Stiglitz, J.E. 1974a. "Demand for Education in Public and Private School Systems." *Journal of Public Economics* 3(November):349–86.

____. 1974b. "Incentives and Risk Sharing in Sharecropping." *Review of Economic Studies* 41(2):219–55.

____. 1974c. "Theories of Discrimination and Economic Policy." In G. von Furstenberg, Bennet Harrison, Ann R. Horowitz, eds., *Patterns of Racial Discrimination.* Lexington, Mass.: D.C. Heath and Company (Lexington Books).

____. 1975. "Incentives, Risk and Information: Notes Towards a Theory of Hierarchy." *Bell Journal of Economics* 6(2):552–79.

____. 1977. "The Theory of Local Public Goods." In M.S. Feldstein and R.P. Inman, eds., *The Economics of Public Services.* London: Macmillan.

____. 1981. "Potential Competition May Reduce Welfare." *American Economic Review* 71(2):184–9.

_____. 1982a. "The Inefficiency of the Stock Market Equilibrium." *Review of Economic Studies* 49(April):241–61.

_____. 1983a. "Public Goods in Open Economies with Heterogeneous Individuals." In J.F. Thisse and H.G. Zoller, eds., *Locational Analysis of Public Facilities.* Amsterdam: North-Holland Publishing Company.

_____. 1983b. "The Theory of Local Public Goods Twenty-Five Years After Tiebout: A Perspective." In G.R. Zodrow, ed., *Local Provision of Public Services: The Tiebout Model After Twenty-Five Years.* New York: Academic Press, Inc.

_____. 1985a. "Economics of Information and the Theory of Economic Development." *Revista De Econometria* 5(1):5–32.

_____. 1985b. "Information and Economic Analysis: A Perspective." *Economic Journal* 95(Supplement):21–41.

_____. 1986a. "Theories of Wage Rigidities." In J.L. Butkiewicz, K.J. Koford and J.B. Miller, eds., *Keynes' Economic Legacy: Contemporary Economic Theories.* New York: Praeger Publishers.

_____. 1986b. "Theory of Competition, Incentives and Risk." In J.E. Stiglitz and F. Mathewson, eds., *New Developments in the Theory of Market Structure.* Houndmills, Basingstoke, Hampshire and Cambridge, Mass.: Macmillan/MIT Press.

_____. 1987a. "The Causes and Consequences of the Dependence of Quality on Prices." *Journal of Economic Literature* 25(March):1–48.

_____. 1987b. "On the Microeconomics of Technical Progress." In Jorge M. Katz, ed., *Technology Generation in Latin American Manufacturing Industries.* Houndmills, Basingstoke, Hampshire: Macmillan.

_____. 1987c. "Pareto Efficient and Optimal Taxation and the New Welfare Economics." In Alan J. Auerbach and Martin Feldstein, eds., *Handbook on Public Economics.* Amsterdam: Elsevier Science Publishers.

_____. 1987d. "Technological Change, Sunk Costs, and Competition." *Brookings Papers on Economic Activity: Microeconomics* 3:883–947.

_____. 1988a. "Economic Organization, Information, and Development." In H. Chenery and T.N. Srinivasan, eds., *Handbook of Development Economics.* Amsterdam: Elsevier Science Publishers.

_____. 1988b. *Economics of the Public Sector.* Second edition. New York: W.W. Norton Publishers.

_____. 1988c. "On the Relevance or Irrelevance of Public Financial Policy." In K.J. Arrow and M.J. Boskin, eds., *The Economics of Public Debt.* Houndmills, Basingstoke, Hampshire: Macmillan.

_____. 1989a. "On the Economic Role of the State." In A. Heertje, ed., *The Economic Role of the State.* Oxford: Basil Blackwell and Bank Insinger de Beaufort NV.

_____. 1989b. "Imperfect Information in the Product Market." In *Handbook of Industrial Organization.* Volume 1. Amsterdam: Elsevier Science Publishers.

_____. 1989c. "Markets, Market Failures and Development." *American Economic Review* 79(2):197–203.

_____. 1990. "Banks as Social Accountants and Screening Devices and the General Theory of Credit Rationing." *Greek Economic Review* 12(Autumn):85–118. Forthcoming in A. Courakis and C. Goodhart, eds., *Essays in Monetary Economics in Honor of Sir John Hicks.* Oxford: Oxford University Press.

____. 1991a. "The Economic Role of the State: Efficiency and Effectiveness." In T.P. Hardiman and M. Mulreany, eds., *Efficiency and Effectiveness in the Public Domain*. Dublin: Institute of Public Administration.

____. 1991b. "Symposium on Organizations and Economics." *Journal of Economic Perspectives* 5(1):15–24.

____. 1992. "Rethinking the Economic Role of the State: Publicly Provided Private Goods." Lecture delivered at University Pompeu Fabra, Barcelona, November 15.

____. 1993a. "Comment on 'Towards a Counter-Counter-Revolution in Development Theory' Krugman." In *Proceedings of the Annual World Bank Conference on Development Economics*. Washington, D.C.: World Bank.

____. 1993b. *Economics*. New York: W.W. Norton Publishers.

____. 1993c. "Perspectives on the Role of Government Risk-Bearing within the Financial Sector." In Mark S. Sniderman, ed., *Government Risk Bearing*. Norwell, Mass.: Kluwer Academic Publishers.

____. 1994a. "The Role of the State in Financial Markets." In *Proceedings of the Annual World Bank Conference on Development Economics 1993*. Washington, D.C.: World Bank.

____. 1994b. *Whither Socialism*. Cambridge, Mass.: MIT Press.

____. 1995. "The Theory of International Public Goods and the Architecture of International Organizations." Paper presented to the Third Meeting of the High level Group on Development Strategy and Management of the Market Economy, Helsinki, July 8–10.

____. 1996. "Some Lessons From the Asian Miracle." World Bank Research Observer 11(2):151–178.

Stiglitz, J.E. and M. Uy. 1996. "Financial Markets, Public Policy, and the East Asian Economic Miracle." *World Bank Research Observer*.11(2):249–76.

Stiglitz, J.E. and A. Weiss. 1981. "Credit Rationing in Markets with Imperfect Information." *American Economic Review* 71(3):393–410.

____. 1986. "Credit Rationing and Collateral." In Jeremy Edwards, J. Franks, C. Mayer and S. Schaefer, eds., *Recent Developments in Corporate Finance*. New York: Cambridge University Press.

____. 1992. "Asymmetric Information in Credit Markets and Its Implications for Macroeconomics." *Oxford Economic Papers* 44(April):694–724.

Tiebout, C.M. 1956. "A Pure Theory of Local Expenditures." *Journal of Political Economy* 64(5):416–24.

Tobin, J. 1970. "On Limiting the Domain of Inequality." *Journal of Law and Economics* 13(2):263–77.

Wade, Robert. 1990. *Governing the Market: Economic Theory and the Role of the Government in East Asian Industrialization*. Princeton: Princeton University Press.

Williamson, O. 1975. *Markets and Hierarchies*. New York: The Free Press.

World Bank. 1993. *The East Asian Miracle: Economic Growth and Public Policy*. New York: Oxford University Press.

Wolf, Charles. 1988. *Markets or Governments: Choosing Between Imperfect Alternatives*. Cambridge, Mass.: MIT Press.

Zodrow, George, ed. 1983. *Local Provision of Public Services: The Tiebout Model after Twenty-Five Years*. New York: Harcourt Brace Jovanovich.

4

The Future of Planning in
Market Economies

EDMOND MALINVAUD AND
MUSTAPHA K. NABLI

In this chapter we will look closely at planning institutions
intended to promote the long-run performance of the economy.
Planning institutions inform public opinion about long-term
prospects. They provide the country with frameworks for designing
and announcing policies or reforms. They offer guidelines for
government intervention and references for private
decision-making. Also, they often play a monitoring role within the
public sector, focusing on the overall efficiency of economic
decisions made by public agents.

The institutional nature of planning that we discuss traditionally
meant in the context of market economies. The chapter will thus
concern not where long-term decisions are made, but rather where
the economic rationale for alternative options is scrutinized before
decisions are made, where long-term views and projections are
prepared and where resulting programmes are explained. We examine the subject in broad terms, leaving much room for variations
among national institutional structures. The substance of development strategies was discussed in chapter 2 of this volume and will
not be considered here except in reference to activities for which

planning is particularly important. But we will survey, again in broad terms, the methods available for the study of long-term options and the respective usefulness of these methods.

FUNCTIONS OF PLANNING

The recent literature on growth and development has focused on the role of institutions in explaining variations in economic performance and growth rates. These institutions can be seen essentially as instruments and mechanisms devised to deal with market failures, on the one hand, and to mitigate government failures on the other. In this chapter we develop the idea that planning can be viewed from this perspective—as a valuable institutional instrument for market economies. So considered, planning is neither the powerful apparatus that some had entertained to build in the past, nor the useless and even detrimental superstructure that others have vilified.[1] Further, we will not suggest a new role for planning. Rather, we will interpret the experience of planning in countries where it has played a positive role as that of an institutional framework for dealing with government and market failures.

The domain

It would make no sense here to focus on a system of pure laissez-faire or full government control of the economy. Neither of the two is feasible. No country has ever restricted the economic role of the state so much that it would be concerned with only the legal and judiciary preconditions for the functioning of markets. The political concern for redistribution, development of infrastructure and many other objectives has everywhere involved a great deal of public intervention. At the other extreme, the pure command economy has failed as a system because it could not really be implemented, even apart from its lack of efficiency. Too much leeway *de facto* remains at the various stages of transmission of orders in large human organizations for a fully centralized economic system to exist. The proper domain of study here is the vast intermediate range of systems sometimes loosely referred to as "mixed economies". But we need not be more precise; the chapter is meant to be meaningful for all countries, because in all countries there are markets, and governments play a direct part in all economies.

In each country, however, or in each region endowed with a good deal of decision-making autonomy, there is a well-defined economic system, and the functions devoted to planning must be correspondingly shaped. The chapter must therefore be read in various contexts. But it is intended to be relevant even where a minimalist view of planning is held.

Many features of a society may influence the type of functions devoted to planning. More or less emphasis may be placed on consensus building. The desired degree of information exchange may vary, particularly if it occurs between agents who are competing with each other; coordination between government agencies may be more or less stressed; more or less reliance may be placed on government regulations; the public productive sector may be more or less important; economic and technical education may be more or less advanced; and so on. But in every country some institutional structures and processes are useful for enhancing the overall efficiency of decentralized economic decisions. We focus on this common core.

Planning in government

The concerns of planning in the context of mitigating government failures can be seen at three levels: the efficiency of decentralized non-market processes that allocate resources within the government sector, the long-term feasibility and sustainability of policies and the enhancement of credibility.[2]

The theories of bureaucracy and public choice show that economic efficiency criteria are often not the main determinants of decisions. Thus it is essential that within the government bureaucracy there be institutional structures and processes concerned with efficiency. A planning institution is of course not meant to replace the political process, nor to act as a central decision-maker within the bureaucracy. Rather, it must be in charge of efficiency-enhancing activities so as to mitigate government failures.

The sustainability of macroeconomic policies, as related to public debt accumulation and foreign debt accumulation, is a major preoccupation everywhere. Long-term forecasting and explorations of debt, including with respect to public social security programmes, are important for managing the public sector and as useful information for the private sector. Of course, this activity is usually part of the domain of interest of any ministry of finance or treasury. But the perspective of a planning institution is specific in that it takes a longer-term view and deals with inter-temporal choice and arbitrage between generations. It is not by chance that planning ministries have been the main initiators of reforms in many developing countries. They are usually carrying out exercises to assess the sustainability and feasibility of policies.

Planning provides a useful framework for announcing long-term government policies. More credibility is achieved through planning, particularly if policies and choices are subject to "concertation" with the private sector (see below) and are validated by some political process such as a debate in parliament. The aim, then, is to mitigate the tendency of the political process to focus on short-term considerations and contingencies. A question is often raised as to why policy-makers should accept a planning framework that limits their discretionary power and commits them over the medium term. But at issue is an institutional set-up, like a constitution, whose objective is to improve the management of society. Imposing medium- and long-term commitments on policy-makers may be viewed as a choice that society has made.

Returning to the first efficiency-enhancing concern, we observe that in any industrial economy and any developing country a significant chunk of resources is not allocated according to the market mechanism. Whether it is through a central bureaucracy, a regionally decentralized bureaucracy or through public enterprises and agencies, economic decisions are made involving between one-quarter and one-half of GDP. Given the importance of these government activities, they are decentralized through a large number of institutions. Resource allocation decisions within the public sector are made mostly by bureaucratic and political processes. But these processes are subject to rent seeking, to non-economic optimization and to other distortions.

Planning institutions improve efficiency within the public sector by providing coordination and coherency. Indeed, whereas strong arguments may be needed to justify cooperation between agents acting in a competitive market, it seems clear that there is scope for such activities when public agents are not subject to market discipline and profit maximization incentives. Such a role is more significant when there are strong interactions between sectoral government activities. As shown by Crémer and Crémer (1993), theoretical support for these functions can be found from the theory of teams, whereby homogenizing the information set between different public agencies can lead to more efficient outcomes. It can also be found from game theory that coordination and cooperation may lead to more efficient outcomes than can uncoordinated Nash equilibrium solutions.

The need to coordinate public investments is seen in a number of convincing cases. Investment programmes in primary and secondary education must be consistent with those in higher education—and those in education with those in vocational training. Investment programmes in transport infrastructures must be coordinated with those in productive activities (industry, tourism, agriculture) or in urban development and environmental protection. The importance of land planning is overwhelming in this respect. Multiple claims are often made on given zones for urban development, agriculture, other production activities and preservation of the environment. Investment programmes in infrastructure for production also must be coordinated, especially when they are carried out mostly by public institutions. The development of a tourism zone must be fully coordinated with the supply of utilities, including water, electricity, telecommunications and transportation. The same issues apply to industrial zones.

Other examples show that more than simple coordination is needed. Efficient choices between alternative uses of resources also must be found in order to answer relevant questions. Is it acceptable to allocate 5 per cent or 7 per cent of GDP to health compared with 3 per cent or 5 per cent for vocational training? Should we allocate 2 per cent of GDP for rural roads compared with 4 per cent for improving roads in the cities?

Answering such questions requires more than what can be directly achieved by cost-benefit analyses (discussed in the last part of this chapter). Negotiation and consultations at the national level, which are an essential part of planning processes, help in determining acceptable social choices. These processes involve comparing projects not only within an activity but also across sectors. Is it more efficient for a society to invest in a dam that costs $200 million or to build an airport? This is the type of question that a planner addresses, but it is one that neither the agriculture department nor the transport department will ask. Individual departments are expected to push for their projects, maximizing their share of government expenditure.

Planning institutions also contribute by insulating government from pressure groups. It is well known that special interests play a significant role in allocating resources, or designing and changing regulations and policies. At the firm or the industry level, trade or industrial policies, regulations relating to competition or the environment and other types of policies are subject to continuous pressure for change and adaptation to please specific interests. Regulators may become captive to the regulated, and politicians tend to cater to these interests. Even in the context of macroeconomic management there is scope for specific interest groups to influence exchange rate and monetary policy.

It is normal that such influence exists in an open and democratic country. Society must, however, not become hostage to such interests. Its institutional structure must contain centers that are not close to interest groups and guard against excessive influence. Planning institutions are part of that set-up. (See also chapter 6, which stresses the role of professional expertise and personal sincerity of government bureaucrats.) World Bank (1993) shows that one of the factors explaining the success of east Asian countries has been their ability to insulate decision-making and government intervention from excessive interest-group influence. This ability stems from various parts of the bureaucracy, but primarily from planning institutions.

Information processing for the private economy

It is not only with respect to public decisions that a valuable service may be offered by institutions insulated from interest groups and studying how to improve the long-run performance of the economy.

Such services should also be provided to private decision-makers. We need not insist on the service to public opinion and citizens when, in the context of planning, a consistent vision of the future, with alternative scenarios, is proposed to the nation. This is essential. But it does not raise problems different from those concerning the examination of public policies, except for the simplicity requirements of any information meant to be widely diffused. The focus of our attention will therefore be on the service to enterprises and other private institutions.

Long-term decisions, whether made by private or by public agents, always involve large uncertainties, which are more troublesome the more decisions become irreversible (and every long-term decision has at least some degree of irreversibility). Thus, having as much information as possible when deciding has a high value.

We now turn to the importance of information and to the role of public planning for gathering, processing and diffusing information. This aspect was already presented in the preceding chapter, among many others. Since the main theme was market failures, as well as limitations on government, the question was more to bring about all elements to be considered when choosing an economic system, than to know how to run a given system. In particular, the extent of public infrastructures, public ownership, public regulations and fiscal interference in the price system was at stake, whereas here we will either take an economic system as given or ask how the government and public opinion can be best informed when contemplating a change. More importantly, we want to think about the information of private agents and about the services they receive from planning institutions.

Private agents may get information from many sources. First and foremost, there is information about their specialization: their techniques of production or exchange, the needs of their customers and so on. In most cases each agent is best placed for knowing about the changes that they must take into account. But not always. With farming, for example, technical stations everywhere are experimenting and diffusing new and more productive practices.

Second in importance is information on market trends, to which we will pay particular attention, considering its real importance and the prominent place given in economic theory to the information conveyed by markets. Third, we must not ignore the other potential sources of information that each decision unit can rely on: the economic and technical press, business or trade associations, courses given by technical schools or universities, government agencies and so on. Finally, we consider the information obtained from planning institutions.

The productivity of an economy depends on the adequacy of these diversified sources. Clearly, the range is wide: from the United States at one extreme, with its developed market system, its rich set of private institutions and its widespread technical and economic education, to a large number of developing countries at the opposite extreme. Also, given this variety of conditions, the best institutional arrangement must be found in each country; what is thought to be best in the United States will not necessarily meet the needs of another country.

Building and maintaining public institutions in charge of gathering, processing and diffusing information is needed particularly where the education of producers and traders is low, and where private sources of information are lacking or conveying inadequate messages about technical knowledge and economic trends. It is with respect to such a diversified background that the following analysis must be interpreted.

In order to sort out issues, we first consider how advantage can be taken of the information conveyed by prices and remuneration rates established in markets. It is appropriate to begin with this question, because critics of planning have often stressed the transmission of information through markets, from which all private agents can benefit. This transmission itself is not a serious objection to good planning because nothing prevents planners from using, at least as well as others, the information transmitted. If transmission was reliable and complete and if decoding was simple, planning would of course be easy—and in hypothetical limit cases, unnecessary.

Markets do transmit some information. But they are particularly insufficient in this respect for making long-term decisions: the transmission is not always reliable, messages transmitted often require expertise to be correctly interpreted and some information is not transmitted. Observation and common sense show these deficiencies; the advanced theory of general equilibrium also provides explanations.

Markets are particularly efficient and reliable for giving information about current trends in the balance between supply and demand. In most cases a falling price reveals sluggish demand. When the fall is due instead to rapid technical progress, it is signalled by an increase in quantities traded. Current production decisions are thus usually well-guided by information coming from markets.

But if the period of production is not short, too much reliance on current market information often leads to mistakes, waste and losses. The persistence of the long-known hog-cycle and the glut of office buildings in large cities around 1990, among other experiences, demonstrate this possibility.

For long-term investment decisions the deficiency of markets in transmitting the most useful information is particularly clear. It is sometimes said that financial markets transmit this information as well as is feasible. A systematic confidence in the market system is required to accept this assertion. We hold that it deserves close scrutiny. First, financial markets are not developed everywhere. Even where they are, they give information only on what is directly related to the values of traded securities. Long-term effective interest rates give information on the forecast of future nominal rates (see, however, Malkiel, 1987) and on risk premia affecting various kinds of bonds. Values of shares give information on the expected profitability of large corporations. Quotations on financial markets quickly reflect the good or bad fortunes of companies. Institutions that developed around stock exchanges contribute to the diffusion of information on the activity and performance of large enterprises; they thus play a role in monitoring managers of these enterprises.

But there is a large gap between such financial information and information that is most needed about future prices and remuneration rates when deciding on physical investments. Financial markets do not give reliable estimates of important indicators such as the real long-term cost of capital, since they do not estimate the course of inflation (bonds indexed on the price level are rare). Markets also do not give an estimate of the future real cost of labour. On two major ingredients of the teaching of economics, investors must either form their own forecast or look at forecasts of others—who are in no better position.

We must recognize that most long-term investments have unique features. Evaluating the future costs of running them and future returns requires a detailed analysis involving a number of components. For some, investors are best placed to judge. But for others, specifically those that concern the overall environment in which future activity will take place, experts and other economic agents often have more knowledge. In order to be most useful, data on this environment must be given in a form directly useful for the investor's project, rather than in a form requiring inference from other indicators. In particular, the information content of market indicators may be obscure (see below), while there is useful information in other, more convenient, forms.

Demographic projections are important, particularly for investment in education or the construction of dwellings, as well as for reforms of (private and public) pension schemes and their regulation. Information on natural resources matters to farmers and urban planners. Diffusion of knowledge about technological potentialities and their likely evolution may be made by specific professions, where they are already well developed, but often has to come from the government, particularly in developing countries. Clearly, such direct information is much more useful than what could be inferred from markets.

As for purely economic conditions, many investors are not well placed to collect all of the relevant information, even that on markets that directly concern them: the chances of a boom in demand or the risk of satiation, the entry of new national and foreign competitors or the projects of existing competitors. Once they collect all of these elements, they still would like to know the trends in foreign prices for their output. In the end they will have to form their own expectations about the prices of the products or services that they sell.

But in order to make decisions about their investments, they will need to be informed about future input prices. Thus projections concerning the evolution of the main input prices (in particular, energy and raw materials), wage rates and interest rates will be necessary. Such medium- and long-term projections are not directly given by markets. In fact, the available information comes from various sources, all of which take advantage of past observations. Time series of real prices and real rates show whether a present price or rate is exceptionally high or low with respect to past trends. Econometric analysis estimates the significance of some main determinants of supply and demand, including some determinants whose evolution is expected to take a special course. Experts may know that important and permanent changes are occurring in some relevant markets. It is useful to synthesize all such information, for instance, in the form of projections, preferably complemented by an assessment of their degree of uncertainty.

In advanced market economies a whole service industry has developed for providing such information to firms. But even there public administrations must offer collective services. Obvious reasons explain why the bulk of statistical information is publicly collected, processed and diffused. Weaker but similar reasons apply to the public provision of basic information from which private consulting firms may derive individualized information services for their clients. In all countries where the information industry is neither developed nor efficient, public provision usefully extends to more specialized services than the most widely needed projections. In this way planning institutions are called on to process information for the private economy.

It is often argued that projections and information provided by public planning institutions may be subject to political influence and lack the objectivity of privately provided information. But while such risk exists, it is not inherent to planning. The issue is how to create an institutional design that insulates planning institutions from undue political influence (we return to this issue in the third section).

The role of planning studies

The functions of planning just discussed, whether they relate to government activity or deal with providing information to private enterprises and institutions, or more generally aim at informing public opinion, are usually carried out by conducting prospective studies with alternative scenarios. The point was just argued while attention was focussed on provision of information to the productive sector. But it applies more generally, as can easily be understood by consideration of long-term policies. In most domains long-term concerns should motivate government action, and good long-term views should inspire policy choices. A full survey could begin with the sectors in which public involvement is widespread. It would then progressively move to domains in which private agents play a more dominant role, but cannot be ignored by public policy. We will look briefly at a few landmarks along such a survey.

Investments in education must be properly allocated. Finely localized demographic projections are needed for making decisions on basic education, in relation to forecasts and plans concerning urban and rural development. Also, some projections about future trends in employment and skill levels are needed for vocational training and higher levels of formal education.

Investments in infrastructure for transport and for urban and rural development must be similarly planned according to prospective maps of housing and industrial settlements, as well as flows of people and goods. The horizon must be two or three decades ahead, particularly for land appropriation and urban regulation.

Technical upgrading of the population, notably the farming population, requires proper networks of research centers, training stations and the like. These must be considered along with long-term prospects for the education system, public infrastructure and agricultural and industrial specialization.

Future specialization in production and international trade is too important a stake for public opinion and government to be indifferent. Not only must it be taken into account in many decisions, but policies must also have some possibility to act upon it (as discussed in chapter 6). A potential comparative advantage might be jeopardized by public action geared to other purposes. Or it might remain ineffective because of lack of public involvement, for instance, because private agents would then not be in a position to invest enough to reach the minimum size required to take advantage of it. Such potentialities and risks must be carefully evaluated, which requires independent studies.

Certainly, the concept of public involvement in the future specialization of the productive system must no longer be as simple-minded
as it was when planning was fashionable. The government in a
market economy has less control over this specialization than was
once thought. Experiences have shown that large public firms seldom succeed in manufacturing industries and that building such
firms in order to gain or to maintain market shares is likely to fail.
But public involvement may be less ambitious, less direct and more
successful—less ambitious, because it no longer claims to have
chosen definitive output targets, even for those industries that retain
its attention; less direct, because public action may bear only on
some conditions required for the birth and growth of private firms;
and more successful, because the proper set of incentives will have
been found, which is seldom the case with large public enterprises
producing for the market. With this new and more realistic concept
of industrial policies, planning studies deserve still more attention,
since they have to be more sophisticated.

Of the many ways open to useful public involvement, a particularly significant one concerns research and development, which may
be, to a large extent, directly assumed by public institutions. Of
course, this activity is exposed to large uncertainties—it may bring
highly profitable results or may fail to discover or implement
anything that is economically worthwhile. Thus each country must
decide how to invest in research and development, realizing also that
part of this activity is directly connected to technical education.
Experience shows that research and development programmes generating successful commercial results share certain features: "They
are insulated from the demands of distributional politics, they
subject potential projects to rigorous technical and economic evaluation, and they recognize that product specifications must be developed with an eye toward manufacturability and a balance between
product performance and cost that will be acceptable to commercial
customers" (US Government, 1994). In order to realize such features, programmes must be monitored at various levels and be
informed by appropriate studies. Indeed, before strategic decisions
concerning the main research and development programmes are
made, careful planning studies, which are the best protection against

an incorrect appreciation of costs and chances of success, must be carried out.

Public finance also deserves long-term analysis. This is becoming more clear as problems with social security become more widespread and more difficult. Often magnified by demographic prospects, these problems also follow from changes in behaviour, which may be induced by changes in rules for entitlements to benefits or for contributions to financing social security systems.

We now turn to the kinds of study required for diffusing relevant information and for adequately preparing public decisions. The foregoing survey stresses the role of long-term views and projections. It must be supplemented in several respects.

First, discussing projections conveys the notion of an exogenously given environment that is independent of planning. Although this may be the case for some important components, such as the main demographic trends, exogeneity does not apply to the full information content of planning projections. More precisely, we can say that most users will find in those projections data that they take as being independent of their own actions. But we must realize that these data concern not only the overall environment of the future economic activity of the country but also the actions of other economic agents. In other words, in order to draw up useful projections, planners must collect a wide range of information, which may be grouped into two categories: information about truly exogenous components and information about individual plans of economic agents. This second category is more complex, because individual plans are "interactive"—each relies on assumptions about the activity of other agents, as well as about truly exogenous elements.

The interactive nature of the information to be gathered is the main reason for stressing the importance of putting together the knowledge, ideas and prospects of a wide array of people, many representing large groups. The term "concertation", coined by French planners, conveys well the image of a gathering in which each participant arrives not only with knowledge that is useful for others and with the expectation to learn, but also ready to revise somewhat his or her intentions depending on what is learned. This image is idealized compared with what can be accomplished in practice. But it nevertheless contains an element of truth. Actually, such an interactive exchange of information often proceeds in two stages— among public actors themselves and then among public and private actors. It is particularly valuable when there are strong interactions, not mediated by markets, among decisions of various actors, for instance when a government has to decide about public investments, about regulations and so on.

Second, to speak of only projections would be to ignore the studies more closely related to public decision-making, all of the medium-term or long-term policy analyses and all of the evaluations of alternative microeconomic projects. Those are, of course, particularly important components of planning, and will be the focus of attention in the fourth part of this chapter. As we will see, macroeconomic projections and macroeconomic policy analyses are made in close association, though this feature need not be more fully examined at this stage.

Cost-benefit analyses of microeconomic projects deserve attention here, because they are not made at the central level as are projections. Like those working for private agents, economists in charge of evaluating public projects should find in planning projections the macroeconomic information they need. This information concerns not only the speed and composition of overall economic growth, but also the main indicators of prices and remuneration rates, which are exogenous with respect to the choice between projects or alternative implementations of the same project. As we will see, the need for indicators often extends to items that are particularly difficult to value, such as exhaustible resources (including environmental resources) or improvements in security. Arguments will then be presented in favour of horizontal consistency between the values given to such indicators in different applications.

Third, projections, as well as policy or cost-benefit analyses, may lead users to underrate the importance of future uncertainties. This concern has been used as an argument against planning. The argument would hold only if there were better ways of making decisions under uncertainty than those that can be followed with planning. Such is not the case. Indeed, planning was often promoted by economists or government officials who wanted to improve the public decision-making process, which was quite sloppy in dealing with uncertainty. These people did not claim that planning would remove uncertainty, though some argued that it would reduce it somewhat. Rather, they insisted on introducing more rationality in the process. One of their contributions was to highlight "contingency planning"—the idea that decisions should not bear directly on actions but rather on "strategies", which predict how future actions will be affected by what will have then been learned about the uncertain world.

It is not easy to introduce a more lucid and rational attitude towards the treatment of uncertainty within the machinery of public administrations and private enterprises. Planners have a direct role to play in this respect within the public sector. But they should also be careful when processing and diffusing information not to mask the uncertainty contained in this information.

Experience shows that it is impossible to make reliable quantitative estimates of uncertainty of information. In some cases it is possible and valuable to provide measures of the effect of one source of uncertainty—measures that in all likelihood underestimate the true overall degree of uncertainty. Examples include random sampling errors in statistics (but not errors coming from other sources) and variances of the forecasts made from an econometric model, but under the false assumption that the model is exact. Thus the degree of uncertainty must be assessed in qualitative terms. In some cases ex post comparisons between forecasts and realizations may suffice. But more often one will have to simply spell out the various sources of uncertainty.

Still, rare events, extending beyond identified uncertainties, may occur, which would greatly perturb the economy and the effects of the chosen strategy. Such events might be major political or social disorders, which would force a full change in the line of action, or they might be external shocks, such as the sharp increases in the price of oil in 1973 and 1980, again changing future prospects. The possibility of such occurrences cannot be fully ignored, but dwelling on them would probably serve little purpose.

PAST EXPERIENCE

In the past decades we have learned a good deal about the potential of public planning and the processes that make it work. But this experience is not easy to assess and summarize. Moreover, what should *not* be done is better characterized than what should be done. Elsewhere in this chapter we examine mainly the positive side of the experience. The negative side, which is well worth remembering in order to avoid repeating well-identified mistakes, must be briefly considered here.

A simple assessment consists of saying that past mistakes of economic planning came, at different times and places, from the association of planning with wrong choices concerning the structures of the economy or the long-term policies to be followed, at other times and places, from an overestimation of what planning could really achieve in a decentralized economy, whose long-term choices were not otherwise misguided. One might argue that, in the first case also, overestimation of the potentialities of planning was at the root of the wrong choices. Distinction between the two cases is, however, worth maintaining because they occurred in different countries and because experience with them suggests different kinds of conclusions.

The Soviet command economy is the clearest case in which planning was associated with widespread public ownership of the productive sector and a hierarchical decision-making structure. One may quarrel over details in deciding on a historical verdict for this system. One robust conclusion, however, stands: whatever the performance may have been after the initial institution of the system, transmission of information and incentives subsequently worked to undermine economic performance. Either the system collapsed because of its increasing inefficiency, or standards of living eventually started to decline.

Such a verdict was reached in advance of the collapse by some economists working in the countries concerned, such as Kantorovitch (1965) and Kornai (1980). It stems from the lack of permanent viability of a system relying on systematic centralization, without any guidance or sanctions coming from market prices. Planning, which first requires gathering, processing and diffusing

relevant information, and then reacting efficiently to this information, failed because economic incentives did not reward the early
detection of relevant information. On the contrary, it induced distortions in whatever transmission was requested, because economic
incentives again were not adequate. Two lessons must be remembered. First, an economy is too complex an organism to be efficiently
run under full centralization. Second, neither faithful and alert
exchange of information nor appropriate decisions can be expected
if agents are not induced to act accordingly. There are incentives
other than purely economic ones, but they have little effectiveness
in comparison and can be relied upon only to a limited extent.

These lessons also concern less centralized systems, which may
have given too large a scope to the public productive sector, extending it far beyond infrastructure and collective services. On the other
hand, we should not push the argument too far—there is no clear
verdict rejecting a moderate share of public ownership in enterprises. Private ownership may lead to a more active search for
enhancing productivity because of the "hard budget constraint", but
also to less information dissemination and to the neglect of positive
or negative externalities.

Are there different kinds of lessons to be learned from the now-
prevailing diagnosis about choosing between inward- and outward-
looking development strategies? Countries that chose the outward
option performed much better in the past few decades. On the whole
they have given a smaller role to planning. Let us accept this reverse
association, although cases like Japan and the Republic of Korea
show that it was far from systematic. What is the explanation? How
should a country avoid repeating the same kind of mistake?

We must recognize that forecasters were often mistaken and that
the general mood was pessimistic about the prospects for exporting
manufactures from developing countries in the 1950s. But two other
reasons also explain the preference for an inward-looking strategy:
a deep dislike of the market economy or a strong preference for
national independence and national control over the economy. Both
reasons led to a more embracing role for planning.

Clearly, a larger degree of openness to the world economy reduces
national independence and makes national control less easily

achieved and less effective. In full awareness of loosing some of the gains from international exchanges, a country is entitled to choose national independence. But the choice may be the wrong one if it is made on the basis of ignorance or underestimation of the large gains that would result from better integration in the world economy, or if it is made on the basis of an overestimation of what the inward-looking strategy can achieve. For example, attempts to build protected heavy industries in small countries turned out to be much more costly than expected, because the protected firms could not reach the minimum efficient size nor the quality of control required by modern technology.

In the years following World War II many economists, particularly those in western Europe, overestimated the potential of planning in decentralized economies. The clearest case was the Norwegian Ragnar Frisch, whose research from the early 1920s had been quite productive and who had been influential as one of the few founders of the Econometric Society. A devoted democrat, Frisch became an active promoter of planning in his country and elsewhere, including in developing countries, which he did not see as essentially different from others. From the late 1940s, he geared most of his research towards the conception and operation of economic planning.[3]

Frisch had very clear views on the main issues. He carefully distinguished between two problems, which he claimed had to be solved in succession: the selection of the plan and the implementation of the plan. His work concerned mainly the selection problem, probably because he never knew exactly how to attack implementation. For selection he expressed great confidence in the techniques of mathematical programming: the plan had to be the optimum solution of a carefully defined model. His research addressed at length the three questions that planners, acting as technicians, would have to answer: how to elicit a preference ordering from political authorities, how to specify the mathematical programme and how to compute the solution. He made concrete proposals in each case. But he was disappointed to see that, even in Norway, no attempt was made to introduce his planning methods into the administration of the country (more common macroeconomic models were used in

Norway by his former students working for the government on short-term forecasting and budgeting).

Although extreme, the case of Frisch is typical of the difficulties faced by economists advocating extensive planning, prepared wholly within public administrations.[4] In retrospect, these economists were overestimating their abilities to gather and process the most relevant information, to elicit from the people and politicians the correct choices among conflicting aims and to propose efficient ways for implementing the calculated solutions. These challenges, of course, also confront any central public decision aimed at improving economic performance. But they will be less exacting the simpler is the decision and the better understood and better accepted it is by those who will have to implement it.

Lessons from this past experience were progressively learned and explain why the functions of planning are presented here somewhat differently from what was common 40 years ago.

It may be worthwhile, now, to reassess how economists serving as planners should view their role. Planners must avoid being too ambitious because they must simultaneously meet the three challenges posed by the collection of information, the elicitation of political choices and the implementation of public decisions. Planners must avoid being too sophisticated because they must be able to persuade those who will have to use the information, make the choices or implement the decisions. Planners must therefore explain the reasoning they used for reaching their assessments, which cannot be perceived as coming from black boxes. But saying so is not pretending that economists working for planning have only a secondary role to play. Quite the contrary: the same lucidity, which should lead us to recognize the difficulties of the task, also brings to the fore what may happen if the task is not performed. In the middle of versatility or ignorance, and sometimes a lack of good will, planners must stand fast on a few well-established assessments and previsions, as well as on a few proposals whose long-run effects are very likely to be positive. They are thus guardians of economic efficiency for the public interest.

INSTITUTIONAL SET-UP

In the preceding discussion we hardly used the word "plan", emphasizing that the functions of planning should not necessarily be associated with the elaboration of periodic plans. Indeed, one can discuss the institutional set-up through three aspects of planning: the planning process, the planning institutions and the plans.

The planning process is the set of rules and procedures through which the planning functions are carried out. Whether it is collecting, processing and diffusing information; concertation and public consensus building; enhancing coordination and cooperation among economic agents or participating in decision-making for public investment and policy, participants must follow a clear set of rules and procedures. This is the complete institutional set-up of planning, which includes rules of different origin that may be constitutional, legislative, regulatory or may come from customs or simple practice. We now turn our attention mainly to planning institutions, which are entities that carry out planning functions. Afterwards, we will consider the role of a plan as an instrument or vehicle for planning.

There are many possible ways to locate planning functions within the public structures of a country. Indeed, a close survey of existing arrangements shows their diversity. This state of affairs is easily understood. Almost everywhere public institutions are the products of a long evolution, which shaped present structures and the respective attributes of those working in these structures. In other words, each country must decide on the character of its planning institutions and their degree of decentralization. But in order to ensure that the planning functions are well served, some general principles and considerations must be kept in mind.

A clear prerequisite for efficiency is an intimate collaboration between planning institutions and operational units. The simple creation of a planning service may not make a significant change if the above prerequisite is not met. Because they are not well integrated with the information and decision processes, studies of a planning bureau may appear to be purely academic. This is well understood in the private economy, where processing information for specific purposes is most often done in close contact with the corresponding decision-making authority, for instance within the planning service or planning directorate of a large firm.

Many government departments have, in addition to operational units, a unit in charge of evaluating the actions of the department and studying options open to it. Projections, policy analysis, control of cost-benefit work and diffusion of information then naturally fall to this unit, which is otherwise involved in the policies of the department.

There are other ways of performing the planning function, in particular, because there is large scope for decentralizing some of the functions. Prospective studies are made in universities and in private or public institutes. The elaboration of a policy may occur under the leadership of a parliamentary committee, a ministerial authority, a group of banks or large industrial firms, a trade association or a trade union. The public planning institutions can increase their efficiency and improve their professional know-how by continuously interacting with and subcontracting to the private sector.

Whatever the institutional set-up, a transversal function of planning should not be forgotten and deserves particular mention. It has three inter-related purposes: ensuring that proper attention is paid to long-term concerns, providing technical assistance for long-term studies, and keeping and updating ethical norms for planners when they deal with matters that are closely related to those belonging to the responsibility of politicians.

As is well known, most politicians are more concerned about short-term difficulties, problems and prospects than about long-term ones. As a result, long-term studies may be neglected in some government departments. Planners, acting as non-political technicians, must ensure that this is not the case in their domain. They must determine whether the projections, policy studies and cost-benefit analyses that are made are as objective as possible and do not need to be better coordinated. They must determine whether sufficient scrutiny of these studies occurred, with public and private partners, including independent experts. And wherever there are lacunas or deficiencies, they must find ways to correct them.

In many cases those in charge of long-term studies are not trained in the full range of methods available. In all countries such expertise is unevenly distributed. Technical assistance should make up for methodological weakness. It may flow from one office to another, or it may be centrally organized. In their concern for methodological improvements, some planners may even search for alternative methods of analysis and test the performance of a new tool that is suggested. They thus contribute to methodological research.

The work on long-term prospects and policies discussed here serves two kinds of purposes: to inform the general public and all economic agents and to provide the technical basis for public decision-making. This work should be done in close contact with policy-makers and often follows their demands. The distribution of roles between politicians and technicians is clear in principle, but not always evident in practice. Similarly, information about contemplated and not-yet-announced policies should be kept confidential. But the extent of this obligation concerning relevant related information may not be evident. In the long run a country benefits from clear, correct and complied-with norms of conduct on the part of both politicians and technicians in their dealings with each other. Planning agencies and governments must be concerned with the emergence and maturation of such norms, as well as with their implementation. The credibility and objectivity of planning depends on the recognition of this ethical concern.

A relevant question is whether a central planning institution creates more advantages than disadvantages. A good argument in favour can be made along the following lines, particularly where the competence and credibility of a number of public administrations remains to be established. In most countries information will be better processed and prospective studies will be better known and examined if a central institution, with recognized public standing, is involved. The competence and objectivity of such an institution can be achieved, as experience shows. Moral authority, which is required when collective discussions on strategies are undertaken, will also come—especially because the institution in question will not be directly involved in the day-to-day operation and implementation of public policy. Finally, within the public administration assessment of broad public projects and their coordination is, in many cases, best performed at the most central level.

Difficulties with a central planning institution may arise precisely because of its influence. Concerned with mitigating government failures, it may have to fight against institutional obstructions. It should have only advisory functions, with governmental authorities remaining responsible for decisions; but these authorities may feel hindered by public statements coming from the planning institution, particularly when long- and medium-term objectives conflict with short-term considerations. Thus hostility against it may arise.

The occurrence of such difficulties is natural. These are among the problems that democracies are used to solving in the current operation of the distribution of roles between respective powers and administrations. For people who know the benefits of constitutions admitting the multiplicity of roles, accepting the existence of a central planning institution is just a new step along a familiar road. Where it is influential, the institution must, of course, have an ethic of responsible behaviour and avoid magnifying the difficulties when they cannot be fully avoided.

In many countries the elaboration of a plan has become a basic feature of planning. The planning process includes the periodic elaboration and production of a document that establishes the main medium-term objectives and policies of the country. It is important to point out that the elaboration of such a document is not a sine qua non for planning. The various roles and activities described in this chapter do not need to be included in a plan.

But there are some arguments for elaborating a periodic plan. Since it is too costly and possibly counter-productive to continuously carry out concertation among various actors, it is more efficient to run such exercises periodically. On such occasions basic policy choices and challenges should be discussed at the national level and orientations selected. A plan is also a good reference for the various agents as to the medium-term programme of the public sector and the overall objectives of society.

Major criticisms can also be leveled against periodic plans. They tend to become outdated soon after adoption because of unforeseen events and changes. Whether for macroeconomic policies, sectoral policies or public projects, major revisions are commonly needed. And the risk of discarding the whole plan is not far removed! Agents will no longer refer to it for information and a return to short-termism by all will follow. Another criticism of detailed periodic plans concerns the capacity to make well-informed decisions about public projects many years in advance. Such capacity is questioned because of the sheer size of the task and because little reliable information is available about future projects when the plan is elaborated.

The preceding discussion shows that an adequate planning process must include a clear and realistic vision of the functions of the plan. There are good reasons for a strict emphasis on fundamental choices and policies—the plan will then involve only those policies and choices that are subject to the wide ranging debate of the consensus-building process. Is the country embarking on a major and determined liberalization programme? Is the country adopting a strong export-push programme? What are the choices about poverty reduction? What are the objectives for human capital accumulation? What are the major objectives for public finances and the extent of government intervention? The plan must then define the "vision" that will underlie public sector policies and constitute the background for private sector activity.

For public sector activities, particularly investment, the plan can be more specific, but not to the point of including detailed projects and decisions. Only the major choices as to the allocation of resources between activities in the public sector must be specified, as well as the basic policies over the medium and long run.

So conceived, a plan can play its role without being strongly subject to the above criticisms. Moreover, such a plan should be viewed in the overall process, which would include yearly "budgets" or programmes, with revisions of the macroeconomic framework, with a detailed public investment programme and with adjustments of policies. After, say, 3 years of implementation a new round of long-term explorations and assessment of prospects, with a 10- to 15-year perspective, can be carried out. It should lay out the "vision" of the next plan and revise the present one if necessary.

The process and institutional set-up, as outlined here, would make a mixture of periodic planning and continuous assessment, evaluation and adjustment. But the main thrust would be to focus on efficiency-enhancing activities with a long-term perspective.

TECHNIQUES USED IN PLANNING

Some doubts about the usefulness of planning came from the realization that the techniques were less powerful than was once thought. Theoretical reflection showed that, when strictly defined, these techniques depended on fairly strong assumptions. Attempts by theorists to relax the assumptions did not often lead to easy revisions. Simultaneously, practical experience showed that when applied, the techniques were exposed to biases, misuses or distortions, which further undermined the validity of the results.

These serious limitations and pitfalls must be recognized. But for lack of better alternatives similar techniques must be used, although on more restricted domains and with greater circumspection. When the methodology is re-examined from its foundations, a renewed and more modest philosophy emerges. Without presenting a full methodological investigation, we will briefly discuss this philosophy for the two main techniques: macroeconometric projections and cost-benefit analyses.

Prospects of macroeconomic conditions, as well as the expected performance of alternative macroeconomic policies must be studied seriously. For this purpose a number of elements must be taken into account:

- Changes in the economic environment, such as demographic trends, or expectations about the world economy.
- The behavior of agents, who will react to changing economic conditions and policies.
- Consistency requirements imposed by markets and, more generally, by economic interdependence.

To examine the interplay of these elements, there is no better way than to build a model that shows what is known and what is assumed. Defining the model is to say which variables are meant to be endogenous and which exogenous (either instruments of policies or variables that are taken as given and whose values must be found independently). When fully specified, particularly with respect to the values of the parameters first introduced in its definition, the model is ready to determine the impact on endogenous variables of changes in either the environment or policies.

No model ever fits perfectly the uses that it serves. The approximations that it provides with respect to actual trends and reactions of the economy are more or less accurate depending on specific circumstances. This imperfection is unavoidable. Model builders have to try to reduce it as much as they can. Model users must wonder in each case which model at their disposal, if any, is suited to the problems they are facing. They must also know how the models were built, never taking them as black boxes.

The macroeconometric movement took the task of model building very seriously. A precise methodology was developed, which was fully consistent and fairly easy to teach, at least in its principles (see Bodkin, Klein and Marwah, 1991). The methodology was then used widely for macroeconomic planning—for both projections and policy analysis.

Some aspects of the methodology, as typically applied, were disputed. First, the relevant domain of a macroeconometric model, once built, was often overestimated: a short-term model was used for long-term projections, notwithstanding the fact that some of its equations had doubtful validity in the long run; a macroeconomic model was used to estimate the effects of a tax reform, not withstanding the fact that it did not recognize the substitutabilities or incentives with which the reform was likely to interact; and so on. Clearly, planners must learn to be more careful and to resist the temptation of relying on an instrument that happens to be available but was not meant to serve all purposes. This recommendation still holds with respect to large, detailed models, which were built in the past decades in order to extend their domain of relevance, though at the cost of making the instrument more difficult to use.

Second, from its introduction the methodology assumed that, for the estimation of parameters, information was coming only from a sample of aggregate time series obtained in the country studied. Econometric estimation relying on such a sample was often imprecise, judging from the values of the standard deviations or test statistics. The precision was usually weaker still because the model provided only an approximation, whereas econometric theory assumed the model to be an exact expression of the real data-generating process. But information on at least some of the parameters is available either from cross-sectional data or from data collected in other countries. The methodology does not help in taking this valuable extra evidence into account. Thus the information is either ignored or introduced on an ad hoc basis, the validity of which is difficult to assess.

Third, the models did not take into account the change in behaviour that could follow any policy change. This was the Lucas critique (Lucas, 1976). Lucas pointed out that agents are likely to revise their expectations, and therefore their behaviour, when a policy change is announced. Estimation on past time series would not capture this change. Further, this behavioural reaction could not only run counter to the purpose of the policy, but in some cases would make the policy wholly ineffective. This last thesis has been the subject of a good deal of research producing complex results—which cannot be discussed here. But, in general, the potential importance of induced revisions in expectations must be remembered. Unfortunately, characterization of these revisions turns out to be uncertain. Even the credibility of policy announcements—a fuzzy notion—must be considered.

These three difficulties must be taken into account by those in charge of providing objective assessments about future trends or policy effects. Briefly stated, today the task is less mechanical and less sure—it requires more reflection and adaptation than was earlier thought. Correspondingly, the role of macroeconometric models has become relatively less central. These models must no longer be seen as fully responsible for prospective studies, but rather as assisting those in charge: models ensure that the main macroeconomic consistency requirements are taken into account, and their results challenge the economic reasoning of planners and politicians, as well as the orders of magnitude that both might have in mind. Models thus contribute to the professional quality and objectivity of macroeconomic studies. Given this more modest role, models no longer have to be as comprehensive and detailed as was originally claimed.

The proper philosophy with respect to macroeconometric projections is thus based on a few firm principles, but also recognizes the limitations of our knowledge. Information about future socio-economic trends, about the options open to a country and about contemplated national strategies is their purpose. But uncertainty about the future must be acknowledged. A minimum requirement, then, is to provide, for each main aspect of future trends, not a single projection but a few alternative projections, giving an idea of the range of possibilities to which the economy may have to adapt. Alternative policy scenarios must also be identified and made explicit. Objectivity, which is expected from planning institutions, and towards which they are aiming, requires that these projections correctly use the accepted outcome of scientific research, concerning both the methods and the phenomena involved. Where this outcome is particularly uncertain, or where more is assumed, it has to be clearly signalled, possibly with presentation of variants following from different theories or methodological approaches.

The first part of this chapter cited the role of planning in promoting the efficiency of decentralized non-market processes. This requires a method for evaluating the consequences of decentralized decisions. Cost-benefit analysis is such a method. Its scope is obviously wide: the development of public infrastructure or collective services, regulation or pricing of their use, protection of the environment and so on.

Evaluating costs and benefits is a natural way to proceed, at least in order to rationalize the decision-making process, whether or not it also involves majority voting or collective bargaining, in addition to the pure use of government power. At first sight evaluation may seem to be a simple operation, which accountants have accomplished in many fields of activity. But accounting rules, as developed for monitoring the normal activity of private business in industry or trade, are not fully appropriate for public decision-making.

Distinct features that make application of these private accounting rules difficult or inadequate often involve the long or distant time period during which benefits will accrue or costs be borne; the significant external effects or the collective nature of the services provided, which are obvious in some cases but subtle in others; the distributive aspects of the provision of benefits or allocation of costs, with the resulting scope for intervention of specific interest groups; and the difficulty of evaluating some qualitative benefits or costs, such as beauty of the environment or health of human beings.

Because of these distinct features, the methodology of cost-benefit analysis in the public sector had to be based on economic theory. The conclusions of this theory then had to be translated into operational evaluation rules to be applied over a wide range of cases. Because covering the whole field would take us too far, we will focus attention here only on the evaluation of public sector investment projects. We will moreover sketch only the evolution of ideas and practices.

Simply stated, the theoretical construction inspiring the rules diffused in the 1950s was built by considering an ideal standard case: that of a new project that could be added to an inter-temporal programme for the allocation of resources. The reference programme was assumed to provide a Pareto-optimal allocation, ignoring the feasibility of the project, and the project was assumed to be small (marginal). The net discounted value of implementing the project was then supposed to be computed from the system of discounted prices supporting the reference programme—the project would be implemented only if the net discounted value was positive.

Translation of this theoretical criterion into an operational rule was direct. The only important point was to say how the supporting system of discounted prices had to be found. Prevailing market prices were said to provide a basis, but one that was subject to lacunas and distortions because of market imperfections. Suitable corrections had to be made on the interest rate, the exchange rate and some other prices. Estimates had to be found for some benefits and costs ignored in the system of market prices. One could then speak of a system of shadow prices. Manuals were written in order to give instructions for a decentralized application of such a cost-benefit analysis (see, for instance, Little and Mirrlees, 1968).

After a wide diffusion and application of the codes of cost-benefit analysis in many countries, the methodology was strongly criticized. Discussion of its theoretical foundations does not concern us here. There was an obvious contradiction between the idea that prevailing market prices were distorted and the assumption that the project would be added to an otherwise Pareto-optimal inter-temporal programme. Theoreticians resolved the contradiction by looking explicitly at the constraints explaining the price distortions and by assuming that the reference programme was not Pareto-optimal but only second-best because of these constraints (see Drèze and Stern, 1987). The reconsideration showed that a well-founded computation of shadow prices needed a good deal of information not easily accessible to planners. However, some qualitative results also showed that the discipline imposed by cost-benefit studies was not misguided. For instance, the proposition that shadow prices should be the same throughout the public sector was recognized to be widely valid. Less general, but still fairly safe, was the proposition that relative shadow prices for traded commodities should coincide with relative world prices.

The main criticism to consider here is that in practice the methodology leaves room for manoeuvre. Proponents of a project can overestimate its benefits, and underestimate its costs, particularly for the qualitative elements or external effects, which are difficult to assess and difficult to value. Critics of the methodology claimed that pressure groups were using it to their advantage and were hiding their interests behind computations tailored for their intended result.

It should strike observers that this criticism is an argument for a system in which planners monitor cost-benefit analyses, are insulated from pressure groups and develop ethical norms of objectivity. For instance, planners must check the quality of their data and the accounting rules, and, occasionally, the econometric procedures used for the evaluation of costs and benefits. They have to question the validity of the projections estimating the demand to be served by the project. They have to ensure that external economies are not overvalued and external diseconomies undervalued. They have to wonder whether shadow prices are consistent across projects and consistent with import and export prices, and so on.

Realizing that cost-benefit analyses are difficult to carry out well and that they need more reflection and investigation than the mechanical aspect of their formulas might suggest, we are led to an inflection of the philosophy, just as in the case of macroeconometric models.

NOTES

1. There are many signs not only of the disrepute that has befallen planning over the last two decades, but also of the excessive impact of this disrepute. A case in point is the otherwise excellent analysis of the East Asian Miracle by the World Bank (1993). The book is largely interested in institutions that contributed to the economic success of the countries concerned, and institutions for improving economic performance of the market and of government intervention. But there is hardly any mention of the role of planning, despite the fact that most of these countries have planning institutions.

2. The points discussed in this section are developed more fully in chapter 7 of volume II.

3. See for instance Bjerve (1996) and Malinvaud (1996).

4. Chapter 7 of volume II reviews the failure of planning models in developing countries to deal effectively with the market failures on the basis of which planning was promoted.

REFERENCES

Bjerve, P.J. 1996. "The Influence of Ragnar Frisch on Macroeconomic Planning and Policy in Norway." In "The Proceedings of the Frisch Centennial Conference." Econometric Society Monograph Series.

Bodkin, R., L. Klein and K. Marwah, eds. 1991. *A History of Macroeconometric Model-Building.* Aldershot, U.K.: Edward Elgar.

Crémer H. and J. Crémer. 1993. "L'apport des théories économiques à la planification indicative." *Revue Economique* 44.

Drèze, J. and N. Stern. 1987. "The Theory of Cost-Benefit Analysis." In A. Auerback and M. Feldstein, eds., *Handbook of Public Economics.* Amsterdam: North Holland.

Kantorovich. L. 1965. *The Best Uses of Economic Resources.* Translated from the 1959 Russian edition. Oxford: Pergamon.

Kornai, J. 1980. *Economics of Shortage.* Amsterdam: North Holland.

Little, I. and J. Mirrlees. 1968. *Manual of Industrial Project Analysis in Developing Countries.* Paris: OECD.

Lucas, R. 1976. "Econometric Policy Evaluation: a Critique." *Journal of Monetary Economics.*

Malinvaud, Edmond. 1996. "How Frisch saw in the 1960s the contribution of economists to development planning." In "The Proceedings of the Frisch Centennial Conference." Econometric Society Monograph Series.

Malkiel, B. 1987. "Term Structure of Interest Rates." In J. Eatwell, M. Milgate and P. Newman, eds., *The New Palgrave.* London: Macmillan.

US Government. 1994. *Economic Report of the President.* Washington, D.C.: U.S. Government Printing Office.

World Bank. 1993. *The East Asian Miracle: Economic Growth and Public Policy.* New York: Oxford University Press.

5

Macroeconomic Policy and the Role of the State in a Changing World

Nicholas Stern

In the Keynesian era a broad consensus emerged on the role of government in an industrial economy. On the macroeconomic front the government had the responsibility of controlling overall demand, using primarily fiscal policy, to secure full employment. Its duty to control inflation was recognized in the 1950s and 1960s, though not seen as the primary challenge. The balance of payments was regarded as a constraint on macroeconomic policy, but one that could be handled, if necessary, by exchange rate devaluations and direct controls on both capital and current transactions. Indeed, capital controls were fairly universal. On the microeconomic and sectoral, or industrial, fronts the tasks included providing basic infrastructure, which was seen as a public responsibility because it was both essential and a natural monopoly; promoting or protecting strategic sectors; and correcting or regulating market failures, such as the establishment or abuse of monopoly positions.

It is, however, important to note that industrial policies were applied in varying degrees in industrial countries during the 1960s— ranging from relatively hands-off policies, at least at the federal level, in the case of Germany, to relatively interventionist policies in the case of France. Concerning income distribution, the state was expected to provide social security in the form of pensions, unemployment insurance, health insurance and a safety net for those outside of such schemes or those who fell below a minimum living standard. Some countries also had population policies, such as the *allocations familiales* in France, which were designed to promote population growth. These tasks went beyond the basic requirement of the state to provide an institutional fabric, including defence, administration, and law and order. In some developing countries, on the other hand, population policy was intended to limit population growth, for example, in India through the promotion of family planning.

Taken together, these responsibilities necessitated a "big government", featuring not only high expenditures and high taxes, but also prominence in most economic activities. The range of tasks for the governments of developing countries was typically seen as broader still, including direct responsibility for investment and the coordination of output decisions, because the market was seen as too frail or fickle to alone determine investment and output in crucial areas.

This consensus began to weaken during the 1970s. The experience of the two oil price shocks demonstrated the inappropriateness of demand stimuli as a response to adverse supply shocks.[1] The steady upward drift of inflation in the OECD countries undermined confidence in the stability or existence of the unemployment-inflation trade-off. Worsening productivity growth and rising unemployment in the OECD countries did not respond as expected to traditional demand management and government intervention.

We have learned from these experiences—and our expectations of government have become more modest. Partly as a result of the success of Keynesian policies in preventing a collapse in demand of the 1930s variety, attention has shifted to controlling inflation and to understanding unemployment as a structural phenomenon. Along with a reduced prescription of what governments should attempt to provide has come an increased appreciation of the potential scope and strength of markets and private provision of some of its services. And the world has changed fundamentally—economies are now more open to trade and capital movements. There has been great technological advance, and economic activities and information are more mobile. Economic concepts and theories have moved in step with these developments and now stress international economics, monetary policy, information, the limitations of government and the importance of structures and institutions in understanding the function of markets and the problems of policy-making.

The purpose of this chapter is to assess macroeconomic policy and the role of the state in light of the experiences in the 50 years since Keynesian ideas were broadly applied, the changing structure of the world economy and the advance of economic ideas. I will not confine myself to the traditional, narrow concerns of macroeconomic analysis—that is, demand management and monetary and fiscal policy in the short run. Institutions will play a central role in this analysis.

I first consider the scale and nature of the responsibilities of the state before proceeding to issues of stability. I examine a number of perspectives on the responsibility of the state, including concern about market imperfections, equity and individual rights. These concerns point to significant roles for the state in funding or providing for health, education, social protection, defence, the rule of law in economic activity and elsewhere, and administration. Together, these activities would call for government expenditure between one-fifth and one-half of national income.[2] Most OECD countries would be clustered between the one-third and one-half mark. Thus major challenges of taxation and expenditure control would arise that must influence, and be influenced by, the responsibilities defined for the state. The nature of those responsibilities and the manner in which, and the institutions through which, they are carried out will have profound consequences for the workings of macroeconomic policy.

Throughout this chapter I emphasize the importance of the link between macroeconomic and microeconomic aspects of policy. I stress, in particular, the importance of macroeconomic stability for microeconomic decision-making and performance in providing credibility, continuity and coherence in policy, and the role of the government in promoting overall performance in the medium and long term. Thus I discuss macroeconomic policy both from the demand and the supply side.[3]

A CHANGING WORLD

In this section I highlight three important ways in which the world has changed since the early post-war period—all have deep implications for macroeconomic policy and institutions. These are growing internationalization, higher real interest rates and a diminished perception of the capabilities and responsibilities of government together with a better understanding of the potential of markets.

Internationalization

The world has internationalized rapidly and along many dimensions in past decades. I focus briefly on five areas: trade, capital, enterprises, labour and information. In each the consequences of change have been radical, and taken together they imply that the economic environment has been profoundly recast. In addition to opening up opportunities, these changes have generated intense competition and strong incentives for performance—there have been winners and losers. These international developments demonstrate the need to understand the constraints that markets place on governments, as well as those that governments place on markets.

In the past two decades world trade has grown at 6 per cent per year in real terms—twice as fast as world GDP.[4] Imports and exports account for a growing share of national expenditure. The ability to impose tariffs is increasingly restricted by international treaties. And the effects of international competition are intense, generating pressures to perform effectively.

The international mobility of capital has increased enormously as, since the 1970s, country after country has abandoned capital controls. In 1995 aggregate net resource flows to developing countries rose 12 per cent from the previous year to US$231 billion (table 5.1). Private flows continued to rise dramatically and now account for 72 per cent of total flows (compared with about 25 per cent in 1985 and 43 per cent in 1990). Official flows, on the other hand, have fallen from 57 per cent in 1990 to 28 per cent in 1995.[5] Increased flows have strong implications for international financial institutions providing development finance. These institutions will have to

Table 5.1: Aggregate net long-term resource flows to developing countries, 1990–95 (US$ billions)

	1990	1991	1992	1993	1994	1995
Aggregate net flows	101.9	127.1	155.3	207.2	207.4	231.3
Official finance	57.9	65.5	55.0	53.0	48.6	64.2
Official grants	29.4	37.5	31.9	29.4	32.5	32.9
Official loans	28.5	28.0	23.1	23.6	16.1	31.3[a]
Multilateral loans[b]	15.0	14.8	12.3	14.2	10.0	12.5
Total private flows	44.0	61.6	100.3	154.2	158.8	167.1
Private debt flows	15.3	19.0	39.6	40.3	43.8	54.8
FDI	25.0	35.0	46.6	68.3	80.1	90.3
Portfolio flows	3.7	7.6	14.1	45.6	34.9	22.0

[a] This figure includes the US$11 billion net disbursement from the exceptional financing package for Mexico from official bilateral and multilateral sources.

[b] Multilateral development banks.

Source: World Bank (1996).

ensure that their strategies complement and enhance opportunities for market-oriented development.

Increased capital mobility has loosened the links between domestic saving and domestic investment, although these links remain strong (and there are, of course, constraints on liquidity and intertemporal budgets). It has also opened the way to diversify investment portfolios. These developments broaden opportunities—and impose constraints. For example, alternative opportunities abroad limit the ability to tax capital income at home.[6] Markets can come close to dictating their views on the appropriateness of exchange rates. And they also bring the problems of instability associated with sudden changes of perception or sentiment.

Enterprises can locate production and other activities where they choose. They look closely at international costs, markets, taxation and government behaviour before making choices. If a country wants to attract foreign investment, it must convince investors that it will provide stability and the right kind of market environment to enable the enterprise to function effectively.[7]

Workers, particularly young workers, are increasingly mobile, notwithstanding the rigidity of immigration regulations in many countries (SOPEMI 1995). This mobility can lead to losses of talent (and a lowering of social returns to some forms of education) in the country of departure (often a developing country). In the receiving country, on the other hand, young immigrants can contribute to relieving the "youth deficit".

Finally, the rapid flow of information allows the aspects of internationalization mentioned above to become increasingly potent. It also constrains the ability of governments to control societies by centralizing and limiting the dissemination of information.

Interest rates

The three decades following World War II saw very low real interest rates, averaging well below 2 per cent, and falling to near zero in 1974–80 (table 5.2). In the past 15 years they have been higher than in any (extended) period since the 1850s. Thus the world has moved suddenly from three or four decades of very low real interest rates to a decade and a half of high interest rates.

Before asserting that high interest rates are here to stay, we must consider the cause of rising interest rates. An examination of saving and investment rates suggests that rising real interest rates are associated with a declining world propensity to save rather than with an increase in returns to capital (see Buiter, Lago and Stern 1997). This declining propensity to save may itself have a number of causes. For private saving major long-term factors are likely to include, changing age structures in industrial countries (a growing elderly population implies more dissaving), and for public saving governments' increasing political difficulties in raising already high taxes. Attempts to reduce the size of government in many industrial countries have influenced taxation more than expenditure. Indeed, in most industrial countries both continued to rise after 1980, with expenditure rising faster than taxation. Public dissaving is compounded by rising real interest rates—which, now that they are significantly higher than growth rates of real GDP, require positive primary surpluses[8] to prevent debt-to-GDP ratios from rising. (Surpluses are not required when real interest rates are lower than real growth rates.) These causes of falling saving rates are basic and will require major policy responses to be reversed. Public saving can be increased by decreasing deficits through cuts in current spending or higher taxes. One possibility for increasing private saving would be to move towards a fully-funded, individually based retirement scheme.[9]

Table 5.2: Long-term interest rates in the major OECD countries, 1850-1993

Four-country average[a]	1850s	1860s	1870s	1880s	1890s	1900-13	1924-29	1930-32	1933-39	1956-73	1974-80	1981-93
Nominal interest rate	4.1	4.2	4.3	3.5	3.1	3.5	5.1	5.1	3.8	6.3	10.0	9.7
Real interest rate[b]	2.5	3.1	4.9	4.1	3.5	2.6	3.7	10.5	1.7	1.7	0.0	5.1
GDP growth rate	2.3	2.5	2.8	2.4	2.8	2.7	2.9	-6.3	5.3	4.1	2.0	2.1
Real interest rate–growth rate	0.2	0.6	2.1	1.7	0.7	-0.2	0.8	16.8	-3.6	-2.3	-2.1	3.0

a. Four-country average includes data from France, Germany, the United Kingdom and the United States.

b. Conversion to real terms is based on the GDP deflator. Note that there are various ways of defining price indices and some conceptual difficulties in choosing between them. Nevertheless, most choices would yield the same general picture.

Source: OECD *Historical Statistics for 1966-1990*; OECD *Main Economic Indicators* (various years) and OECD *National Accounts* (various years), supplemented as required by data on interest rates from Homer (1991). Pre-World War II data on interest rates from Homer (1991); pre-World War II data on GDP and prices are from Mitchell (1992).

Diminishing expectations for government

The 1980s saw powerful political movements—in the form of the Reagan and Thatcher administrations in the United States and United Kingdom—to diminish both the scale of government spending and the role of the government in economic life. In India enthusiasm for planning had evaporated by the 1970s,[10] and there have been various movements to liberalize (including the administration of Rajiv Gandhi in the 1980s and the Narasimha Rao-Manmohan Singh reforms of the first part of the 1990s). China began to dismantle its planning system and total state economic control with agricultural reforms in 1979–83 and then industrial reforms from the mid–1980s. There have been many other recent examples in Latin America and elsewhere. Most dramatic, however, have been the experiences of the communist regimes in eastern Europe and the former Soviet Union, culminating in their dramatic collapse between 1989 and 1991.

Diminishing expectations for government were not generated by a sudden realization that market failures were not as bad as previously thought or that new solutions had been found. Rather, the decline resulted from both an increasing awareness of the inadequacies of governments, which attempted to take on too much, and a resistance to higher taxation. The appalling waste and low productivity of the communist systems of eastern Europe and the former Soviet Union offer the most powerful example.

There is now widespread acceptance that ownership of or detailed interference with ordinary production processes are not sensible functions for government. Private entrepreneurship and incentives do the job much better. The same principles also apply to some parts of infrastructure—an area seen in the Keynesian era as a public sector domain. Two examples that have great potential for private sector provision are telecommunications and power generation. Changes in these areas have, in part, arisen from technological advances undermining natural monopolies, as well as from the inadequacies of government control and the performance of public finances.

The desire to bring back the involvement of government seems to have been stronger on the taxation side than on the expenditure side.

Indeed, a major part of the drive for smaller government was motivated by opposition to high tax rates. Undoubtedly, scepticism as to the real value of government expenditure played a part, but the loudest noises have been associated with a desire to reduce taxes. And, in fact, expenditure in industrialized countries has risen faster than taxes. As a result public deficits and debt-to-GDP ratios have risen sharply over the last two or three decades in many industrial countries (figure 5.1, table 5.3).

Figure 5.1: Revenues and expenditures as a share of GDP in major industrial countries

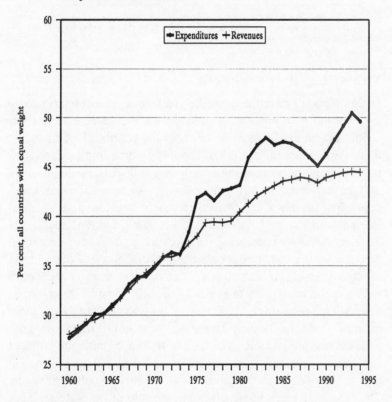

Source: IMF (1996).

Table 5.3: Government debt net of government financial assets
            (percentage of GDP)

Country	Average 1978–80	1995
Austria	35.7	54.6
Belgium	62.7	127.9
Canada	12.6	66.7
Denmark	2.3	54.5
France	−0.6	35.1
Germany	11.0	49.1
Ireland	71.6	86.3
Italy	54.4	108.9
Japan	14.4	9.8
Netherlands	21.9	60.5
Norway	8.8	−21.5
Spain	5.2	50.3
Sweden	−19.5	27.0
United Kingdom	46.3	40.8
United States	25.6	56.4

Note: The change in net financial assets of governments depended in some cases on the privatization policy that was implemented (privatization being defined as a transformation of physical assets into, at least at a first stage, financial assets).

Source: IMF (1981 and 1996).

THE ROLE OF GOVERNMENT

In this section I describe the tasks that I think governments should take on and then argue that although we should be cautious, we should not be overly pessimistic about the possibility of financing them through the tax system. It should be borne in mind however, that the issue of designating appropriate tasks for the government will be answered by different countries in very different ways, depending on initial conditions, economic structure and a host of internal and external political and economic circumstances. For instance, when we consider general government spending and revenue totals of the transition economies, two distinct types of problems seem to be emerging. In a number of advanced transition economies public spending appears to be unsustainably high due, for example, to very large pension rights. On the other hand, in a number of other countries, principally those in the earlier stages of transition, government revenues appear to be too low to finance basic government functions, due in part to the decline in the traditional tax base and in part to the decline in the government's ability to collect revenue. Thus the challenges in transforming the role of the state are very different in these two types of transition economies.

The tasks for government

Maintaining macroeconomic stability is a prime task for government. Stability can be viewed as a public good, which no other economic agency can provide.[11] It is essential for the effective operation of the price mechanism, for efficient enterprise decision-making, for investment and for growth. As will be argued in the next section, these arguments make sense from first principles and are borne out by experience. Here, I identify other areas where the government should take responsibility based on microeconomic theory, distributional values, rights and paternalism. I will be brief since I (along with my colleagues) have developed some of these arguments elsewhere[12] (and they are raised by other authors in this book), and the prime focus of this chapter is macroeconomics. My purpose is to say enough to indicate that the scale of government responsibilities and, although this is not the same thing, the scale of expenditure, should be large enough to go beyond a "night-watchman" state and will place significant challenges on raising revenue.[13] It is important to recognize that what I call government here may also include local authorities, especially in countries with a federal structure.

From standard microeconomic theory we can identify the first two areas below. The remaining are largely concerned with distribution rights and responsibilities and are derived from a broader philosophical perspective.

- The government should provide the rule of law, basic administration and external defence. These responsibilities include protecting the system of private property and contracts. These are basic to the functioning of a market system based on decentralized, private decision-making.
- Market failures or imperfections will require government action, in some cases through regulation, taxes or subsidies (for example, concerning monopoly and environmental issues) and in others, public provision. Overambition must be avoided, however, since some causes of market failure—for example, moral hazard issues connected, say, with insurance or financial markets—may also lead to government failure if government attempts to correct them.

- Government will likely want to pursue distributional objectives, particularly protection from poverty or destitution. But these are much more effectively tackled on the expenditure rather than the tax side of the budget.[14]
- There are important arguments for government actions concerning individual rights. The notion of rights is not straightforward and requires careful discussion of its philosophical underpinnings. On this there is a voluminous literature—and I will not review it in detail here. Briefly, it can be argued that in return for compliance with laws and taxes, governments should ensure that all citizens have the opportunity and freedom to participate effectively in the economy or, more generally, in society.[15] The perception of what constitutes basic rights emerges from notions of liberty and equality within society. Arguments for state intervention to guarantee equality of opportunity can have several dimensions.
- From this perspective the state has a central role in protecting individuals from basic deprivations (for example, illiteracy, poor health, hunger, homelessness) that would exclude or inhibit participation in society. Effective alternative mechanisms may not be available either through the market mechanism alone, or at the community or household level.[16] In particular, these considerations point to interventions in the areas of education, health, nutrition and housing. Broadly, we can summarize these notions by saying that the state has a responsibility to help citizens achieve a basic standard of living. The right to vote and the right of freedom of speech and religion can be viewed from similar perspectives.
- The government must take some responsibility for future generations, particularly in maintaining a safe and habitable environment.
- There are also some important paternalistic or merit-good issues: the government may have the responsibility of protecting citizens from their own inadequacies, including in drug-abuse, pensions, education, and health.

Clearly, more than one of these arguments can apply to any given area of economic activity. For example, in the case of health, education, pensions and the environment, market failure, individual rights and paternalism may all be relevant.

Not all of these responsibilities require that the government provide a particular good or service. The government can deal with market failure in infrastructure, for example, by regulating private provision. It can require saving for old age without providing pensions itself. It is sensible to ask in each case whether the government is likely to be able to supply the good or service as well as or better than the private sector before allocating provision to government.[17] We must also look carefully at the internal structure of a sector. For example, in the power sector the arguments for private ownership and investment are much stronger for some parts of the system (generation) than for others (transmission and distribution). Telecommunications is, for the most part, no longer a natural monopoly and is best supplied privately.[18] But given problems of administering pricing systems, roads should probably stay in the public domain.

Nevertheless, the provision of the basic services described above will surely involve spending more than one-fifth of GDP—possibly much more. And social protection and other responsibilities assumed by governments in industrial countries take these expenditures to two-fifths of GDP and beyond. While expenditure control and efficiency should be high priorities, the task of financing these expenditures in as non-distortionary and equitable a way as possible represents a major challenge.

Financing of expenditure

Over the medium term most expenditure must be financed by taxation.[19] The alternatives—borrowing and seigniorage—each have strong limitations. In a world in which real interest rates are greater than growth rates, borrowing is limited by the fact that the government must have a primary surplus to prevent debt-to-GDP ratios from rising in the short run and to ensure solvency in the longer run.[20] And seigniorage is closely linked to the inflation tax, which is limited in that the population substitutes away from money in inflationary environments.[21] Further, privatization can raise only limited revenues for only a short period. It can, however, stop the heavy drain on budgetary revenue that arises from losses incurred in state-owned enterprises.

It has become fashionable to be pessimistic about the ability to raise large fractions of GDP from taxes. The problems of disincentives to effort and high incentives for tax evasion and corruption of tax administrations are invoked. These are serious issues. But the pessimism can be overdone. Consider a hypothetical tax structure and revenue level (table 5.4). While the generation of 50 per cent of GDP may be viewed as an upper limit of the potential of taxation, in revenue terms it is not hopelessly ambitious for an industrial country.[22] Whether it is desirable is another question. While lower levels must be expected in developing countries, substantial revenue generation is possible there as well. These totals do not take into account revenue from trade taxes, property or rent taxes, special mineral taxes and so on. The pattern reflects, broadly speaking, tax structures found in many industrial countries.[23]

Broadly speaking, the type and range of taxes described here can find support in terms of the basic analytics of public economics. This approach combines the principles of efficiency/incentives, equity and revenue.[24] They also reflect key criteria for tax administration, including transparency and simplicity. The levels suggested are on the borderline of what is possible but are actually achieved in some countries.

From this simple table a number of straightforward observations emerge. First, if revenues in the region of two-fifths to one-half of

Table 5.4: A notional tax structure

Tax	Description	Revenue (percentage of GDP)
Value-added tax or sales taxes	20 per cent rate; base 60 per cent of GDP	12
Excise duties on cigarettes, alcohol and petroleum products	Average rate 50 per cent; base 10 per cent of GDP	5
Personal income tax and social security contributions	32 per cent average rate on 80 per cent of GDP	26
Corporate income tax	35 per cent rate; base 20 per cent of GDP	7
Total		50

GDP are to be raised, a number of tax sources must be used. Second, revenues of this magnitude are possible to obtain, though the magnitudes in table 5.4 should be viewed as upper limits.[25] Third, an examination of the rates and bases presented in the table reveals that earning much more than this amount of revenue will present major challenges to tax administrations if they are to maintain bases broad enough to keep rates manageable.

The patterns for developing countries are different, with indirect taxes becoming relatively more important. Also, import taxes generally make a larger contribution to revenue. The ratio of revenue from indirect plus trade taxes to that from direct taxes would be, on average, roughly 2:1. Among direct taxes corporate income taxes are generally more important than the personal income taxes and social security contributions.[26] Variations of the pattern among industrial and developing countries are substantial, particularly among developing countries.

Tax collection in some developing countries, particularly those in South America, have advanced impressively over the past decades (figure 5.2). Tax administration has improved in many cases, notwithstanding the pervasive problems of evasion, the black market economy and corruption. In general, the fraction of the economy coming under the tax net grows as development proceeds—but not without close attention and political will. Resources and technical assistance devoted to tax administration can, with the right political commitment and support, bring great rewards.

MACROECONOMIC STABILITY

This section concerns the importance of macroeconomic stability and how it can be promoted. For both I will begin with some theoretical considerations and then discuss the evidence.

The importance of macroeconomic stability

The costs of inflation are embodied mainly in uncertainty and distribution. If inflation is fully anticipated and indexed and if a range of financial instruments is broadly available, then its costs would not be large. These residual costs would be of the "shoe-leather" (frequent trips to the bank) and "menu" (frequent relabelling in restaurants) variety. Inflation, however, tends to be associated with uncertainty in both aggregate and relative prices. Inflation at the aggregate level may ultimately be rooted in social conflict over public spending and its financing. The way that such conflict might be resolved is likely to be uncertain and will thus generate cautious investment plans. Economic agents may anticipate future fiscal or monetary policy actions to control inflation. These may directly affect business profitability through changes in taxes, subsidies, public sector infrastructure investment and so on. Such actions could involve declining demand and depreciation of the real exchange rate.

Figure 5.2: Government revenues and expenditures in Latin America, 1975–95

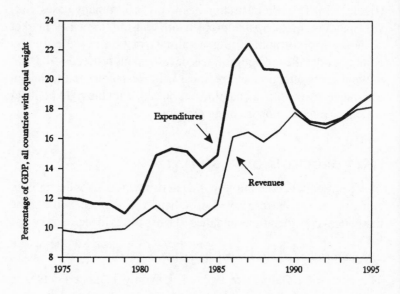

Source: IMF (1996).

The above factors will spur cautious production and investment decisions. Investments involve sunk costs—costs that cannot easily be recovered or allocated to alternative uses if anticipated profits do not materialize. Greater uncertainty increases the "option value" of waiting and lowers investment.[27] This wait-and-see approach may make investors cautious about committing themselves following the implementation of a stabilization plan.[28] They will want to be convinced (especially if there have been a number of failed attempts in the past) that the commitment to stabilization and reform is real and enduring.

The relevant uncertainty here concerns not only the macroeconomic considerations described above, but also relative prices. Uncertainties concerning relative prices and future policies can reduce the quality, as well as the quantity of investment. And quality of investment is crucial to the productivity and dynamism of capitalism—that it is undermined by a weakly functioning system of relative prices has long been recognized.[29]

The costs of uncertainty for production and investment go further. High inflation diverts scarce entrepreneurial resources to short-term financial management and rent-seeking. The most talented employees of companies and economies in highly inflationary environments are likely to move towards such activities.

Inflation creates severe problems in capital markets: it erodes the volume of outstanding debt. For real interest rates to be positive nominal interest rates must be very high. Individual borrowers are effectively forced by inflation to pay off loans very quickly, thus making loans short-term and causing severe liquidity problems. If nominal interest rates are high enough to make real interest rates positive, then lenders see their resources devalued.

Distributional costs of inflation are associated with the regressive nature of the inflation tax. The poor do not have easy access to the kind of financial protection mechanisms available to the better-off, and are much more dependent on cash. The regressive effect of both the inflation tax and the effects of inflation on real wages have been extensively documented for Argentina, Brazil and Mexico.[30]

Inflation can also profoundly affect the tax system, since indexation is always limited (the challenges to accounting of a fully-indexed system are formidable). Inflation can then make official tax burdens crippling, resulting in the erosion of tax payer compliance (the choice may be between honesty and bankruptcy on the one hand, and evasion on the other).[31] Inflation also weakens public finances through the Tanzi effect (a delay in tax payments reduces their value in real terms).

In all of these ways inflation has very real costs for efficiency, growth, equity, and public finances and administration. Their effects can be illustrated by macroeconomic relationships between growth and inflation and microeconomic consequences of investment decisions. In a sample of 109 countries, Levine and Renelt (1992) found that countries with faster growth rates than the mean had significantly lower inflation and significantly higher investment. Similar results were found in a number of other cross-sectional studies of inflation and growth. [32]

In speaking about the empirical evidence on the detrimental effects of inflation on economic performance, I should emphasize that there is less evidence at lower rates of inflation (say, below 20 per cent) of any clear pattern of covariation between inflation and growth or between inflation and other observable indices of efficiency, such as total factor productivity. The damage to economic performance caused by very high rates of inflation emerges strongly in the evidence. But at rates below 20 per cent or 25 per cent per year the relationship is less clear.[33] Interestingly, these broad generalizations taken from a large sample of countries over the past decades seem to be consistent with the experience of the last six years in the transition economies of eastern Europe and the former Soviet Union.[34]

The detrimental effect of macroeconomic instability on economic performance is also brought out in microeconomic studies. World Bank (1991) argues that rates of return on World Bank and International Finance Corporation (IFC) projects were systematically higher where macroeconomic distortions associated with fiscal deficits and foreign exchange premiums were lower.[35] These conditions were also associated with countries that had lower inflation.

The promotion of macroeconomic stability

How can macroeconomic stability be promoted? The short answer is through responsible fiscal and monetary policies. It is, of course, necessary to be more explicit about the nature of responsible policies and the institutions that can deliver them.

Sustainable deficits

There is no simple theory dictating the "right" level of fiscal deficit. In the longer term the issue is that of government solvency and of future tax burdens or spending cuts to pay for interest on borrowing. Often, this longer-term solvency constraint is expressed in terms of controlling the debt-to-GDP ratio. I illustrate this in the Appendix with a simple calculation. This calculation indicates that the debt-to-GDP ratio falls only if the primary surplus as a fraction of GDP exceeds the difference between the real interest rate and the growth rate, where this difference is multiplied by the debt-to-GDP ratio itself. Intuitively, if we want to prevent the debt-to-GDP ratio from rising, the primary surplus must cover the interest payable on bonds, less an allowance for GDP growth.

This calculation can be complicated in a number of ways, in particular to allow for seigniorage and to distinguish between internal and external debt.[36] But the essentials of the argument are clear. The higher is existing debt and the higher is the excess of the real rate of interest over the growth rate, the higher must be the primary surplus. Some hypothetical numbers can illustrate orders of magnitude. If the real interest rate is 5 per cent, the growth rate 3 per cent and the existing debt-to-GDP ratio 0.5, then the primary surplus must be 1 per cent of GDP to stabilize the debt-to-GDP ratio.

The simple calculation underlines the significance of the international rise in real interest rates to the challenge of stabilizing debt-to-GDP ratios. As we saw from table 5.2, the four-country average of the difference between the real interest rate and the growth rate was of the order of –2 per cent in the 1950s, 1960s and 1970s, but has been +3 per cent thereafter. For a government with a modest debt at, say, 50 per cent of GDP, this jump of 5 percentage points means that the primary surplus must rise, or the deficit be reduced by, 2.5 percentage points of GDP, simply to keep the debt-GDP ratio from rising (assuming it was stable under the old regime). The high real interest rates that now seem to be a longer-term feature of the international environment surely dictate that for most countries a primary surplus will be essential to keep debt-GDP ratios from rising further—and that in many cases the required surplus could be of the order of 2 or more percentage points of GDP.

Increased recourse to the inflation tax in the face of an otherwise unfinanceable public sector deficit is unlikely to provide a lasting solution to the problem of an inconsistent fiscal-financial-monetary programme. The amount of real resources that can be appropriated through the inflation tax is limited and will ultimately decrease when the rate of inflation becomes sufficiently high. Experience has shown that seigniorage (or, ultimately, the inflation tax) is unlikely to raise more than 2–3 per cent of GDP over any period of time with acceptable rates of inflation—even in economies with weak financial institutions. The seigniorage Laffer curve reflects both direct international currency substitution (away from the local currency and towards hard currencies) and a shift into domestic non-monetary assets that are better hedges against inflation.

We must be careful to avoid asserting that debt-to-GDP ratios must be prevented from rising in all circumstances. It is possible, for example, that if returns to public investment are very high, it may be sensible to borrow in the short term. But the rising indebtedness over the past 20 years in many countries should indicate the need for great caution in further borrowing.

Policies and institutions for macroeconomic stability

The argument above focused on the requirements of fiscal policy. I now turn to the monetary side and focus on the problems of macroeconomic policy in an open economy and on institutions, including the role of the central bank. I look first at the banking side and then at the issue of setting targets or using anchors for nominal variables. My final topic is coping with capital flows.

Hard budget constraints are a sine qua non of a market economy. The banking sector is fundamental to their establishment. The central bank has the responsibility of imposing hard budget constraints on commercial banks, thereby forcing them to impose hard budget constraints on their borrowers. Banking supervision will play a crucial role in restricting the development of non-performing loans, which are a key manifestation of soft budget constraints. Without hard budget constraints, stabilization will fail—sooner or later the subsidies or transfers that are softening the constraints will show up in the fiscal deficit or in the quasi-fiscal deficit of the central bank. Their appearance may force the government to take at least partial responsibility for insolvent banks or enterprises. Governments are now attempting to impose the necessary discipline on themselves, as well as on the rest of the economy by passing constitutional amendments regulating the ability to borrow, spend or tax or by establishing independent central banks.

A variety of nominal anchors have been proposed as devices for establishing price stability. These include controlling or targeting a monetary aggregate, the general price level or nominal income, or, from an open economy perspective, the nominal exchange rate. An external nominal anchor, however, cannot substitute for sound underlying domestic and monetary policies.[37] For example, the pursuit of a nominal exchange rate target constrains domestic credit expansion to the growth of money demand at the target exchange rate— otherwise, the country will ultimately run out of reserves. Similarly, domestic unit cost inflation cannot exceed indefinitely the foreign rate plus the target depreciation rate of the nominal exchange rate. If it did, the country would become so uncompetitive that the target nominal exchange rate would have to be abandoned.

Income policies or overall price controls can, in a sense, be seen as providing nominal anchors if the average money wage or general price level is targeted. They may also be used, on a temporary basis, to support another nominal anchor, such as the money stock or the exchange rate. Again, they cannot be a substitute for overall fiscal and monetary discipline in the medium term. For example, if real wages get too far out of line in the controlled sector, the result will either be drastic and disruptive reallocation in the labour market (with no obvious economic rationale) or labour unrest. The control of any single macroeconomic parameter against other economic developments or policies will eventually break down.

International capital flows

In principle, lending or borrowing abroad expands the choices open to a country. For example, it can finance a high investment period or smooth shocks to consumption. If a country can borrow at rates substantially below the productivity of investment, the wealth of the country will increase over time. Also, the establishment of facilities to make international transfers allows for international risk sharing.

There are potential disadvantages of international capital movements, however. Large capital inflows, for example, following a reform that is believed to bring more favourable economic conditions, can drive up real exchange rates very rapidly. These inflows may simply reflect a revaluation that acknowledges the improved economic position—which is not a problem. But the real exchange rate can easily overshoot, either because the positive sentiments are exaggerated or because domestic markets react more slowly than international markets to the changed economic situation. In these circumstances sentiments can change rapidly—in the opposite direction—forcing huge capital outflows and putting downward pressure on the real exchange rate. Sudden capital outflows can also put considerable strain on the domestic banking system.

Such dramatic reversals of financial movements can have large real costs in terms of the uncertainties they create for relative prices, exchange rates and interest rates. Such uncertainty brings, as I argued above, waste in terms of sunk costs and strong discouragement for investment.

The response to the dangers of these disruptive flows can be both domestic and international. Attempts to "speed up" responses of other markets, such as domestic factor prices, have their own costs, and, in any case, could never match the speed of capital markets. Another response might be to try to "slow down" capital markets—through, for example, Tobin's (1982) suggestion to impose a tax on foreign exchange transactions. But given the scale and sophistication of markets relative to effectiveness of international cooperation among national tax authorities, such attempts are unlikely to be workable.

Alternatively, a country could attempt to impose administrative controls on capital movements. The potential for success of this type of procedure depends on the development of capital markets. The more sophisticated they are, the more difficult are controls to impose. There are so many ways to attack a currency in an advanced system that direct controls are unlikely to be effective—particularly because they are likely to be imposed precisely when markets are anticipating rewards to such attacks.[38] On the other hand, such controls could be effective in the relatively less sophisticated markets of some developing countries.

Capital controls should not interfere with current account transactions (and it must be recognized that some capital transactions would be concealed as current transactions—through, for example, leads and lags in payments and over- and underinvoicing). It is also important to avoid discouraging foreign direct investment. The administrative difficulties and potential corruption associated with these controls would pose real problems. If they were to be imposed, simplicity and transparency would be needed to minimize side-effects.

One possible reaction to net capital inflows in excess of the current account deficit is to avoid appreciation of the currency by allowing an increase in foreign exchange reserves. If no attempt is made to cut domestic credit (sterilization), then this increase in reserves corresponds to an increase in domestic money stock. If there has been no corresponding shift in the demand for money, then real appreciation can occur through a rise in domestic prices. When capital mobility is perfect, sterilization is not an option—it will not be possible to maintain the necessary interest rate differentials. If mobility is imperfect, sterilization can work for a while. But the required higher interest rates can create further problems of inflows and losses for the central bank if the foreign exchange reserves carry lower interest rates than the central bank is paying on the debt it issues to sterilize the inflows. These problems suggest that sterilization should be attempted only if the flows are seen as short term. Otherwise, it is probably more sensible to let the currency appreciate or to accept an increase in the domestic rate of inflation for a while.

Sudden large capital outflows can create problems that are the mirror-image of those associated with inflows—depletion of foreign exchange reserves, downward pressure on the currency, incomplete sterilization of the outflows, contraction of the domestic money stock and a temporary deflationary impulse. In addition, the effect of large international portfolio shifts on the domestic banking sector can be very disruptive, especially if banks' liquid foreign currency liabilities have as their counterpart illiquid loans to domestic enterprises. Unless the central bank stands ready to satisfy banks' sudden demand for foreign currency, a full-fledged banking crisis can result. Countries with currency boards, in which the central bank fixes the exchange rate and does not engage in domestic credit expansion, are especially vulnerable to such banking crises, as the central bank cannot act as lender of last resort. The recent Argentine banking crisis is an example.

BEYOND STABILIZATION

In this section I examine macroeconomic priorities for times other than those of crisis or adjustment. How should countries take advantage of these periods? The response is simple. At such times governments have opportunities to plan and act for the future by making certain types of basic investments or structural changes. In particular they should examine policies to promote longer-term saving or investment. There are many arguments (some have been presented here) why markets might not perform well in provisioning for the future (uncertainties, moral hazard, the lack of concern for future generations and so on). Governments may be able to boost saving and investment to the advantage of both current and future generations.

Savings can be raised by increasing public (cutting deficits) or private saving. As for public saving the prescription is simple—tax more or spend less. This will involve difficult decisions, and one can try to propose administrative structures that will improve tax collections and make it harder to raise spending. Some aspects of private saving were discussed briefly in the third section. Government revenues could also be enhanced by introducing more efficient user chargers and limiting deficits in public firms (here, privatization or commercialization may have an important role to play in ensuring future revenue flows). The methods that have been proposed to limit expenditures include tighter review procedures, zero-based budgeting (all expenditures must be justified annually, not just increments to expenditures), line-item vetoes, time-limited subsidies that require an act of parliament for renewal and cash limits. But at the end of the day there is no substitute for the determination to make difficult decisions.[39]

It is interesting that some have argued—for example, Healey (1989, p. 432) in his autobiography when reflecting on his period as Chancellor of the Exchequer—that it is more difficult to run a tight budget in a democracy than in other governmental systems. On the other hand, fiscal rectitude may be seen as a vote winner if the population has been scarred by the experience of very high inflation (for example, Germany before World War II, or Argentina more recently). Pressures to curb inflation also seem high on the agenda of voters in the transforming economies of eastern Europe and the former Soviet Union.

It is not easy to promote private saving through interest rates—aggregate effects seem to be small. Where financial intermediaries are weak, saving could be promoted, or at least allocated more effectively, by building financial institutions and markets. Where government pension promises are grand relative to resources and are not linked to personal contributions, saving can be promoted through personalized accounts.[40] Linking individual contributions to individual benefits rewards the marginal decision to save more. If personal contributions (linked to benefits) are introduced at the same time as current entitlements to benefits are reduced (for example, through raising retirement ages), then public and private saving may rise together.

The problems of making grand promises for pensions are more serious for advanced and transitional countries. Developing countries have avoided these problems by offering limited coverage and often small rewards for those who are covered. Indeed, in a number of cases pension contributions have been subjected to de facto capital levies since the pension funds are obliged to hold a large fraction of assets in government bonds, which yield only low returns. Given this state of affairs, it would seem that in developing countries policies to promote saving are best channelled through greater diversification and development of financial intermediaries, and the promotion of government saving.

On the investment front some government programmes do show high returns. These include primarily health and education.[41] Similar comments apply to the right kind of infrastructure.[42] Although increasing commercialization and private sector contributions can contribute to greater efficiency in some areas of infrastructure only some of this commercialization can or should arise through privatization.[43] It is probably sensible that, for the most part, roads, some of power (except generation) and, in many cases, water stay in the public sector. These will constitute a large part of total infrastructure.

Environmental investments are often squeezed out when axes are falling and should thus be remembered all the more after crises or stabilization. Government must take responsibility for many of these investments often, but not always, paying for them out of the public budget.[44]

Strengthening competition and budget constraints are generally crucial to a well-functioning market economy and areas in which the government has a strong role to play. The necessary attention from senior politicians and government servants in these areas of detailed and long-term institution building will be more easy to capture in better times.

There is no doubt that the agenda for strong government action in good times is substantial. But in good times as well as bad times, difficult choices must be made. It is important to avoid spurious macroeconomic policies. Short-term fiscal incentives to boost investment are far from being efficient in the medium term since they undermine continuity and credibility. In the same vein attempts to promote household saving through fiscal incentives typically result in substitution among different forms of financial assets without any increase in overall saving. Much of the reforms and investment I have discussed are long term. It is important to prepare early.

CONCLUDING COMMENTS

In a number of respects the developments and ideas that I reviewed have made the tasks facing governments more subtle and more difficult. Governments are under stronger pressures to balance budgets and, indeed, to bring down debt-GDP ratios, which have risen sharply in the past 20 years. They have to blend their policies with the market. Such a blending involves much deeper conceptual issues than those, in principle, facing the managers of command economies. Their actions are scrutinized constantly by increasingly unconstrained and well-informed public debate. Their macroeconomic policies have to take account of the challenges of integrated world capital markets. It has in many ways become more difficult to be a policy-maker, policy adviser or policy administrator.

On the other hand, these are exciting times. World barriers are breaking down. Economic instabilities are better understood and hence, to some extent, more manageable. Democracy has advanced strongly in many countries. The experience of government, and market imperfections and failures are now combined and interpreted in a more subtle way—the issues are not presented as an artificial horse race between the two.

I have argued that experience has taught us a great deal. I stressed throughout this chapter the importance of a strong, democratic but limited state—one that takes on responsibilities for which there are analytically strong theoretical and empirical arguments for doing so, and those that it is capable of delivering. This may involve refocussing or playing only a minor role in tasks that may be, in principle, important but for which adequate policies have not been formulated. But the areas identified go clearly beyond a night-watchman or minimalist state—they include health, education, social security, infrastructure, environment, defence, administration and rule of law in economic activities and elsewhere. And I have especially stressed the importance of macroeconomic stability as a necessary condition for the effective functioning of the market economy. However difficult the circumstances, the government has a responsibility to deliver this stability.

APPENDIX: SUSTAINABLE DEFICITS

Consider a primary deficit D (that is, a deficit before interest payments), which is entirely financed by bonds paying interest rate r. The price level is P, real GDP is Y, the stock of bonds is B, the debt-to-GDP ratio is β, and the deficit-to-GDP ratio (D/PY) is α. Then:

$$(1) \qquad \dot{B} = D + rB \text{ or } \frac{\dot{B}}{B} = \frac{D}{B} + r$$

where dots denote time derivatives. Equation 1 says that outstanding debt rises by the sum of the primary deficit and the interest payments. The debt-to-GDP ratio β is defined as:

$$(2) \qquad \beta \equiv \frac{B}{PY}$$

so that its rate of change is given by the rate of change of the numerator less that of the denominator:

$$(3) \qquad \frac{\dot{\beta}}{\beta} = \frac{\dot{\beta}}{\beta} - \frac{\dot{P}}{P} - \frac{\dot{Y}}{Y}$$

From equations 1 and 3 we have:

$$(4) \qquad \frac{\dot{\beta}}{\beta} = \frac{D}{B} + \left(r - \frac{\dot{P}}{P}\right) - g$$

or

$$(5) \qquad \frac{\dot{\beta}}{\beta} = \frac{\alpha}{\beta} + \hat{r} - g$$

where $\hat{r}$ is the real rate of interest ($\hat{r}$, less the rate of inflation) and g is the growth rate of real GDP. Thus the debt-to-GDP ratio falls only if:

$$(6) \qquad -\alpha > \beta(\hat{r} - g)$$

that is, if the primary surplus ($-\alpha$) as a fraction of GDP exceeds the difference between the real rate of interest and the rate of growth, where this difference is multiplied by the debt-to-GDP ratio.

NOTES

I am very grateful for the guidance and contributions of my colleagues at the EBRD, namely Kasper Bartholdy, Robin Burgess, Willem Buiter, Vanessa Glasmacher, Rika Ishii, Ricardo Lago and Andrew Tyrie, and the helpful comments that were provided by participants at various meetings of the UN High Level Group on Development Strategy and Management of the Market Economy. The views expressed are not necessarily those of the EBRD.

1. The first part of chapter 7 in this volume is devoted to this problem.
2. See, for example, table 10 of World Bank (1995).
3. This chapter draws heavily on Buiter, Lago and Stern (1997).
4. Indeed, trade growing faster than GDP has been an important feature of world growth since World War II. See, for example, Bhagwati (1988).
5. The fall would have been more drastic if one excluded from official bilateral and multilateral sources in 1995 the exceptional financing package for Mexico (which amounted to $11 billion of net disbursements).
6. The Mexican authorities are keenly aware that the (risk-adjusted) post-tax rate of return in Mexico cannot fall to a level systematically below that in Miami or New York. See, for example, Gil Díaz (1987).
7. See, for example, EBRD (1995), chapter 4.
8. See the fourth section for further discussion.
9. See, for example, Buiter, Lago and Stern (1997).
10. This decline could be dated somewhat earlier—the death of Nehru in 1964, war with Pakistan in 1965 and a series of poor harvests caused the abandonment of the Third Five-Year Plan in the mid–1960s.
11. It is non-rival and non-excludable in the usual sense, but it is not a direct input or output. Rather, it influences the quality of decision-making. Hence, I am stretching the term public good a little.
12. See, for example, Stern (1991), or Buiter, Lago and Stern (1997).
13. See Stern (1991) and Burgess and Stern (1993).
14. For evidence from industrial countries, see, for example, UK Government, *Economic Trends*, and from developing countries see, for example, Drèze and Sen (1989).
15. See, for example, Nozick (1974), Dworkin (1977), Rawls (1972) and van Parijs (1995).
16. See Sen (1987), Drèze and Sen (1989) and Burgess and Stern (1991).
17. And in doing this we must take account of the advantages and availability of competition, and of differential incentives and accountability.
18. In both telecommunications and power, the ability to enforce revenue collection through disconnection is basic to successful commercialization.
19. This section is based on my work on taxation issues over the past 20 years, including close involvement with the tax administrations and policy-makers in a number of industrial and developing countries.
20. A primary surplus means that government revenue exceeds expenditure before allowing for interest on public debt. See, for example, Buiter, Lago and Stern (1997).
21. Again, see Buiter, Lago and Stern (1997).

22. See, for example, the Netherlands in table 11 of World Bank (1995) and Burgess and Stern (1993).
23. See, for example, Burgess and Stern (1993).
24. See, for example, Ahmad and Stern (1991), Kay and King (1978). and Newbery and Stern (1987).
25. See Burgess and Stern (1993) for an analysis of tax structures in developing and industrial countries.
26. For revenue/GNP figures and breakdowns see table 11 of World Bank (1995).
27. See, for example, Dixit and Pindyck (1994).
28. See Dornbusch (1990).
29. See, for example, von Hayek (1935) and Schumpeter (1942).
30. See, for example, Gil Diaz (1987), Cardoso (1992), Cardoso, Paes de Barros and Urani (1995), and Kane and Morisset (1993).
31. See, for example, EBRD (1994).
32. See, for example, Fischer (1993), Bruno (1993, 1995), Cooper and others (1993) and Ramey and Ramey (1995).
33. Recently, some studies have argued that inflation damages growth at lower levels of inflation. See for example, Barro (1995) and Sarel (1996). While the argumentation in these papers is less than convincing, the issue is an open one.
34. See below and, for example, EBRD (1994, 1995).
35. Kaufmann (1991) and World Bank (1991, p. 82).
36. See, for example Anand and van Wijnbergen (1989), Joshi and Little (1995) and Stern (1996).
37. Other than if a country joins a currency union and gives up its domestic currency altogether. Even then, the rules of the union are likely to guard against any free riding associated with lax fiscal policies in a given member country.
38. Still, there are some ways, for example, by making it harder for foreigners to buy treasury bills.
39. Narrowing state spending to areas where it has clear comparative advantages over markets (see the third section) can also help to contain expenditures.
40. See Buiter, Lago and Stern (1997).
41. See, for example, Drèze and Sen (1989), Drèze and Sen (1995) or World Bank (1990, 1993).
42. See World Bank (1994).
43. See World Bank (1994), EBRD (1996).
44. See, for example, World Bank (1992).

REFERENCES

Ahmad, E. and N. Stern. 1991. *The Theory and Practice of Tax Reform in Developing Countries*. Cambridge, U.K.: Cambridge University Press.

Anand, R. and S. van Wijnbergen. 1989. "Inflation and the Financing of Government Expediture: An Introductory Analysis with an Application to Turkey." *World Bank Economic Review* 3(January):17–38.

Barro, R. 1995. "Price Stability is the Path to Prosperity." *Financial Times*. Wednesday, May 17, p. 19.

Bhagwati, J. 1988. *Protectionism*. Cambridge, Mass.: MIT Press.

Bruno, M. 1993. "Inflation and Growth in Recent History and Policy: Applications of an Integrated Approach." Hebrew University, Department of Economics, Jerusalem.

_____. 1995. The Kuznets Lectures. New Haven: Yale University Press.

Buiter, W., R. Lago, and N. Stern. 1997. "Promoting an Effective Market Economy in a Changing World: Economic Institutions and Macroeconomic Policies." In *Development Strategy and Management of the Market Economy*, Volume II.

Burgess, R. and N. Stern. 1991. "Social Security in Developing Countries: What, Why, Who and How?" In E. Ahmad, J. Drèze, J. Hills and A. K. Sen, eds., *Social Security in Developing Countries*. Oxford: Oxford University Press.

_____. 1993. "Taxation and Development." *Journal of Economic Literature* 31(2):762–830.

Cardoso, E. 1992. "Inflation and Poverty" NBER Working Paper 7006. Cambridge, Mass.

Cardoso, E., R. Paes de Barros and R. Urani. 1995. "Inflation and Unemployment as Determinants of Inequality in Brazil: the 1980s." In R. Dornbusch and S. Edwards, eds., *Reform, Recovery and Growth: Latin America and the Middle East*. Chicago: University of Chicago Press.

Cooper, R., W. Corden, I. Little and S. Rajapatrana. 1993. *Boom Crisis and Adjustment: The Macroeconomic Experience of Developing Countries, 1970–1990*. New York: Oxford University Press.

Dixit, A. and R. Pindyck. 1994. *Investment under Uncertainty*. Princeton: Princeton University Press.

Dornbusch, R. 1990. "Policies to Move from Stabilization to Growth." In *Proceedings of the Annual World Bank Conference on Development Economics*. Washington, D.C.: World Bank.

Drèze, J.P. and A. K. Sen. 1995. *India: Economic Development and Social Opportunity*. Oxford: Clarendon Press.

_____. 1989. *Hunger and Public Action*. Oxford: Oxford University Press.

Dworkin, R. 1977. *Taking Rights Seriously*. London: Duckworth Press.

EBRD (European Bank for Reconstruction and Development). 1994. *Transition Report*. London, October.

_____. 1995. *Transition Report*. London, October.

_____. 1996. *Transition Report*. London, October.

Fischer, S. 1993. "The Role of Macroeconomic Factors in Growth." *Journal of Monetary Economics* 32(3):485–512.

Gil Díaz, F. 1987. "Some Lessons from Mexico's Tax Reform." In D. Newbery and N. Stern, eds., *The Theory of Taxation for Developing Countries*. Oxford: Oxford University Press.

Healey, D. 1989. *The Time of My Life*. London: Michael Joseph.

Homer, S. 1991. *A History of Interest Rates*. London: Rutgers University Press.

IMF (International Monetary Fund). 1996. *World Economic Outlook*. Washington, D.C., May.

_____. 1981. *Government Finance Statistics Yearbook*. Washington, D.C.

_____. 1996. *Government Finance Statistics Yearbook*. Washington, D.C.

Joshi, V. and I. Little. 1995. "Macroeconomic Stabilization in India, 1991–1993 and Beyond." In V. Joshi and R. Cassen, eds., *India. The Future of Economic Reform*. Oxford: Oxford Universtity Press.

Kane, C. and J. Morisett. 1993. "Who Would Vote for Inflation in Brazil? An Integrated Framework Approach to Inflation and Income Distribution." World Bank Policy Research Working Papers 1183. Latin America and the Caribbean Country Department, Washington, D.C.

Kaufmann, D. 1991. "The Forgotten Rationale for Policy Reform: The Productivity of Investment Projects." Background paper prepared for *World Development Report 1991*, World Bank, Washington, D.C.

Kay, J.A. and M.A. King. 1978. *The British Tax System*. Oxford: Oxford University Press.

Levine, R. and D. Renelt. 1992. "A Sensitivity Analysis of Cross-Country Growth Regressions." *American Economic Review* 82 (September):942–63.

Mitchell, B. 1992. *International Historical Statistics: Europe 1750–1988*. London: Macmillan.

Newbery, D. and N. Stern. 1987. *The Theory of Taxation for Developing Countries*. New York: Oxford University Press.

Nozick, R. 1974. *Anarchy, State and Utopia*. New York: Basic Books.

van Parijs, P. 1995. *Real Freedom for All*. Oxford: Clarendon Press.

Ramey, G. and V. Ramey. 1995. "Cross-Country Evidence on the Link Between Volatility and Growth." *American Economic Review* 85(December):1138–51.

Rawls, J. 1972. *A Theory of Justice*. Oxford: Oxford University Press.

Sarel, M. 1996. "Nonlinear Effects of Inflation on Economic Growth." *International Monetary Fund Staff Papers* 33(March):199–215.

Schumpeter, J. 1942. *Capitalism, Socialism, Democracy*. New York: Harper and Brothers.

Sen, A.K. 1987. *The Standard of Living*. In C. Hawthorn, ed., *Tanner Lectures*. Cambridge, U.K.: Cambridge University Press.

SOPEMI. 1995. *Trends in International Migration*. Annual report. Paris: OECD.

Stern, N. 1991. "Public Policy and the Economics of Development." *European Economic Review* 35(2/3):241–71.

———. 1996. "Tax Reform in Sri Lanka." In M. Blejer and T. Ter-Minassian, eds., *Macroeconomic Dimensions of Public Finance*. Routledge: Washington D.C.

Tobin, J. 1982. "A Proposal for International Monetary Reform." In *Essays in Economic Theory and Policy*. Cambridge, Mass.: MIT Press.

UNICEF. 1994. "Crisis in Mortality, Health and Nutrition." *Regional Monitoring Report,* No. 2, Florence.

von Hayek, F. 1935. *Prices and Production*. New York: Augustus M. Kelley.

World Bank. 1990. *World Development Report 1990*. New York: Oxford University Press.

———. 1991. *World Development Report 1991*. New York: Oxford University Press.

———. 1992. *World Development Report 1992*. New York: Oxford University Press.

———. 1993. *World Development Report 1993*. New York: Oxford University Press.

———. 1994. *World Development Report 1994*. New York: Oxford University Press.

———. 1995. *World Development Report 1995*. New York: Oxford University Press.

———. 1996. *World Debt Tables*. Washington, D.C.

6

Industrial Policy in Developing Market Economies

KOTARO SUZUMURA

An industrial policy is an economic policy that is designed to improve the long-run welfare performance of a national economy by intervening in the allocation of resources between industrial sectors, or in the industrial organization of a specific sector, if the competitive market mechanism fails to function efficiently. Because market failures often arise from imperfect information; the cost of information acquisition, transmission and coordination; factors generating Marshallian externalities; and imperfections in risk and capital markets, the relevance of industrial policy as a strategy for developing market economies and economies in transition seems to be beyond dispute. Indeed, industrial policies have played a substantial part in the economic development of Japan, the Republic of Korea and other countries of east Asia, where the government has actively complemented the market mechanism.[1] As Stiglitz emphasized in chapter 3 of this book, "the government simply cannot replace the market—or any significant part of it. [But it] can play a critical role *through markets* in promoting economic growth" (Stiglitz, 1997, p. 1). The purpose of this chapter is to evaluate the role of industrial policy as a development strategy, paying due attention to its distributional implications, side effects that may be generated and prerequisites for its successful implementation.

Where it is useful to lend concrete substance to my highly stylized exposition, I will supplement my analysis by invoking the experience of postwar Japanese industrial policy. As is well known, a fairly sophisticated system of industrial policies, which evolved in postwar Japan on the basis of prewar and wartime legacy, has often been given credit for Japan's economic reconstruction and rationalization in the immediate postwar period, rapid economic growth in the late 1950s and 1960s, and smooth adjustment to international competition in the presence of frequent external shocks in the 1970s. It is also noteworthy that the Japanese government's industrial policy initiatives have met, more often than not, cooperative response from private agents. Needless to say, the prima facie success of Japanese postwar industrial policy does not prove anything about the workability, effectiveness and transplantability of industrial policy as a development strategy. Thus I am not recommending postwar Japanese industrial policy as a model to be applied to developing market economies and economies in transition. Rather, its relevance is strictly as a collection of concrete historical experiences that may help us identify the factors responsible for the successful application of industrial policies, as well as the dangerous traps that could swallow up the benefits of industrial policies.

A BASIC CONCEPTUAL FRAMEWORK

Given the recent upsurge of concern about industrial policies, it is somewhat perplexing that a standard definition of the concept has never been firmly established in the literature.[2] In the context of the postwar Japanese industrial policy at its zenith in the late 1950s and 1960s, Kaizuka (1973, p. 167) expressed his concern about this conspicuous lack of precision: "[i]t is surprising to note that the term 'industrial policy', to the best of my knowledge, has never been clearly defined". This elusive nature of industrial policy was echoed later by Hindley (1984, pp. 277–8), according to whom, "[t]he term 'industrial policy' has an entirely spurious sound of precision. Over the past ten or fifteen years, the term has become a portmanteau catchword for that broad range of governmental actions which directly affect the structure of production in an economy. From a political point of view, this very lack of precision in definition is a major attraction of support for industrial policy". Consequently, arguments for or against a nation's industrial policy may be addressing entirely different issues.

In view of this lack of conceptual precision, I began this chapter with an explicit definition of industrial policy. Several remarks are in order at this early juncture. First, since the task of industrial policy is to complement the competitive market mechanism when market failures occur, a prerequisite of industrial policy is that the basic legal framework and administrative authority for establishing and maintaining competitive market order already exist. It is also pre-supposed that private agents and government bureaucrats are fairly accustomed to rules and morals that underly competitive market behaviour. I am keenly aware that these prerequisites are not easy to secure in developing market economies and economies in transition. Nevertheless, I contend that we should carefully distinguish two fundamental tasks that a development strategist should confront. The first is the task of designing and implementing institutions to establish a framework for a fully competitive market economy. The second is the task of complementing the competitive market mechanism in the presence of market failures.[3] This chapter focuses exclusively on the latter, leaving the former to other chapters of this book, especially chapters 2 and 3.

Second, industrial policies may be classified more concretely into four major categories. The first category consists of policies affecting the nation's industrial structure. Policies in this category either nurture and promote industries that are of strategic importance or regulate and facilitate the shift of resources away from declining industries towards more promising ones—either by restricting trade and direct foreign investment, or by providing pecuniary incentives such as subsidies and favourable tax treatments, with the purpose of improving the nation's long-run welfare performance. The second category consists of policies designed to correct market failures associated with technology development and imperfect information. Policies in this category encourage and promote the shift towards more appropriate use of research and development (R&D) resources and knowledge by providing a public information exchange, and transmission and dissemination mechanisms, or through the use of favourable tax/subsidy measures. The third category consists of policies seeking to raise economic welfare by means of administrative intervention in the industrial organization of specific industries. Industrial policies in this category, which are exemplified by entry and exit regulations, depression cartels, rationalization cartels and investment adjustment cartels, intervene either in the competitive structure of industries or in the allocation of resources among industries through the use of administrative authority or guidance. The fourth category of industrial policies are those based on political considerations rather than economic considerations. Voluntary export restraints and other bilateral trade-restricting agreements designed to deal with harsh trade frictions are notable examples.

A wide spectrum of other economic policies—such as fiscal and monetary policies designed to control swings in macroeconomic variables like GNP, the general price level and employment over the course of business cycles; policies aimed at equitable income distribution or pollution control; region-specific policies; and policies for small- and medium-size businesses—are often included under the loose umbrella of industrial policies. Such policies, though closely related to industrial policies, will not be considered in this chapter.

Third, to design and implement industrial policies for a specific economy, it is necessary to determine the nature and causes of market failures that justify their use. Furthermore, in considering a nation's long-run welfare performance, it is necessary to specify the nature and scope of welfare judgements that will be applied. There is no way to eschew this task—a nation always consists of groups with conflicting interests, such as consumers and producers, the young and the old, the rich and the poor. In addition, we should also weigh the concerns of the present generation against those of future generations. Policy measures employed in pursuit of industrial policy objectives will vary depending on which interest group receives top priority and which interest group receives only cursory or secondary attention. It goes without saying that in designing and implementing industrial policies, it is often politically difficult to address distributional implications explicitly; doing so almost inevitably uncovers latent conflicts among interest groups, which may be disruptive to the nation's political and social stability. For this reason we often find subtle emphasis in the literature—especially among official documents prepared by the authority in charge of industrial policy—on such ambiguous concepts as "economic rehabilitation", "industrial rationalization", "economic independence", "stable growth", "international competitiveness" and "improvement of work and living conditions", which, in effect, obscure the conflicts of interest that lurk behind each policy decision. Nevertheless, a development strategist should not lose sight of the distributional implications of industrial policies other than the effects on total welfare—that is, their efficiency implications.

Feasibility of policy measures

For an industrial policy to be feasible, it must satisfy two basic conditions. First, the government must be equipped with a rich choice of policy measures that enable the authority in charge of industrial policy to substantiate the policy objectives effectively and efficiently. We facilitate our analysis if we classify industrial policy measures according to two criteria. The first is that of applicability. According to this criterion industrial policy measures can be classified as discretionary measures or universal measures. Discretionary measures are those policies that are used to confer differential treatment to different firms, or firm groups, within the same industry. In contrast, universal measures are those policy measures that are uniformly applied to all firms within the same industry. The second criterion is that of the rights of administrative authority. According to this criterion industrial policy measures can be classified into incentive-providing measures and regulatory measures. The former, which are exemplified by tax/subsidy measures, are designed to induce private firms—through pecuniary or non-pecuniary incentives —to adopt "voluntarily" a behaviour pattern that conforms with industrial policy objectives. The latter, exemplified by administrative guidance, are used to force private firms to comply with industrial policy objectives, even against their wishes.

Second, the feasibility of an industrial policy is also constrained by the extent to which domestic compliance with the government's initiatives is warranted, as well as by the extent to which a nation's industrial policy is accepted internationally. When an industrial policy objective is pursued in terms of discretionary and regulatory measures, some administrative arbitrariness and compulsion arise inevitably. To what extent are private agents willing to put up with such administrative arbitrariness and compulsion? Will they be satisfied if such a policy brings about "good" consequences measured in terms of their attained material well-being, or will they also be concerned about the non-consequential features of a nation's industrial policy, such as procedural fairness, transparency and objective accountability? When a nation's pursuit of an industrial policy objective generates negative spillovers that affect other nations, we should also ask: to what extent will the affected nations tolerate this nation's unilateral pursuit of an industrial policy objective?

The answers to these questions hinge squarely on the stage of a nation's social and economic development. Except possibly in the embryonic and infant stages of development, private agents will not acquiesce to bureaucratic paternalism. Likewise, an industrial policy that is permissible for a nation in her early stage of development will meet harsh international criticism and retaliation if it is pursued by a nation that has already matured into a full-fledged world competitor.

First-best and second-best industrial policies

Are industrial policy interventions always justified when there are market failures? My answer is no: there is no guarantee that an industrial policy can invariably improve the long-run welfare performance of a nation in the face of market failures. Quite often industrial policies fail, just as competitive markets fail. What, then, are the conditions necessary for the complete rectification of market failures? At least three crucial conditions must be satisfied.

First, government must have accurate information regarding the segment of the economy in which market failures have occurred, as well as the causes and consequences of distortions thereby generated. This condition is necessary for the successful diagnosis of market failures. Second, government must be equipped with enough administrative authority to take effective and efficient actions to deal with each market failure diagnosed. This condition is necessary for the appropriate treatment of market failures. Third, government must be capable enough to look far beyond the direct and immediate effects of the remedial policy adopted, taking into account its indirect and long-term effects and making policy decisions to deal with these side effects. This condition is necessary for the appropriate aftercare of the industrial policy.

These conditions are obviously demanding. The first requires, among other things, that government is capable of gathering and making effective use of basic information, such as technology, consumer preferences and initial resource allocation, which is owned by numerous private agents. Note that the initial holders of this information may be unable to transmit what they know in a clear and consistent way to other economic agents, including government, even when they have no incentive to hide or distort their private information and knowledge. This being the case, it is difficult practically, if not impossible logically, for government to order the original holders of private information to divulge that information accurately and quickly for public use, and to then manage and apply it centrally. This is an important insight attributable originally to von Hayek (1948).

The second condition is related to the feasibility problem discussed in the previous section. The regulatory power and authority needed to implement an industrial policy may infringe upon basic economic freedoms, like the freedom to do business and the freedom to choose one's own occupation, and may occasionally turn out to be inconsistent with a nation's competition policy. The third condition requires that government anticipates complex and subtle causal linkages and perceive the future through a thick veil of uncertainty.

Let us call the all-knowing, all-powerful and far-sighted government that satisfies these stringent conditions the first-best government, and industrial policies implementable by only such an ideal government first-best industrial policies. First-best industrial policies can resolve all problems related to market failures in one stroke. But for the purpose of designing a system of industrial policies for developing market economies and economies in transition, first-best industrial policies do not constitute an interesting standard of reference. A real world government is never a first-best government, and it is surely inappropriate to justify interventions by an imperfect government simply because an ideal first-best government can perform miracles. Indeed, policy interventions by an imperfect government may result in the deterioration, rather than the improvement, of a nation's economic welfare. Imagine a situation in which an ideal arbitrator can neatly resolve a harsh dispute among members of a group to the complete satisfaction of all parties involved, yet an imperfect arbitrator may aggravate, rather than resolve, the dispute to the bitter disappointment of all parties involved.

In what follows, I call an imperfect government that must follow the dictates of physical, ability, institutional, political and international constraints a second-best government. Industrial policies that are implementable by such a less-than-perfect government are called second-best industrial policies. In sharp contrast with first-best industrial policies, second-best industrial policies take the realistic constraints on government as given and attempt to generate gradual and piecemeal welfare improvements.

POTENTIALLY JUSTIFIABLE INDUSTRIAL POLICIES

Among the four identified categories of industrial policies, some are justified at least in principle, while others are hardly justified even in principle. Even if some industrial policies are justifiable in principle, they must be implementable by the second-best government before they can qualify as a part of the nation's development strategy. This section is devoted to the issue of theoretical justifiability, leaving the issue of implementability to the next section.

Policies affecting the nation's industrial structure

Industrial policies in this category either nurture and promote industries of strategic importance or regulate and assist resource shifts away from declining industries and towards more promising ones. First, I examine industrial policies that nurture and promote industries of strategic importance. The standard trade policy literature describes this as infant-industry protection. An infant industry, by definition, is an industry that cannot survive under free trade conditions, but may grow into an industry with a competitive edge against foreign rivals once it accumulates production experience (learning by doing) or exploits economies of scale under temporary protection during the early stage of development. Note, however, that standard trade theory maintains that the protection of an infant industry can be justified only under stringent conditions.[4]

For the required protection to be temporary, the industry in question must eventually become self-sustainable. And, the future social benefits obtainable from the industry after maturity should more than compensate for the social costs incurred during the initial period of protection. But this double criterion, known as the Mill-Bastable test, is only a necessary, not a sufficient, condition for protection to be justified. If firms within the industry can appropriate the benefits of the learning process, there is, in principle, no need to provide protection, because firms can make up for their initial private losses with their future private profits.[5] On the other hand, if the outcome of the learning process spills over to other firms, including late-comers who have never contributed to this learning process, firms that sustained the initial losses may not be compensated in the future—and industry output may be less than what is socially desirable, or the industry may fail to get started in the first place. Thus it is the non-appropriability of learning-induced technological progress and accumulation of knowledge capital that constitutes a legitimate reason for protecting infant industries.[6]

Even when the learning process and its outcome are internal to firms, so that they can directly control the process and appropriate the benefits, there may still be a clear case for protecting infant industries, provided that the country is large (in the jargon of trade theory). Suppose that the expansion of output by an infant industry reduces the international relative price of its product in the future. Then, even when firms' private calculus (after taking into account the appropriable private benefits from learning by doing) incurred deficit, the falling international price may increase future consumer surplus, which may cancel out the social costs of covering firms' initial deficits. If this is the case, protecting an infant industry may yield a higher overall level of economic welfare.[7]

In addition to these well-known classical reasons for protecting infant industries, there are several other justifications for promoting the development of a new industry. A good case in point, which is acutely relevant in the context of developing market economies and economies in transition, is the situation in which several industries, say the steel industry and the machinery industry, or the automobile industry and parts suppliers, stand in a relationship of strategic complementarity, and at least one industry is characterized by economies of scale.[8] In such a situation the interaction among industries may generate Marshallian externalities in the sense that a firm operating in an industry experiences an external downward shift in its average cost curve whenever output of the whole industry expands. As a result, multiple equilibria may exist that are Pareto-rankable. With multiple equilibria, government policy may have a substantial impact on the long-run welfare performance of the economy by helping it to escape a low-level equilibrium trap and to settle into a higher-income equilibrium with industrialization. Murphy, Schleifer and Vishney (1989) presented several theoretical explanations for justifiable government activities. Their study is reminiscent of the classical theses of Rosenstein-Rodan (1943) and Nurkse (1953).

Using the example of the steel industry and the machinery industry, we can illustrate a role for government in this context. If demand for steel products is low (high), scale economies in the steel industry will be left underexploited (effectively made use of), and steel products will remain expensive (become less expensive). Accordingly, average cost in the machinery industry, which uses steel products as major inputs, will also remain high (become lower) and as a result the demand for machinery will remain low (become higher). In turn, the derived demand for steel products will also remain low (become higher). Thus, there are two stable equilibria, high steel production, high machinery production and low steel production, low machinery production, in which the first is Pareto-superior to the latter.[9]

In order for this economy to escape from the low-level equilibrium trap and realize the high-level equilibrium, a big push for industrialization through coordination of investments among sectors is required. And industrial policy may be of great help in coordinating expectations about investments by other firms around the high-level equilibrium.

A more sophisticated explanation of coordination failures is provided by Rodríguez-Clare (1993, 1996), who visualizes a situation in which multiple equilibria arise from strategic complementarities among sectors and cumulative processes generated by increasing returns to scale in the sector producing support services and complex inputs. Suppose that the manufacturing sector producing tradeable final goods requires the domestic availability of non-tradeable support services and complex inputs. The efficiency of the manufacturing sector will be enhanced by the well-diversified availability of these services and inputs, but the extent of their availability is limited by the size of the market. In such a situation the economy may get stuck in a low-level equilibrium, in which the manufacturing sector uses primitive technology that does not require highly diversified support services and complex inputs, and, accordingly, the extent of input specialization remains shallow. The potential role of industrial policy in this context is to help the economy escape from the historical trap of low-efficiency specialization by facilitating linkages between the manufacturing sector and the intermediate inputs sector.

Three remarks are worth making at this juncture. First, although Rosenstein-Rodan (1943) used the idea that coordination failures are the main obstacle to economic development as a plea for large-scale development planning, the necessary government action for circumventing coordination failures need not be comprehensive planning. As was acutely observed by Nurkse (1953, p. 249), coordination of investments among private firms may be achieved through "the infectious influence of business psychology", which, in turn, may be generated through information exchange, coordination and dissemination among private firms under the auspices of an industrial policy authority.

Second, a big-push theory à la Rosenstein-Rodan and his descendants meets a common objection to the effect that their model presupposes that foreign trade is costly. But in an open economy that faces an international competitive market, the size of the domestic market need not hinder the adoption of technologies that promote increasing returns to scale. It is true that the big-push theory is essentially based on a closed-economy model reflecting the "export pessimism" at the time and that "[t]he East Asian success stories have given credence to the belief of many economists in a positive relationship between outward-orientation and economic development" (Bardhan, 1995, p. 2986).[10] Nevertheless, it would be wrong to neglect the size of the domestic market altogether in choosing a nation's development strategy, even in an open economy. After all, the development of the Japanese automobile industry was largely a function of the size of the domestic market, which enabled firms to exploit economies of scale and strengthen their competitive edge before the Japanese market was finally opened to international competitors.

Third, it may be informative to cite a few concrete cases from postwar industrial policies in Japan in order to illustrate the coordinating role of industrial policy. The first case is the priority production system (1946–48). It was aimed at industrial rehabilitation in the war-devastated economy, which had been closed since the outbreak of the war. The specific focus of industrial policy was the resumption of production in mining and manufacturing through the joint expansion of the strategically important coal and steel industries.

Note that the steel industry, characterized by strong economies of scale, could be expanded if coal output could be expanded and allocated to the steel industry on a top-priority basis—but not otherwise. The coal industry, in turn, could be expanded if steel output could be expanded and allocated to the coal industry on a top-priority basis—but not otherwise. To break this impasse, which is a typical case of coordination failure, the priority production system brought into full play the direct control measures left over from the wartime economy—materials rationing, government financing, price controls, price support subsidies and import allocations. To the extent that these direct control measures, rather than indirect, indicative and incentive-providing measures, were invoked in the priority production system, this policy is more a vestige of wartime control than a precursor of market-complementing industrial policies.

It is true that the priority production system helped Japan to initiate the process of economic rehabilitation fairly quickly, but the resulting resource allocation lacked any guarantee of economic efficiency. Furthermore, the financing method of this system—the Reconstruction Finance Bank secured funds by issuing bonds that were accepted by the Bank of Japan—exerted serious inflationary pressures, coupled with the lack of competitive discipline in the strategically important industries. In this sense the priority production system, which effectively coped with the problem of coordination failure, left a negative legacy of its own.

The second case is the adjustment of investment allocations to the industries of strategic importance during the rationalization and rapid growth era of the 1950s. Electric power, ocean transportation, coal and steel were recognized as the four major industries of strategic importance. They were identified for their crucial role in providing industrial infrastructure. Because of coordination failures and insufficient private incentives, however, it was felt that these industries would be left underdeveloped, thereby deterring the smooth development of general industrial activities, unless systematic public assistance in the form of allocating investment funds on a priority basis could be provided.

For this purpose the Sub-Committee on Industrial Funds Allocation was established in December 1957 within the Industrial Rationalization Council. It played an official role in adjusting, coordinating and authorizing investment plans for these industries. Prior to and during the official deliberations within the Sub-Committee, the *genkyoku* (the section of the bureaucracy within the government having primary responsibility for developing and supervising policies for a given industry) prepared the investment plan of each industry under its jurisdiction in close contact with the industry association (the industrial counterpart to the genkyoku).

Through this iterative adjustment and coordination process the banking sector could collect reliable information on the direction of industrial policy initiatives, thereby orienting their private loans in coordination with low-interest public loans. The macroeconomic consistency of investment plans for each industry was secured through negotiations among the genkyoku bureaus. The possibility of rent seeking and the incentive to manipulate this mechanism by submitting false information were effectively contained by the expertise of the banking sector in screening industrial and financial information, coupled with the expertise of technocratic government bureaucrats in checking the credibility and consistency of investment plans.

In sharp contrast to the priority production system, which invoked directly interventionist policy measures, the investment allocation scheme used an indirect incentive-generating public-assistance device that provided an information exchange, coordination and dissemination mechanism. Several economists have maintained that among the many policy measures that the Japanese government undertook as part of its postwar industrial policy, those that explicitly or implicitly manipulated industrial information flows within the economy were the most, if not the only, successful ones. For example, Komiya (1975, p. 221) wrote about deliberation councils under the auspices of government ministries:[11]

Whatever the demerits of the system of industrial policies in postwar Japan, it has been a very effective means of collecting, exchanging, and propagating industrial information. Government officials, industry people, and men from governmental and private banks gather together and spend much time discussing problems of industries and exchanging information on new technologies and domestic and overseas market conditions. People at the top levels of the government, industries, and banking circles meet at councils, and junior men meet at their sub-committees or less formal meetings. Probably information related to the various industries is more abundant and easily obtainable in Japan than in most other countries. Viewed as a system of information collection and dissemination, Japan's system of industrial policies may have been among the most important factors in Japan's high rate of industrial growth, apart from the direct or indirect economic effects of individual policy measures.[12]

We now turn to industrial policies aimed at declining and ailing industries and the problems of adjustment assistance.[13] A nation's industrial structure is anything but fixed. For an economy to develop rapidly, its industrial structure must be able to transform itself in response to external changes and shocks. But structural adjustment is almost always accompanied by substantial costs and pains for the people involved. It shifts labour and capital from declining industries to industries with higher growth potential and a sharper competitive edge—a transfer that takes place neither spontaneously nor smoothly. Workers released from declining industries are not easily absorbed into other industries, and the adjustment process, more often than not, ends up producing unemployment. Not only workers, but also productive capacities are often industry-specific and not adjustable to use in other industries. Thus there is a great amount of room for policy interventions—such as unemployment benefits, subsidies for retraining workers, trade controls to eliminate foreign competition in the short-run, collective purchase and disposal of excess capacity, and structural improvement programs, including exempting rationalization cartels from the antimonopoly law—to assist private firms with the problems of structural adjustment.

Are these structural adjustment policies justifiable, at least in principle? In answering this question, attention should be given to fairness considerations along with efficiency considerations. Indeed, in the process of adjustment workers employed in declining industries must bear substantial losses in the form of unemployment. Or, if adjustment assistance policy takes the form of trade restrictions, consumers lose.[14]

To crystallize my points, I examine the effect on a nation's economic welfare of shifting productive factors from declining to non-declining industries, using a highly stylized two-good model. The economy is small, and both goods are traded. In Figure 6.1 the horizontal (vertical) axis measures production and consumption of good 1 (good 2). The long-run production frontier is described by AB, and curves denoted by u_1, u_2 and u_3 are indifference curves of a representative individual. All factors of production are fully employed, so that the optimum resource allocation results in production at a point on AB. The slope of the line q^1 represents the initial terms of trade faced by the economy. If the economy is in its long-run equilibrium under this terms of trade, production and consumption

Figure 6.1: Factor movements and economic welfare

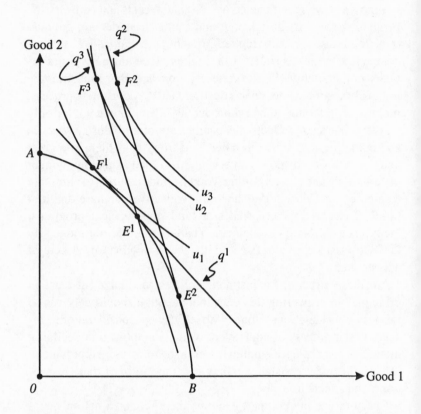

points are denoted by E^1 and F^1, respectively, and the economy is exporting good 1 and importing good 2.

Suppose that domestic firms in the industry that produces good 2 face keener competition from foreign rivals, whose price is gradually falling. As a result this industry is declining. Because of the fall in the foreign price of good 2, the terms of trade for the economy improve to the slope of straight lines q^2 and q^3. If adjustments to this change are made instantaneously, production and consumption points will shift to E^2 and F^2, respectively, and domestic economic welfare will be improved from u_1 to u_3. Because the process of structural adjustment is seldom quick and smooth, however, the shift in production and consumption may take long time. The structural adjustment problem becomes severe if the production point moves inside the frontier because of the emergence of unemployment during this process.[15]

As was made clear in disequilibrium trade theory, pioneered by Haberler (1950), some rigidities in factor prices can drive the production point inside the production frontier. For example, assume that the price of good 1 and wages in the sector producing good 1 remain unchanged, while the price of good 2 falls. The relative wage for the firms producing good 2 rises accordingly, and a portion of the workers employed in the production of good 2 must lose their jobs. This loss does not create any problem if the workers released by firms producing good 2 are immediately employed by firms producing good 1. But because the price of good 1 and wages in this sector remain unchanged, there is no incentive for the firms producing good 1 to increase employment. If unemployment leads to a decline in wages in the sector producing good 1, the producers of good 1 may employ a portion of the unemployed workers, but this mechanism does not function in the presence of wage rigidities. Despite an improvement in its terms of trade, therefore, the economy may suffer a loss in economic welfare if the production point moves inside the frontier. Here, there is ample room for industrial policies aimed at adjustment assistance.

Possible remedial measures abound—for example, restricting trade through tariffs or import controls, implementing employment and wage subsidies and establishing policies directed at business switchovers. The first two measures are more concerned with finding a solution to the unemployment problem rather than promoting a shift of production factors away from declining industries. The third measure, on the other hand, directly promotes the shift of production factors. Two remarks on the pros and cons of these policy measures are warranted.

First, let us compare trade restriction by means of a tariff and by means of a wage subsidy. In Figure 6.2, G denotes the production point in the presence of unemployment in the sector producing good 2 (which was induced by a change in the terms of trade). The corresponding consumption point is given by H, where economic welfare is lower than at F^1. Suppose that government imposes a tariff on the import of good 2 that is just enough to nullify the effects of

Figure 6.2:   A comparison of adjustment policy measures

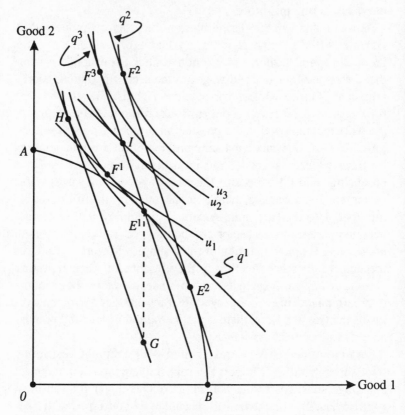

the change in the terms of trade. Then, the production point remains at E^1 and the domestic relative price remains at the previous level. In Figure 6.2 the consumption point I denotes the equilibrium under a tariff—economic welfare is higher than that in the absence of tariff. Thus, not only does this policy prevent unemployment accompanying a change in the terms of trade, but it can also secure higher economic welfare.

Alternatively, if government introduces a wage subsidy, which is just enough to induce firms producing good 2 to maintain current employment, then the production point and the consumption point become E^1 and F^3, respectively. Note that under a wage subsidy consumers gain from the improved terms of trade, because they can attain point F^3 with a wage subsidy compared to point I with a tariff. This occurs because a wage subsidy may affect the unemployment problem without imposing a distortion, whereas a tariff distorts domestic consumer prices.[16]

Second, both a tariff and a wage subsidy effectively mitigate the shock arising from a change in the terms of trade in the short run. But the long-run implications of these policies are problematic. With a change in the terms of trade, factors of production must eventually move from the declining industry to other industries. However, the required resource transfer may be difficult to realize if trade restricting policies hinder changes in domestic prices that might otherwise signal producers that such an adjustment is inevitable. Likewise, producers may not be motivated to facilitate resource transfers if their potential loss may be effectively offset by a wage subsidy.

Experiences in a number of countries show that adjustment assistance policies usually end up preserving declining industries, and required resource transfers may never be made. This result points to the existence of a trade-off between the short-run unemployment problem and the long-run structural adjustment problem. It is impossible to make a general recommendation as to which of the two targets should receive priority. This choice hinges on the nation's time preference, as well as on the prevailing inter-temporal distributional equity.

It can be suggested that a trade restricting policy or an employment maintenance policy implemented for a limited period of time may be useful in dealing with problems of short-run unemployment and structural adjustment. The argument goes as follows. If an adjustment assistance policy is applied for a limited period of, say, five years to rescue a declining industry, the understanding that this assistance will be dismantled after five years can reduce mid- to long-term investment in the declining industry, thereby promoting inter-industrial resource transfers. This strategy sounds good, but the real issue is whether the government can make the time limits proposed credible. All too often when the time-bound adjustment assistance policy is introduced, the private sector does not take the stipulated time limit very seriously. Also, the government may find it too difficult to dismantle the assistance when the time arrives, since removing assistance may lead to a serious unemployment problem if factor movements have been insufficient.

Because in the long-run a shift of production factors from a declining industry to other industries is desirable, active policies designed to promote a voluntary shift in industrial structure may be important. Public provision for technical training to facilitate job switching by workers, provision of incentives to move firms away from areas with a preponderance of declining industries and subsidies for scrapping excess capacities are salient examples of such public policies. Still, however, care should be taken. The deteriorating performance of declining industries by itself is a signal for factors of production to move out. Thus factors of production are bound to move even if the government does not seek recourse in a public policy to promote structural adjustment. Policy interventions are justified only if they outperform, in terms of economic welfare, the autonomous adjustment in response to market signals.

Policies associated with research and development

Research and development is one of the major economic activities vulnerable to market failures. Indeed, because R&D is an activity that creates new technological information that may be easily diffused to other agents in the absence of an effective patent system, private agents who succeed in R&D may be unable to protect the new information they have created against free riding by other agents. Thus there may be socially insufficient private incentives to invest in R&D. But there may be a socially excessive rush to invest in R&D in the presence of an effective patent system, since private agents who succeed in R&D ahead of other competing agents may be able to enjoy exclusively the economic rents from establishing a strong competitive edge against rivals. Thus private R&D may, more often than not, be socially suboptimal, but it cannot be decided a priori whether R&D will be socially insufficient or excessive.

This theoretical indeterminacy notwithstanding, policy-makers in many industrial economies seem convinced that public assistance for promoting private R&D is justified. Indeed, protective and supportive policy measures for private R&D abound, including lenient enforcement of the antimonopoly law for R&D cartels. There is a vast literature on the potentially justifiable measures for promoting private R&D, including subsidizing private R&D and assisting the formation of R&D cartels.[17] But I will refrain from discussing this interesting issue further because the empirical relevance of this class of industrial policies is not warranted in the context of developing market economies and economies in transition. It would be far more relevant for developing market economies and economies in transition to design and implement public assistance promoting the efficient importation of intra-marginal best-practice technology and its smooth adaptation to local needs and environments.

A casual observer may think that industrial policies for technology importation and adaptation are easier to design and implement than industrial policies for promoting private R&D because of the abundant supply of intra-marginal technologies in industrial economies. But an embarassment of riches is a real possibility. Although the formal elements of technology may be transplanted through the purchase of technology licenses and/or capital goods embodying the technology in question, tacit circumstantial knowledge à la von Hayek (1948) associated with the transplanted technology is often crucial for its efficient and effective application to industrial use. More often than not, however, such circumstantial knowledge, being deeply rooted in the peculiarities of local resources, institutions and practices, is difficult to transplant. And this difficulty will be greater, the more options there are. In this situation those who dare to risk considerable capital in attempt to ascertain whether a particular technology will function after international transplantation may be unable to appropriate fully the returns to their innovative attempt. The regrettable consequence is that, despite an abundant supply of intra-marginal technologies, there is little private incentive to make use of them.

On the other hand, if the best-practice technology is easy to identify and transplant across national boundaries, competition for its exclusive importation may raise the price of technology beyond reasonable bounds—to the detriment of developing economies and economies in transition. Thus industrial policies towards technology importation and adaptation have great practical relevance. They may take the form of allocating licenses for technology importation and/or international know-how contracts. However, note that this controlling power over international technology transfer may produce a problem of its own by providing the industrial policy authority with an effective measure for regulating private firms with a view to keeping competition under control. It goes without saying that the regulation of competitive market forces can be a risky venture.

Administrative regulation of competition

There are three instrumental roles of competition. First, competition abhors waste, just as nature abhors a vacuum. If there is waste in the current allocation of scarce resources, an unambiguous signal is sent that there are unexploited profit opportunities, and unfettered inter-firm competition will soon drive waste out. Thus competition plays an instrumental role in promoting economic efficiency. Second, competition is a spontaneous mechanism through which innovations are introduced into the market economy. Firms will be motivated to introduce new innovations in order to sharpen their competitive edge against rivals and also to protect themselves from rivals' challenges. Thus competition plays an instrumental role in promoting long-run economic progress. Third, competition is a discovery procedure (von Hayek, 1978) through which a decentralized economic system finds a way to make efficient use of dispersed information that is privately owned. Because no agent, the government included, owns enough information to calculate the efficient use of resources in one stroke, it is left to market competition to determine who is most capable of meeting market demand. Thus competition plays an instrumental role in promoting and facilitating privacy-respecting, decentralized decision-making.

In addition to these instrumental roles, competition also has an intrinsic value of its own. It is the unique mechanism through which each economic agent can test his/her own life chance on his/her own initiative and responsibility. It is true that the mechanism of competition can be very cruel and wasteful in weeding out the winners from the losers. It is also true that the freedom rendered by this mechanism is crucially conditioned by the initial distribution of assets and capabilities. But these valid reservations do not change the fact that competition is a process that provides each agent with an equal and free opportunity to pursue his/her own aspirations.

In view of these important services, it is widely believed that, except possibly in the embryonic and infant stages of economic development, the guiding principle of industrial policies in developing market economies and economies in transition should be to make the maximum use of the competitive market mechanism. Note, however, that one of the alleged functional impediments of the market mechanism, which is frequently invoked in rationalizing government intervention in the organization of several industries, is excessive competition. It is worth examining the rationale of this allegation in some detail, as it can shed light on the insidious nature of this type of argument.

Those well-accustomed to the standard theory of welfare economics and industrial organization may find the term "excessive competition" dubious. As Baumol (1982, p. 2) has put it, "the standard analysis leaves us with the impression that there is a rough continuum, in terms of desirability of industry performance, ranging from unregulated pure monopoly as the pessimal [*sic*] arrangement to perfect competition as the ideal, with relative efficiency in resource allocation increasing monotonically as the number of firms expands". Reflecting this indoctrination, "a widespread belief that increasing competition will increase welfare" (Stiglitz, 1981, p. 184) is commonly held. Thus it is quite natural to ask: how can competition ever be excessive?

To provide at least one partial answer to this intriguing question, consider an imperfectly competitive industry in which firms are earning higher-than-normal profits. If "a widespread belief" that the "relative efficiency in resource allocation [increases] monotonically as the number of firms expands" is correct, profit-induced entry of new firms must improve economic welfare. By examining whether or not this conjecture is valid, we can check if competition can ever be excessive.

With this purpose in mind, consider Figure 6.3, which describes a long-run Cournot-Nash equilibrium among identical firms. *MM* denotes the market demand curve for the industry as a whole, whereas *RR* denotes the residual demand curve for the individual

Figure 6.3:   Excess entry theorem at the margin

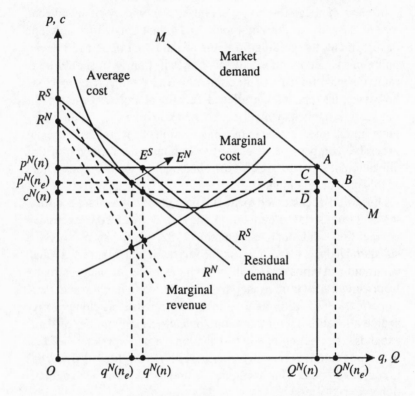

firm. It is clear that $q^N(n_e)$ and $Q^N(n_e)$ denote, respectively, individual firm output and industry output at the long-run Cournot-Nash equilibrium, where n_e denotes the number of firms in the long-run equilibrium. By definition, we have $Q^N(n_e) = n_e q^N(n_e)$. To verify these facts, we only have to notice that the marginal cost curve crosses the marginal revenue curve, derived from the residual demand curve $R^N R^N$, at $q^N(n_e)$, and profits at $q^N(n_e)$ are zero.

Suppose now that the number of competitors is lowered marginally from n_e to n. Since a smaller number of firms are sharing the same market demand, the residual demand curve for an individual firm must shift up to $R^S R^S$, so that the new Cournot-Nash equilibrium, denoted by $q^N(n)$ and $Q^N(n) = n q^N(n)$, satisfies $q^N(n_e) < q^N(n)$ and $Q^N(n_e) > Q^N(n)$.

It is clear that this decrease in the number of firms generates two conflicting effects on social welfare measured by the net market surplus, that is, the sum of consumer surplus and producer surplus. The first is the effect on allocative efficiency, which is due to the concomitant decrease in consumer surplus, resulting from the increase in equilibrium price from $p^N(n_e)$ to $p^N(n)$. In Figure 6.3 this negative effect is measured by the area $Ap^N(n)p^N(n_e)B$. The second is the effect on production efficiency, which is due to the better exploitation of residual scale economies, resulting from the increase in individual equilibrium output from $q^N(n_e)$ to $q^N(n)$. In Figure 6.3 this positive effect is measured by the area $Ap^N(n)c^N(n)D$. The net effect on potential social welfare is given by the difference between two—the area $Cp^N(n_e)c^N(n)D$ less the area ABC. Because the latter is clearly of an infinitesimally higher order than the former, the net effect turns out to be positive, vindicating the excess entry theorem to the effect that the number of firms in the long-run Cournot-Nash equilibrium is socially excessive at the margin.[18] In other words, contrary to the conventional wisdom of neoclassical economics, there is a clear welfare-theoretic sense in which market competition can be socially excessive.[19] Thus we must admit that "regulation by enlightened, but not omniscient, regulators could in principle achieve greater efficiency than deregulation" (Panzer, 1980, p. 313). But this theoretical result falls short of justifying actual intervention into the industrial organization of specific sectors for at least two reasons.

First, restricting competition to control excessive competition in this sense boils down to protecting producer benefits at the expense of consumer benefits. To understand this point, we only have to notice that the excess entry theorem holds as a decrease in consumer surplus is overcompensated by an increase in producer surplus, yet the losses incurred by consumers are not actually compensated by the gains accruing to producers.

Second, the regulation of competition, which was indeed implemented in postwar Japan to keep excessive competition under control by allocating, for example, import quotas or mandatory authorization of new productive facilities, was pursued by assigning priority to firms according to their rank-order based on some simple indices of productive capacity or market share. Thus import quotas for crude oil were allocated in accordance with the rank-order of refining capacity at a certain time.[20]

The effect of using such a rule of thumb on regulation was remarkable. Instead of keeping excessive competition under control as intended, this practice aggravated the situation by motivating firms to expand their productive capacity or market share beyond the level justified by prevailing market conditions. This was done in the obvious hope of securing favourable treatment by government officials in future rounds of allocating privileges: "[T]hat productive capacity has actually been used or referred to for administrative or allocative purposes in direct controls, administrative guidance, or cartelization, and that companies rightly or wrongly expect this to be repeated in future, seem to be the real cause of the 'excessive competition in investment' " (Komiya, 1975, p. 214).

It seems to me that the best way to conclude this subsection is to cite an acute observation made by Dixit (1984, p. 15): "Vested interests want protection, and relaxation of antitrust activity, for their own selfish reasons. They will be eager to seize upon any theoretical arguments that advance such policies in the general interest. Distortion and misuse of the arguments is likely, and may result in the emergence of policies that cause aggregate welfare loss while providing private gains to powerful special groups".

Policies based on political considerations

The second class of industrial policies that are hardly justifiable even in principle from a purely economic point of view are exemplified by voluntary export restraints (VERs), voluntary import expansions (VIEs) and other bilateral agreements to deal with trade frictions. I use VERs as an example.

A VER, which is a quota on trade imposed by the exporting country instead of the importing country, is often introduced at the request of the govenment of the importing country and is accepted by the exporting country to forestall other trade restrictions.[21] Since a VER is a variant of an import quota in which license is assigned to foreign exporters rather than to domestic importers, it is a very costly protective measure to the importing country. Thus a natural question to ask is: why is this form of bilateral agreement requested by the government of the importing country, and why should it be accepted voluntarily by the exporting country? The answer is simple.

Instead of accepting a VER agreement, the importing country could use a tariff or import quota that would limit imports by the same amount. If these alternative import-restricting measures were invoked, rents earned by foreign exporters under a VER would remain in the importing country either as tariff revenue or import license fees. Using this alternative scenario as a standard of reference, let us consider how stakeholders are affected by agreeing to a VER arrangement.

First, by agreeing voluntarily to a VER, the foreign country may secure rents that would otherwise remain in the importing country. Second, domestic producers, who would otherwise have to face challenges from foreign exporters, are protected by the VER cartel and can reap extra profits from price increases, which foreign exporters can also enjoy. Thus domestic producers and foreign exporters are able to simultaneously increase their profits at the cost of an overwhelming decrease in domestic consumers' benefit. I recall an insightful passage from Pareto (1927, p. 379): "A protectionist measure provides large benefits to a small number of people, and causes a very great number of consumers a slight loss. This circumstance makes it easier to put a protection measure into practice". It is for this reason that the VER arrangements (and their import-side counterpart, VIE arrangements) are presumably the worst forms of protectionism.[22]

Before concluding this subsection, a remark on the free trade regime and the associated dispute settlement mechanism may be in order. In addition to the welfare-based criticism against bilateral VER arrangements, there is a non-welfare-based or procedural criticism that also casts serious doubt on the legitimacy of bilateralism in international conflict resolution. More often than not bilateral agreements are prepared and concluded in complete neglect of third parties that have no way of representing themselves in the procedure, even though they would most likely be affected by spillover effects. Furthermore, this problem will not be alleviated even when the nature of bilateral agreements is such that the third parties can enjoy equally the beneficial outcomes of bilateral agreements in full accordance with the most-favoured-nation treatment stipulated in the GATT/WTO agreements. As Berlin (1958, pp. 15-16) aptly put it, "[t]he desire to be governed by myself, or at any rate to participate in the process by which my life is to be controlled, may be as deep a wish as that of a free area for action, and perhaps historically older". The problem of bilateralism becomes worse when it is enforced by unilateral aggression and/or extra-territorial application of domestic laws.

As Stiglitz rightly emphasized in chapter 3 of this book, the institutional infrastructure defines the "rules of the game", and the rules of the game thus defined, in turn, have a major impact not only on efficiency, but also on equity. It goes without saying that one of the most important components of institutional infrastructure is the free trade regime with its associated multilateral dispute settlement mechanism. It is worth remembering that the future of an outward-oriented development strategy hinges on the successful provision of this component of institutional infrastructure and the collective commitment by all parties involved to the successful functioning of this public dispute-settlement mechanism.

Implementation of potentially justifiable industrial policies

Even when an industrial policy can be justified in principle, there is no a priori guarantee that such a legitimate policy is actually implementable by the second-best government. Partly for lack of accurate information and partly for lack of ability to understand the causes and consequences of market failures, coupled with the lack of clearly defined and unanimously supported social objectives, the problem faced by the second-best government is not simply that of constrained optimization of a given social objective. Instead, the real issue faced is that of designing and managing a public mechanism for information exchange, coordination and dissemination, through which disparate and potentially conflicting objectives of private agents and government officials are made compatible, and voluntary compliance by all parties involved with the second-best industrial policy is eventually secured. Certainly, this is no simple task.

Making this task even more difficult is the ultimate cause of government failures: human fallibility. Government interventions—be they directly interventionist measures, administrative order or guidance, or incentive-providing measures—inevitably favour some industries over others. Thus there is always potential room for corruption, opportunistic behaviour and rent-seeking activities—and government-assisted market economies may ultimately perform worse than laissez faire with market failures.

There are no magical formulas to resolve all of these difficulties. The best we can do is to examine the experiences of industrial policies in several well-performing countries and ask how their industrial policies escaped serious government failures. Our current state of knowledge falls far short of answering this question in sufficient detail, but some parts of our answer may be found in the postwar Japanese industrial policies.

First, when industries of strategic importance were selected and favourable tax treatments, low-interest public loans and other measures for promotion and protection were applied on a priority basis, the criteria for industry selection were impartial, transparent and objectively accountable. Depending on the stage of economic development, the exact nature of these selection criteria differed substantially. For example, the criteria for industry selection invoked during the rapid growth era in Japan were explained in the relevant official document as follows:

The industrial vision...placed increased emphasis on the sophistication of the industrial structure through more strengthening of the heavy and chemical industries than ever, in order to enhance the country's international competitiveness. In defining the optimal industrial structure of the future, two criteria were adopted: one was the rate of productivity growth, and the other, income elasticity. The income elasticity criterion led to greater appreciation of the importance of developing export industries with high demand elasticity relative to world growth in real income. On the other hand, the productivity increase rate purported to examine the prospects for relative superiority on the basis of improved productivity. These criteria were in effect an application of a theory of comparative production [*sic*] with long term consideration on dynamic development of international trade". (Industrial Structure Council, Ministry of International Trade and Industry, 1980)

It is doubtful that the strategic industries were in fact selected meticulously in accordance with the two main objective criteria—the productivity improvement criterion and the income elasticity criterion.[23] But the fact that the selection of industries had to be accounted for in terms of such objective criteria reveals that the government bureaucrats in charge of industrial policy had to pay careful attention to the objective accountability of industries selected for preferential promotion. In such a situation there was little room for excessive administrative arbitrariness, opportunistic behaviour and rent-seeking activities.

Second, a cooperative mechanism for exchanging, coordinating and authorizing activity plans of various industries was meticulously developed for the purpose of implementing second-best industrial policies, in which government bureaucrats, industry associations, and private and government banks participated, exchanged information and negotiated with each other. Through this interactive coordination mechanism, reliable information on the direction of industrial policy initiatives and the macroeconomic constraints the economy was facing were effectively disseminated and shared, thereby motivating and helping private firms to adjust and coordinate their plans and expectations accordingly. The possibility of rent-seeking and manipulation through false information submission could be effectively checked by the expertise of the participating banking sector, as well as by technocratic bureaucrats. It was clearly understood by all parties involved that this game would be repeated sufficiently many times, and the attempt to squeeze out private benefits in the short run through strategic manipulation would vitiate one's reputation in the long run beyond rectification. It was this mechanism that left little room for rent-seeking activities by, and corruption of, government bureaucrats.[24]

The more we emphasize the role of a cooperative mechanism for information exchange, coordination and sharing, however, the more we are exposed to further questions like:

• Cooperative behaviour among competitive firms may prepare the stage for collusive behaviour to the detriment of social welfare. How could this subtle and dangerous shift from cooperation to collusion be detected and contained?

- Cooperation among competitive firms may easily dull the edges of their competitive swords, and may even inhibit effective competition itself, leading to managerial slack or a more general loss of economic efficiency. How could this foreseeable danger be alleviated and harsh inter-firm competition be maintained?
- Frequent and informal negotiations and persuasions among government bureaucrats and people in business may pave the road towards encouraging firms to seek favours from government bureaucrats in exchange for pecuniary or non-pecuniary compensations. How could this easy progression to corruption be blocked?

In full awareness of these crucial questions, the third ingredient of my reasoned answer to the original question is: the institutional structures were deliberately developed so that firms within the cooperative mechanism had to compete with each other for prizes in the form of preferential access to favourable tax/subsidy measures, permission of international know-how contracts or exclusive import licenses. Examples of such contest-based competition abound in the postwar Japanese economy and some other highly performing economies in east Asia. The most widely applied contests were export contests for favourable access to credit and foreign exchange. Likewise, the government's authority to grant licenses to firms that complied with government policy was invoked to generate contest-based competition among firms. It was this contest-based competition that effectively prevented inefficiency and favouritism. Put differently, even within the context of a cooperative mechanism for coping with coordination failures, the key word is, again, competition. In the absence of market failures it is market-based competition that matters, whereas in the presence of market failures it is contest-based competition within the coordination mechanism that matters.

It is obviously important for the successful implementation of second-best industrial policies that the nation has a well-organized, highly motivated and sincere group of government bureaucrats promoting industrial policies. It is much safer, however, if a well-designed and well-managed public mechanism for implementing industrial policies exists, in which private agents and government agents iteratively interact, and that is robust enough to ward off the potential danger of rent-seeking activities, opportunistic behaviour, strategic manipulation and bureaucratic corruption.

OUTCOMES AND PROCEDURES: THE CONCEPT OF DEVELOPMENT RE-EXAMINED

In an insightful paper that compared the government-business relationships in Japan, the Republic of Korea and Taiwan (province of China), Johnson (1987, p. 141) rightly pointed out that "an indispensable element in any model of the capitalist developmental state [is] the commitment by the political elite to 'market-conforming' methods of intervention in the economy...One of the things a state committed to development does is [to] develop a market system, and it does this to the extent that its policies reduce the uncertainties or risks faced by entrepreneurs, generate and disseminate information about investment and sales opportunities, and instill an optimistic psychology in the people".[25] To this extent, Japan, the Republic of Korea and Taiwan (province of China), as well as some other high-performing countries in east Asia, have much in common. The real difference, if any, lies in the methods these countries used in implementing their industrial policies. For example, it is well-known that "[t]he Japanese economic bureaucracy has long found that its most effective powers are tailor-made, verbal, ad hoc agreements implemented through 'administrative guidance" (Johnson, 1987, p. 159),[26] whereas in Korea "[t]he hand of government reaches down rather far into the activities of individual firms with its manipulation of incentives and disincentives" (Mason and others, 1980, p. 254).[27]

In any case, because they are interventionist, industrial policies inevitably interfere with private economic activities. In order to motivate private agents to comply with industrial policy initiatives, it is desirable that the objectives and instruments of industrial policies do not conflict outright with private objectives and incentives. Suppose, for the sake of argument, that these conditions are fully satisfied. A basic fact still remains that the process of policy design and implementation is exclusively controlled by government bureaucrats in charge of industrial policies. This is so even when private agents are actively involved in the public information exchange, coordination and dissemination mechanism for implementing second-best industrial policies, since such a mechanism is not only designed, but also managed, by government bureaucrats.

If we are devoted consequentialists exclusively concerned with the outcomes of industrial policies, such heavy dependence on the capability and sincerity of the government bureaucrats in charge of industrial policies may not bother us at all. But if we care not only about outcomes, but also about the procedures through which these outcomes emerge, we should pay attention to procedural considerations, as well as outcomes. Instead of focusing on outcomes of politico-economic mechanisms, we should pay attention to the pair of an outcome and the politico-economic mechanism that generates this outcome.

People seem prepared to accept this extended viewpoint and make judgements as follows. Let x and y be the outcomes of politico-economic mechanisms m^1 and m^2, respectively. According to Mr. A's judgements, having x through m^1 is better than having y through m^2. In effect, one is making such judgements when one says that it is better to obtain whatever commodity bundle the free market enables one to choose than to be assigned another commodity bundle by the central planning board, even when the latter bundle contains more of all commodities. One is also making such judgments when one asks for more bread, more wine and so on, irrespective of how these commodities are made available. In the former case the politico-economic mechanisms have clear lexicographic priority over the outcomes emerging from these mechanisms, whereas, in the latter case, the outcomes have lexicographic priority. While such extreme lexicographic judgements are certainly not inconceivable, it is presumably more realistic to suppose that individuals care not only about social decision-making mechanisms, but also about outcomes that emerge from them, and they are prepared to strike a balance between these two considerations.[28]

The point to be made here is the importance of judging a nation's stage of social and economic development within this extended conceptual framework. Unfortunately, the traditional framework of development economics focuses exclusively on outcomes and, more often than not, neglects procedural considerations altogether.

Although our point was made in rather abstract terms, the importance of procedural considerations along with outcome considerations in the appropriate understanding of social and economic development is acutely relevant in developing market economies and economies in transition. Often it is said that, for the sake of promoting rapid social and economic development, an authoritarian, if not an outright despotic, developmental state may be more suitable. This is a view that judges the form of a state from the exclusive peephole of its instrumental value. What I am suggesting is that we should take the intrinsic value of a state and its decision-making procedures into proper consideration along with their instrumental value.

CONCLUDING REMARKS

Industrial policy is an amalgamation of many complicated policies. In order to categorize these policies according to whether they are justifiable at least in principle or not justifiable even in principle, I have abstracted historical backgrounds and political contexts from the concrete experience of the Japanese postwar industrial policies. As Alfred Whitehead once observed, "[t]he utmost abstractions are the true weapons with which to control our thought of concrete fact". Nevertheless, if the postwar experience of Japanese industrial policies could be valuable to developing market economies and economies in transition as a model for development strategy, the most precious part of such a transplantation exercise would be a detailed historial account of the success and failure of each policy within its concrete socio-political context, rather than a neatly edited book of blue-prints that are taken out of historical context. In this chapter I tried to draw a map that development strategists could use for working out their own industrial policy design on the basis of concrete experiences in the past. Like any map, this map is an abstraction.

In concluding this chapter, two fictitious stories about the role of industrial policy may be suggestive. First, a race horse may run well if it is given the right amount of water at the right moment, but water given in untimely fashion or in excess tires the horse, so that it may even fail to complete a race. Industrial policy is just like water. It may be useful in supplementing the competitive market mechanism if it is properly applied, but it may be detrimental if misapplied. Second, a mountain hut is useful for mountaineers as it provides them with shelter from storms. However, the knowledge that there is a dependable mountain hut may precipitate more reckless mountaineering. Likewise, industrial policy may induce firms to invest more than what may be rationalized on the basis of fundamental market conditions, because firms may be led to expect that industrial policy will come to the rescue if their reckless competitive behaviour brings about excess capacity and declining profitability. Both stories are meant to highlight side effects of industrial policy, which should never be overlooked, whatever the merits of industrial policy as a development strategy.

APPENDIX: ENTRY BARRIERS AND ECONOMIC WELFARE

Consider an oligopolistic industry producing a homogeneous product, where n firms compete in terms of quantities. Let $\pi_i(q)$ be the profit of firm i, which is defined by

(A1) $\pi_i(q:) = q_i f(Q:) - c(q_i), (i = 1, 2 ..., n)$,

where f is the inverse demand function, q_i is the output of firm i, $q: = (q_1, q_2, ..., q_n)$ is the output vector, $Q: = \Sigma_{i=1}^n q_i$ is the industry output and c is the cost function, which is the same for all firms.

Throughout this appendix, I assume that $f'(Q) < 0$ for all $Q > 0$, $c'(q) > 0$ and $c''(q) > 0$ for all $q > 0$, and $(\partial^2/\partial q_i \partial q_j) \pi_i (q) < 0$ $(i \neq j; i; j = 1, 2, ..., n)$ for all $q > 0$. The last assumption is what Bulow, Geanakoplos and Klemperer (1985) called "strategic substitutability". To see the crucial role of this assumption, let the reaction function of firm i, $r_i(q_{-i})$ with $q_{-i}: = (q_1, ..., q_{i-1}, q_{i+1}, ..., q_n)$, be defined by

(A2) $q_i = r_i(q_{-i})$ if and only if $(\partial / \partial q_i)\pi_i(r_i(q_{-i}), q_{-i}) = 0$.

It is clear that the reaction function is downward sloping if and only if the strategic substitutability is satisfied.

For each n, I assume that the symmetric Cournot-Nash equilibrium exists. Let $q^N(n)$ and $Q^N(n)$ be, respectively, the individual firm's output and the industry output at the symmetric Cournot-Nash equilibrium with n firms. To see how $q^N(n)$ and $Q^N(n)$ will be affected by a change in n, we define the cumulative reaction function, $R_i(Q)$, by

(A3) $q_i = R_i(Q)$ if and only if $q_i = r_i(Q - q_i)$.

It is easy to check that the cumulative reaction curve is downward sloping if and only if the reaction function is downward sloping. Note also that, by the definition of the Cournot-Nash equilibrium, we have $q^N(n) = R_i(Q^N(n))$ for all $i = 1, 2, ..., n$. Adding up these n equations, we obtain $Q^N(n) = \Sigma_{i=1}^n R_i(Q^N(n))$. Thus $Q^N(n)$ is nothing other than the fixed point of the aggregate cumulative reaction function $\Sigma_{i=1}^n R_i$. Noting this fact, figure A1 describes the displacement of the Cournot-Nash equilibrium when the number of firms increases from n to $n + \Delta n$. As is clear from this figure (see Suzumura, 1995 for analytical proof, if necessary), we have $q^N(n) > q^N(n + \Delta n)$ and $Q^N(n) < Q^N(n + \Delta n)$.

Let $\pi^N(n)$ be the profit earned by each incumbent firm at the Cournot-Nash equilibrium with n firms, which is defined by

Figure A1: Firm entry and output response

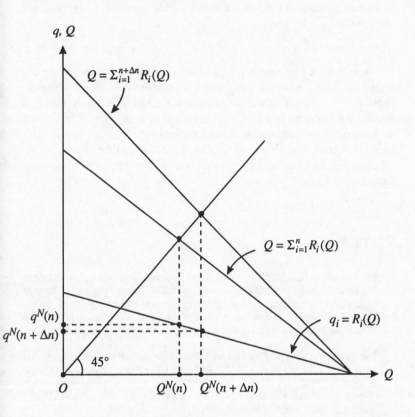

(A4) $\quad \pi^N(n) := q^N(n) f(Q^N(n)) - c(q^N(n))$.

If $\pi^N(n) >$ (or < 0), potential firms (incumbent firms) will be motivated to enter into (exit from) this industry, so that the *long-run Cournot-Nash equilibrium* will be attained when there are n_e firms in the industry, each producing the output $q^N(n_e)$, where n_e is defined by $\pi^N(n_e) = 0$. If this industry is left unregulated, this is the outcome we should expect to observe in the long run.

As in the main text I adopt a welfare criterion of net market surplus, which is defined by

(A5) $\quad W^N(n) := \int\limits_0^{Q^N(n)} f(Q)dQ - nc(q^N(n))$.

Suppose that we are at the long-run Cournot-Nash equilibrium, and let there be a small decrease in the number of firms. This marginal change in n will affect the net market surplus by:

$$(A6)\quad (d/dn)W^N(n_e) = \pi^N(n_e) + n_e\{f(Q^N(n_e)) - c'(q^N(n_e))\}(d/dn)q^N(n_e).$$

It is clear that the first term in the right side of equation (A6) is zero by the definition of n_e, whereas the second term thereof is unambiguously negative. Thus the social welfare measured in terms of net market surplus *increases* when there is a marginal *decrease* in the number of firms from the long-run equilibrium level n_e, which vindicates that there is a socially excessive firm entry at the long-run Cournot-Nash equilibrium.

Further generalizations of the excess entry theorem may be found in Suzumura (1995).

NOTES

I have greatly benefited from comments by, and discussions with, Edmond Malinvaud, Jean-Claude Milleron, Amartya Sen, Arjun Sengupta, Nicholas Stern and Joseph Stiglitz. I am also grateful to Bhaskar Dutta, Ryutaro Komiya, Masahiro Okuno-Fujiwara, Prasanta K. Pattanaik and John Vickers, with whom I had joint work and/or discussion on the topics covered in this chapter.

1. See Amsden (1989), Itoh and others (1991), Johnson (1982, 1987), Jones and SaKong (1980), Komiya (1975), Komiya, Okuno and Suzumura (1988), Krueger (1984), Lall (1994), Mason and others (1980), Mutoh and others (1986), Pack and Westphal (1986), Rodrick (1992, 1995), Wade (1990), Westphal (1990) and World Bank (1993), among many others.

2. The exposition in this section capitalizes on Itoh and others (1991, chapter 1) which in turn is based on Komiya, Okuno and Suzumura (1988).

3. During the occupation period (1945–52) in postwar Japan a series of economic reforms aimed at Japan's democratization were implemented under strong order and control of the occupation authorities. These reforms, which include the dissolution of the *zaibatsu* (family-dominated combines) and elimination of excessive concentration in production as well as property ownership in general, the transplantation of the US Antitrust Law into Japan (Antimonopoly Law of December 1947), land reform and labour democratization, undoubtedly shaped the basic competitive framework of postwar Japan. These postwar economic reforms correspond to what we called "designing and implementing institutions", or the provision of "institutional infrastructure" in Stiglitz's terminology, which are surely not part of the Japanese industrial policy per se. Those who are interested in the postwar reforms in Japan are referred to Suzumura and Okuno (1987) and Teranishi and Kosai (1993), among many others.

4. For further details of the legitimate and illegitimate reasons for infant-industry protection, see Corden (1974), Itoh and others (1991, chapter 4), Kemp (1960), Krugman and Obstfeld (1994, chapter 11) and Negishi (1972, chapter 6). See also Grossman and Horn (1988) for a refutation of the case of establishing informational barriers to entry for infant-industry protection.

5. If capital markets are imperfect and firms that are willing to take the risk of making up initial losses with future profits are unable to finance their attempt to do so, there may be an apparent case for protection. But what is needed is not the provision of protection by such measures as tariff or non-tariff barriers, but rectification of imperfect markets. In this sense the creation of development banks for the sake of allocating low-interest public funds may be one of the crucial industrial policies for the promotion of industries of strategic importance. But there is a strong case for making such allocation of public funds transparent, as well as contest-based. I will discuss this issue more in detail in the fourth section below.

6. This argument is drawn essentially from Kemp (1960). It is well recognized that an appropriate tax-subsidy scheme may improve economic welfare if one industry is exerting favourable external effects on other industries. Kemp's reasoning for infant-industry protection may be regarded as an example of this argument.

7. This argument is attributable originally to Negishi (1972, chapter 6). Despite its logical appeal, however, it may be less relevant in the context of developing market economies, where the large country assumption often does not apply.

8. Strategic complementarities are said to prevail when two industries reinforce each other in such a way that an expansion of industry A leads to an expansion of industry B, which in its turn leads to further expansion of industry A. See Matsuyama (1995) and Rodríguez-Clare (1997).

9. For further details of this mechanism, see Bardhan (1995), Murphy, Shleifer and Vishny (1989), Rodríguez-Clare (1997), Krugman (1991), and Matsuyama (1991, 1992, 1995). Note that this mechanism works through what Scitovsky (1954) christened pecuniary externalities. As such, government intervention is not indispensable for the resolution of the Pareto-inferior equilibrium trap. Nevertheless, government intervention may well be the only feasible option if market institutions (especially capital and risk markets) are highly incomplete, and private agents lack confidence in the invisible hand of competitive markets.

10. However, Bardhan (1995, p. 2986) was careful enough to add that "a rigorous empirical demonstration of the causal relationship between some satisfactory measure of outward-orientation and the rate of growth is rather scarce." See Dollar (1992) for an example of attempted empirical demonstrations of the statistical relationship between a measure of outward orientation and the rate of growth of a nation.

11. Historically speaking, it was the US occupation authorities who strongly encouraged participatory democracy in order to reduce and rectify the arbitrary nature of the prewar administration in Japan. With the implementation of the National Administrative Organization Law in 1949, the ministries began to establish advisory bodies at the levels of cabinet ministers, bureau chiefs and section chiefs. These bodies are classified as consultative bodies, which deliberate on policies, and examining bodies, which, by participating in

administrative decision-making, ensure that laws are fairly administered. A report submitted by a consultative body is not legally binding, whereas the resolution of an examining body can act as a formal constraint on bureaucracy. Thus, examining bodies are far stronger than consultative bodies in terms of independent authority.

A system of using deliberation councils on major policy matters has gradually evolved in postwar Japan. These councils are consultative bodies whose deliberations are referred to in the process of policy formation and whose members are private agents, including former bureaucrats, who are formally nominated by the minister in charge. The majority of these members are industry leaders, corporate executives and former bureaucrats, and a small number of scholars (academics) and newspaper journalists are included. To the extent that these members are nominated by government bureaucrats, a danger inherent in this public decision-making mechanism is that not only the agenda, but also the deliberation process and final conclusion are almost completely controlled by government bureaucrats. Thus the mechanism may turn out to be a process for rationalizing policies that the bureaucrats intend to pursue anyway, rather than a forum for sincerely gathering public opinion through open discussion. See Suzumura (1996a) for a case study of the modus operandi of this public decision-making mechanism.

12. Despite their obvious importance to the theoretical understanding of industrial policies, theoretical analyses on the role played by the gathering, transmission and dissemination of private information for public use are few. See, however, Okuno-Fujiwara, Postlewaite and Suzumura (1990) and Vives (1990).

13. The following discussion on adjustment assistance draws from Itoh and others (1991, chapter 21). See also, Komiya, Okuno and Suzumura (1988, chapter 14).

14. It goes without saying that industrial policies intended to promote and protect industries of strategic importance also create serious distributional issues, since giving favourable treatment to some industries inevitably implies disfavour to others. Thus the problem is that of emphasis, not of principle.

15. If factor shifts between industries involve costs, the production point may move inside the production frontier even when full employment of all factors of production is guaranteed. On this point, see Mussa (1974, 1978, 1982) and Mayer (1974). See also Neary (1982).

16. Note that a tariff enables the government to collect tariff revenue, which may be transferred to consumers, whereas intervention by means of a wage subsidy requires the government to pay just enough subsidy to maintain continued full employment in the declining industry, which requires that tax be collected from consumers to finance this subsidy. Thus in addition to their difference in efficiency, the two policy measures also contrast in their distributional implications.

17. Those interested in this literature are referred to d'Aspremont and Jacquemin (1988), Itoh and others (1991, part V), Jorde and Teece (1990), Kamien, Muller and Zang (1992), Kamien and Zang (1993), Katz (1986), Katz and Ordover (1990) and Suzumura (1992, 1995, part II and appendix B) among many others.

18. This result is proved rigorously by Mankiw and Whinston (1986), Suzumura (1995, part 1) and Suzumura and Kiyono (1987). See also the appendix at the end of this chapter.

19. It may be suggested that what is called excessive competition in Japan is a phenomenon that is concerned not with the welfare effect of an increase in the number of firms within an oligopolistic industry, but with the socially excessive aggregate investment within an oligopolistic industry. It may also be suggested that excessive competition in this sense develops in industries characterized by three features—heavy overhead capital, homogeneous output and oligopolistic competition. Is there any reason why such excessive competition should be expected to emerge in an oligopolistic industry? To answer this question analytically, a model incorporating these three features was built, and it was examined whether such a model generates an intrinsic tendency towards socially excessive investment in fixed overhead capital. See Suzumura (1995, part 2), where the previous statement on the theoretical possibility of excessive competition was essentially vindicated.

20. Quite apart from its easy enforceability due to the simplicity of informational requirements, this rule of thumb to the effect of remunerating each agent in proportion to past accomplishments has an intuitive appeal with an equitable flavour, so that it is rather hard to argue against its application. This was presumably the reason why Japanese government officials took recourse to this rule of thumb in their regulatory practice.

21. Designed to cope with trade frictions triggered by excessive and disrupting exports from Japan, formal VER agreements have been concluded on a large number of manufactured goods. In the wake of a rapid increase in exports of cotton products in the 1950s, temporary voluntary restraints on Japanese exports to the United States were introduced. These export (import) controls on textile products were gradually formalized and came to cover a large number of countries other than Japan and the United States, and international trade in textile products came to be carried out within the framework of the Multi-Fiber Arrangement (MFA). This is an international arrangement to manage textile trade, which has not only blocked export opportunities for developing countries, but has also delayed industrial adjustments in more developed countries.

Managed trade in iron and steel was introduced in the late 1960s in response to a rapid increase in exports from Japan. Although in a modified form, this measure had been in place subsequently, and indications of further strengthening and continuation of managed trade may be found in the extension of such trade-restricting measures in the automobile and integrated circuits industries. As managed trade spread to more and more industries, the system of free trade, meticulously built up in the postwar period within the General Agreements on Tariffs and Trade (GATT) framework, was on the verge of breaking down completely. It was in view of this gloomy prospect that these grey measures came to be prohibited under the World Trade Organization (WTO) Safeguard Agreement.

On the problem of protectionism and unilateral aggression, see Bhagwati (1988, 1995) and Bhagwati and Patrick (1990).

22. Capitalizing on the pioneering attempt by Harris (1985), Suzumura and Ishikawa (1993) explored the welfare implications of a VER agreement within a simple model of duopoly with product differentiation and conjectural variations. We show that a VER imposed at the free trade equilibrium level of exports is welfare-improving for the importing country only if the foreign exporter is forced to comply with the restraint involuntarily. In other words, it

is impossible to improve home-country and foreign-country welfare simultaneously with a VER agreement. See Kemp, Shimomura and Okawa (1996) for a re-examination of the Suzumura-Ishikawa thesis within a simple general equilibrium framework.

23.   This point was made by Komiya, Okuno and Suzumura (1988, p. 8) as follows: "Although heavy and chemical industries (like iron and steel, general machinery, heavy electrical equipment, and chemicals and petrochemicals), which were actually chosen and promoted, satisfied these criteria, there were many other industries (camera, bicycle, watch, tape recorder, magnetic tape, tourism, supermarkets, and restaurants) that were not promoted, despite their clear 'success' in passing these tests. Besides, almost no theoretically satisfactory explanations were provided justifying these criteria. To be sure, the well-known infant industry argument and other arguments based on market failures were sometimes invoked to defend them. However, the productivity improvement and income elasticity criteria seem to have little, if anything, to do with non-appropriable external economies that are key elements of the infant industry argument."

24.   This is surely not to say that there was no government and political corruption in relation to the implementation of industrial policy in postwar Japan. The most controversial corruption case was the ship-building bribery case, which broke out in 1954. Presumably, it was in response to the dangerous possibility of rent-seeking activities and corruption, which unambiguously came to the fore in this case, that the sophisticated system of checks and balances was developed.

25.   The term, "developmental state", was coined by Johnson (1982, p. 19), according to whom "[a] regulatory, or market-rational, state concerns itself with the form and procedures—the rules, if you will—of economic competition, but it does not concern itself with substantive matters...[such as] what industries ought to exist and what industries are no longer needed. The developmental, or plan-rational, state, ..., by contrast, has as its dominant feature precisely the setting of such substantive social and economic goals. ... In the [developmental] state, the government will give greatest precedence to industrial policy, that is, to a concern with the structure of domestic industry and with promoting the structure that enhances the nation's international competitiveness. The very existence of an industrial policy implies a strategic, or goal oriented, approach to the economy."

26.   It was only in 1993 with the enforcement of the Administrative Procedure Law that the opportunity for rectifying the discretionary application of administrative procedures in Japan was officially opened. With the implementation of this law, it became obligatory for government bureaucrats in charge of administration to define transparent standards and procedures for administrative guidance. People to whom administrative guidance is addressed are now in the legal position to request that the guidance be given in the form of an official document that specifies the purpose of the guidance and the name of the bureaucrat(s) to be held responsible for that guidance. Whether this law will bring about more transparent and less arbitrary government administration is yet to be seen, but it surely testifies to the wide range of administrative discretion that existed before the implementation of this law. Thus, "administrative guidance...is obviously open to abuse and has been abused on occasion, but it

is also much faster than the rule of law and avoids the unpredictable impact of new legislation and court decisions on sectors that do not require adjustment but that are affected anyway because of the universal scope of laws" (Johnson, 1987, p. 160).

27. Writing on the Park Chung Hee regime, which began with the military coup of May 16, 1961 and ended with the assassination of President Park on October 26, 1979, Mason and others (1980, p. 265) observed that "[a] firm that does not respond as expected to particular incentives may find that its tax returns are subject to careful examination, or that its application for bank credit is sturdiously ignored, or that its outstanding bank loans are not renewed. If incentive procedures do not work, government agencies show no hesitation in resorting to command backed by compulsion. In general, it does not take a Korean firm long to learn that it will 'get along' best by 'going along'. Obviously, such a system of implementation requires not only cooperation among the various government agencies that administer compliance procedures but continuous consultation between firms and public officials. Such a system could well be subject to corruption, and there is some evidence that payments are, in fact, made and received for services rendered, but again it must be emphasized that there is very little evidence that such corruption ... interferes in any serious way with production processes." See also Jones and SaKong (1980), Rodrick (1992) and Westphal (1990) on this and related points.

28. Although this extended conceptual framework is somewhat novel, it is worth pointing out that the origin of this framework, like many other basic aspects of welfare economics and social choice theory, can be traced back to Arrow (1963, pp. 90–1) who wrote: "[A]mong the variables which taken together define the social state, one is the very process by which the society makes its choice. This is especially important if the mechanism of choice itself has a value to the individuals in the society...If the decision process is interpreted broadly to include the whole socio-psychological climate in which social decisions are made, the reality and importance of such preferences, as opposed to preferences about the distributions of goods, are obvious." Some formal implications of this extended approach are explored by Pattanaik and Suzumura (1994; 1996) and Suzumura (1996b), where the politico-economic mechanisms are specified by individual rights modelled as game forms.

REFERENCES

Amsden, A.H. 1989. *Asia's Next Giant: Late Industrialization in South Korea.* Oxford: Oxford University Press.

Arrow, K.J. 1963. *Social Choice and Individual Values.* Second edition. New York: John Wiley & Sons.

Bardhan, P. 1995. "The Contributions of Endogenous Growth Theory to the Analysis of Development Problems: An Assessment." In J. Behrman and T. N. Srinivasan, eds., *Handbook of Development Economics.* Volume IIIB. Amsterdam: Elsevier.

Baumol, W.J. 1982. "Contestable Markets: An Uprising in the Theory of Industry Structure." *American Economic Review* 72(1):1–15.

Berlin, I. 1958. *Two Concepts of Liberty.* Oxford: Oxford University Press.

Bhagwati, J. 1988. *Protectionism.* Cambridge, Mass.: MIT Press.

_____. 1995. *Free Trade, 'Fairness' and the New Protectionism.* IEA Occasional Paper 96, Institute of Economic Affairs, London.

Bhagwati, J. and H.T. Patrick, eds. 1990. *Aggressive Unilateralism: America's 301 Trade Policy and the World Trading System.* Ann Arbor: University of Michigan Press.

Bulow, J.I., J.D. Geanakoplos and P.D. Klemperer. 1985. "Multimarket Oligopoly: Strategic Substitutes and Complements." *Journal of Political Economy* 93(3):488–511.

Corden, M.W. 1974. *Trade Policy and Economic Welfare.* Oxford: Oxford University Press.

d'Aspremont, C. and A. Jacquemin. 1988. "Cooperative and Non-cooperative R&D in Duopoly with Spillovers." *American Economic Review* 78(5):1133–7.

Dixit, A. 1984. "International Trade Policy for Oligopolistic Industries." Supplement to *Economic Journal* 94:1–16.

Dollar, D. 1992. "Outward-Oriented Developing Economies Really Do Grow More Rapidly: Evidence from 95 LDCs, 1976–1985." *Economic Development and Cultural Change* 40(3):523–44.

Grossman, G. and H. Horn. 1988. "Infant Industry Protection Reconsidered: The Case of Informational Barriers to Entry." *Quarterly Journal of Economics* 103(4):767–87.

Haberler, G. 1950. "Some Problems in the Pure Theory of International Trade." *Economic Journal* 60(2):223–40.

Harris, R. 1985. "Why Voluntary Export Restraints Are 'Voluntary'." *Canadian Journal of Economics* 18(4):799–809.

_____. A. 1978. *New Studies in Philosophy, Politics, Economics and the History of Ideas.* London: Routledge & Kegan Paul.

Hindley, B. 1984. "Empty Economics in the Case for Industrial Policy." *The World Economy* 7(3):277–94.

Industrial Structure Council, Ministry of International Trade and Industry, Japan. 1980. "Industrial Policy—Japan", position paper presented at the Positive Adjustment Policy Special Group in the OECD Economic Policy Committee, October.

Itoh, M., K. Kiyono, M. Okuno-Fujiwara and K. Suzumura. 1991. *Economic Analysis of Industrial Policy.* San Diego: Academic Press.

Johnson, C. 1982. *MITI and the Japanese Miracle: The Growth of Industrial Policy, 1925–1975.* Stanford: Stanford University Press.

_____. 1987. "Political Institutions and Economic Performance: The Government-Business Relationship in Japan, South Korea, and Taiwan." In F.C. Deyo, ed., *The Political Economy of the New Asian Industrialism.* Ithaca: Cornell University Press.

Jones, L.P. and I. SaKong. 1980. *Government, Business, and Entrepreneurship in Economic Development: The Korean Case.* Cambridge, Mass.: Harvard University Press.

Jorde, T. and D. Teece. 1990. "Innovation and Cooperation: Implications for Competition and Antitrust." *Journal of Economic Perspectives* 4(1):75–96.

Kaizuka, K. 1973. *Agenda for Economic Policy.* Tokyo: University of Tokyo Press. (In Japanese).

Kamien, M.I., E. Muller and I. Zang. 1992. "Research Joint Ventures and R&D Cartels." *American Economic Review* 82(5):1293–306.

Kamien, M.I. and I. Zang. 1993. "Competing Research Joint Ventures." *Journal of Economics & Management Strategy* 2(1):23–40.

Katz, M.L. 1986. "An Analysis of Cooperative Research and Development." *Rand Journal of Economics* 17(4):527–43.

Katz, M.L. and J. Ordover. 1990. "R&D Cooperation and Competition." *Brookings Papers on Economic Activity.* Microeconomics:137–191.

Kemp, M.C. 1960. "The Mill-Bastable Infant-Industry Dogma." *Journal of Political Economy* 68(1):65–7.

Kemp, M., K. Shimomura and M. Okawa. 1996. "Voluntary Export Restraints and Economic Welfare." Paper presented at Kobe Conference on Trade and Welfare, Kobe University, January.

Komiya, R. 1975. "Planning in Japan." In M. Bornstein, ed., *Economic Planning: East and West.* Cambridge, Mass.: Ballinger.

Komiya, R., M. Okuno and K. Suzumura, eds. 1988. *Industrial Policy of Japan.* San Diego: Academic Press.

Krueger, A.O. 1984. "Trade Policies in Developing Countries." In R.W. Jones and P.B. Kenen, eds., *Handbook of International Economics.* Volume I. Amsterdam: North-Holland.

Krugman, P.R. 1991. "History versus Expectations." *Quarterly Journal of Economics.* 106(2):651–67.

Krugman, P.R. and M. Obstfeld. 1994. *International Economics.* Third Edition. New York: Harper Collins.

Lall, S. 1994. "*The East Asian Miracle*: Does the Bell Toll for Industrial Strategy?" *World Development* 22(4):645–54.

Lucas, R.E. 1988. "On the Mechanics of Economic Development." *Journal of Monetary Economics* 22(1):3–42.

Mankiw, N.G. and M.D. Whinston. 1986. "Free Entry and Social Inefficiency." *Rand Journal of Economics* 17(1):48–58.

Mason, E.S., M.J. Kim, D.H. Perkins, K.S. Kim and D.C. Cole. 1980. *The Economic and Social Modernization of the Republic of Korea.* Cambridge, Mass.: Harvard University Press.

Matsuyama, K. 1991. "Increasing Returns, Industrialization, and Indeterminacy of Equilibrium." *Quarterly Journal of Economics* 106(2):617–50.

_____. 1992. "The Market Size, Entrepreneurship, and the Big-Push." *Journal of the Japanese and International Economies.* 6(4):347–64.

_____. 1995. "Complementarities and Cumulative Processes in Models of Monopolistic Competition." *Journal of Economic Literature* 33(2):701–29.

Mayer, W. 1974. "Short-Run and Long-Run Equilibrium for a Small Open Economy." *Journal of Political Economy* 82(5):955–67.

Murphy, K.M., A. Shleifer and R.W. Vishny. 1989. "Industrialization and the Big Push." *Journal of Political Economy* 97(5):1003–26.

Mussa, M. 1974. "Tariffs and the Distribution of Income: The Importance of Factor Specificity, Substitutability, and Intensity in the Short and Long Run." *Journal of Political Economy* 82(6):1191–203.

____. 1978. "Dynamic Adjustment in the Heckscher-Ohlin-Samuelson Model." *Journal of Political Economy* 86(3):488–510.

____. 1982. "Government Policy and the Adjustment Process." In J. Bhagwati, ed., *Import Competition and Response*. Chicago: University of Chicago Press.

Mutoh, H., S. Sekiguchi, K. Suzumura and I. Yamazawa, eds. 1986. *Industrial Policies for Pacific Economic Growth*. Sydney: Allen & Unwin.

Neary, J.P. 1982. "Intersectoral Capital Mobility, Wage Stickiness, and the Case for Adjustment Assistance." In J. Bhagwati, ed., *Import Competition and Response*. Chicago: University of Chicago Press.

Negishi, T. 1972. *General Equilibrium Theory and International Trade*. Amsterdam: North-Holland.

Nurkse, R. 1953. *Problems of Capital Formation in Underdeveloped Countries*. Oxford: Basil Blackwell.

Okuno, M. and K. Suzumura. 1986. "An Economic Analysis of Industrial Policy: A Conceptual Framework through the Japanese Experience." In H. Mutoh and others, eds., *Industrial Policies for Pacific Economic Growth*. Sydney: Allen & Unwin.

Okuno-Fujiwara, M., A. Postlewaite and K. Suzumura. 1990. "Strategic Information Revelation." *Review of Economic Studies* 57(1):25–47.

Pack, H. and L.E. Westphal. 1986. "Industrial Strategy and Technological Change: Theory vs. Reality." *Journal of Development Economics* 22:87–128.

Panzer, J.C. 1980. "Regulation, Deregulation and Economic Efficiency: The Case of the CAB." *American Economic Review: Papers and Proceedings* 70(2): 311–15.

Pareto, V. 1927. *Manual of Political Economy*. New York: A.M. Kelley.

Pattanaik, P.K. and K. Suzumura. 1994. "Rights, Welfarism and Social Choice." *American Economic Review: Papers and Proceedings* 84(2):435–9.

____. 1996. "Individual Rights and Social Evaluation: A Conceptual Framework." *Oxford Economic Papers* 48(2):194–212.

Rodríguez-Clare, Andrés. 1993. "The Division of Labor, Agglomeration Economies and Economic Development." Unpublished Ph.D. Dissertation, Department of Economics, Stanford University.

____. 1997. "Positive Feedback Mechanisms in Economic Development: A Review of Recent Contributions. In Richard Sabot and István P. Székely, eds., *Development Strategy and Management of the Market Economy*. Volume II. Oxford: Clarendon Press.

Rodrick, D. 1992. "Political Economy and Development Policy." *European Economic Review* 36(2/3):329–36.

____. 1995. "Trade and Industrial Policy Reform." In J. Behrman and T.N. Srinivasan, eds., *Handbook of Development Economics*. Volume IIIB. Amsterdam: Elsevier.

Rosenstein-Rodan, P.N. 1943. "Problems of Industrialization of Eastern and South-Eastern Europe." *Economic Journal* 53(2):202–11.

Scitovsky, T. 1954. "Two Concepts of External Economies." *Journal of Political Economy* 63(2):143–51.

Stiglitz, J.E. 1981. "Potential Competition May Reduce Welfare." *American Economic Review: Papers and Proceedings* 71(2):184–9.

____. 1997. "The Role of Government in the Economies of Developing Countries." In Edmond Malinvaud et al., eds., *Development Strategy and Management of the Market Economy*. Volume I. Oxford: Clarendon Press.

Suzumura, Kotaro. 1992. "Cooperative and Non-cooperative R&D in an Oligopoly with Spillovers." *American Economic Review*. 82(5):1307–20.

____. 1995. *Competition, Commitment, and Welfare*. Oxford: Oxford University Press.

____. 1996a. "Japanese Industrial Policy for Telecommunications: Anatomy of the 1985 Institutional Reform and Its Aftermath." In K. Odaka and J. Teranishi, eds., *Market and Government: Foes or Friends?* Tokyo: Maruzen.

____. 1996b. "Welfare, Rights, and Social Choice Procedure: A Perspective." *Analyse & Kritik*, forthcoming.

Suzumura, Kotaro and J. Ishikawa. 1993. "Voluntary Trade Restraints and Economic Welfare." Discussion Paper 272, Institute of Economic Research, Hitotsubashi University, Tokyo.

Suzumura, Kotaro and K. Kiyono. 1987. "Entry Barriers and Economic Welfare." *Review of Economic Studies* 54(2):157–67.

Suzumura, Kotaro and M. Okuno. 1987. "Industrial Policy in Japan: Overview and Evaluation." In R. Sato and P. Wachtel, eds., *Trade Friction and Economic Policy*. New York: Cambridge University Press.

Teranishi, J. and Y. Kosai, eds. 1993. *The Japanese Experience of Economic Reforms*. New York: St. Martins Press.

Vives, X. 1990. "Information and Competitive Advantage." *International Journal of Industrial Organization* 8(1):17–35.

von Hayek, F. 1948. *Individualism and Economic Order*. Chicago: University of Chicago Press.

Wade, R. 1990. *Governing the Market: Economic Theory and the Role of Government in East Asian Industrialization*. Princeton: Princeton University Press.

Westphal, L.E. 1990. "Industrial Policy in an Export-Propelled Economy: Lessons from South Korea's Experience." *Journal of Economic Perspectives* 4(3):41–59.

World Bank. 1993. *The East Asian Miracle: Economic Growth and Public Policy*. New York: Oxford University Press.

7

Global Aspects of a
Development Strategy

JEAN-CLAUDE MILLERON

From the end of World War II until the mid–1960s the United States held a dominant position in the world economy, characterized by its relative importance in world GDP (more than one-third in 1950 compared with less than one-fourth today), a system of fixed exchange rates related to gold through the dollar and post-war hegemonic power with respect to Japan and Europe. The Cold War clearly reinforced US leadership within the western hemisphere, and the actions taken by the United States affected—often in a positive way, such as through Marshall Aid—the welfare of the rest of the world much more than any country in the rest of the world could affect the United States. But the progressive emergence of the European Community in the 1950s represents an important step towards more economic and social coordination.

A first wave of changes took place between the end of the 1950s and the beginning of the 1970s. Decolonization increased significantly the number of governments present on the international scene. In 1971 the suspension of conversion of the dollar to gold and the devaluation of the dollar that followed marked a first step towards a less asymmetrical relationship. The two oil shocks of 1973 and 1979 were at the origin of serious economic and social turmoil. In the mid–1970s, however, there was a first attempt towards more coordinated policy-making within the G–5 and G–7 nations.

A second set of events is related to the end of the Cold War and the emergence of many independent states from the former Soviet Union. Transition economies became a new concern for the international community, and the previous east-west political balance became meaningless for the industrial and developing world. At the same time some countries, especially in east and south-east Asia, enjoyed considerable progress in a single generation. For instance, since the early 1960s, Japan's rank in per capita income went from thirtieth to second and that of the Republic of Korea went from ninety-ninth to fifty-fourth.

The first half of the 1990s may be characterized by the complete recognition of general economic integration throughout markets—the Uruguay Round was completed successfully at the end of 1994—and by an increased awareness of the importance of globalization, with more concern about the environment, population, some aspects of peace and security, and the emerging "global commons". Following these evolutions, it has become very difficult to accept the simplifying assumption of a closed economy. In most countries today policy-makers aim at adapting economic and social policies to changes in the international environment and participating actively in international forums. In the international market economy a government strategy must be defined with reference to these dimensions.

Within the limits of this chapter, it is not feasible to address these issues comprehensively. I focus on only two aspects. First, I illustrate how countries may adapt to the international environment by using the example of changes in terms of trade. This change is considered as given, and the problem is to find the right way to react to it. In the second part I present a brief survey of the main concerns of managing the international market economy. I cover issues related to trade, the provision of international public goods, international equity and coordination of economic policies.

At the risk of being pedantic, I will summarize by making an analogy with the theory of imperfect competition. In the first part the actors will be examined as "environment takers" and in the second as "environment makers". Or, by analogy with game theory, the strategy described in the first part is a Nash-type and in the second a cooperative-type.

ADAPTING TO EXTERNAL SHOCKS

Here, I will simplify the picture, considering national policies without discussing the complex issues related to the elaboration of the national strategy itself. Moreover, what I present would have to be carefully reexamined before it is applied to least developed countries or to one of the major economies of the world. In particular, I will not try to analyze the possible consequences of the policy orientations of a large country (United States) or a group of countries (European Union) on the international environment. Still, the stories told might be relevant to more than 100 countries.

I start by assuming a smooth development process that is sometimes affected by external shocks, which call for reactions from policy-makers. Here, I am interested in the case of a country confronted with a significant disturbance: either an adverse external shock that has negative effects or a windfall gain that creates new room for manoeuvring among economic and social policies. I will try to show that there is no symmetry—different policies should be applied in each case, and one cannot be considered the converse of the other.

Before beginning the analysis itself, I must define a "shock": it is a change that is discrete, unexpected and, in general, sudden. It is important to make a distinction between a temporary shock, which will last for a relatively short time, and a permanent shock. By temporary shock I mean one that is expected to last for one or two years, after which conditions will return to their initial state. By contrast, a permanent shock will last for a long time and, as a consequence, could affect the medium- or long-term outlook of the economy.

Many possible shocks could affect an economy. In a useful contribution Krugman (1988) presents what he calls an "anatomy of external shocks". He distinguishes between the shocks arising from the goods market (exports, imports, exchange rates and trade, terms of trade) and those originating in the capital market (interest rates, inflation and debt, real interest rates, new constraints on borrowing). It would not make sense to elaborate on each of these categories given the limits of this chapter. Rather, I explore the case of a real shock—I choose a change in terms of trade—and present the main elements of the policy response to such a shock. The analysis could apply to the oil shock in 1973 or 1979, or to the counter oil shock that occurred when oil prices collapsed in 1986. Or, it may be used to discuss the more conventional case of a developing country that must react to a significant change in the international price of a commodity that it produces (Gavin 1988).

In this section I describe a decision tree that is applicable to many contexts. First, according to a simple static general equilibrium model, following a shock, a crucial choice must be made between changes in external indebtedness and adjustments in internal absorption. Second, the content of absorption—investment versus current expenditures—matters from a dynamic point of view and, because it is related, I discuss possible changes in the internal/external price structure through devaluation. Then, I examine, within this context, the possible deflationary effects of risk aversion when risks are asymmetric. Finally, I summarize what the role of government should be in adjusting to changes in the international environment.

A static analysis of a simple shock

Suppose, first, that the economy has just one resource, say, labour. If a country is confronted with, for example, an increase in the price of exports and a decrease in the price of imports (an improvement of the terms of trade) and if the country maintains its external trade balance, then it gets more imports per unit of labour than previously. One possible interpretation is that the activity of trade—the exchange of imported for exported commodities—increases productivity. It is essential to understand that such a change in terms of trade is comparable to a change in factor productivity as long as external disequilibrium is ruled out. From a microeconomic point of view such a change generates a windfall gain that must be divided among economic agents. I estimate this windfall in a very simple general equilibrium model in the annex.

Within such a framework the windfall gain is the product of the relative change in terms of trade and the "size" of trade, properly defined. For a country in which trade represents 20 per cent of GDP, if a 10 per cent change in the terms of trade occurs, the corresponding gain (loss) is 2 per cent of GDP. In the simple static economy that we are talking about, this positive (negative) change can be allocated in the following ways (see equation 15 in the annex):

• Increasing (reducing) the internal absorption of the economy.
• Reducing (increasing) the labour supply.
• Using less (more) of the nation's natural resources.
• Reducing (increasing) the real trade deficit, that is the nominal deficit deflated by the simple mean of export and import prices.

If one starts from an equilibrium and if one wants to reach another equilibrium given the new terms of trade, then the changes that one considers must be linked to the estimated windfall gain by the allocative mechanism. In particular, if the policy-maker wants to avoid any change in the trade deficit (or surplus), the labour supply or the rate of exploitation of natural resources, then the necessary change in absorption is precisely equal to the windfall gain generated by the change in the terms of trade (2 per cent in our example).

Through this mechanism we can also understand how disequilibria can be generated: if the decisions—centralized or decentralized—about absorption, labour supply, natural resources and trade balance do not fit with the level of the surplus related to the change in terms of trade, then some disequilibria will appear in markets that can generate price dynamics, which may be inconsistent with a return to equilibrium.

Finally, two questions related to the scope of this model must be examined. First: are there limits to my model because of the simplifying assumptions made? It is easy to generalize the analysis I present in the annex to a case of m non-producible resources and n goods. Such an exercise, however, does not add much to the depth of economic analysis, as is often the case. Second: is there full employment given the initial allocation of resources? And is there some rigidity in production factors, implying that the reallocation of resources that should take place cannot? If there is not full employment, it is necessary to start from a theory explaining unemployment and providing prices associated with the initial allocation. Today, there is no good answer to the question "where do prices associated with unemployment come from?" A correct theoretical answer to this question would be a prerequisite to undertaking a cost-benefit analysis with unemployment. If there was such a theory, its policy recommendations would have to be implemented in any case, whether or not the windfall gain takes place.

The problem of rigidity is examined in detail by Suzumura (1997). It is one of the cases in which an accompanying industrial policy makes sense.

Dynamics: allocating a surplus windfall gain

Now, I will go one step further. Suppose an economy is confronted with a shock arising from goods markets (keep in mind the example of a change in terms of trade). What is the best policy response?

If the shock is anticipated to be temporary, there are many good reasons for recommending a hands-off policy, which is not a benign-neglect policy. Nor does it imply that faced with a temporary shock that may be very harmful to the weakest and poorest people, solidarity should not play its role at the national or international level. It does mean, however, that if the country is not under heavy pressure because of its external imbalances, the result will be a change in external indebtedness that may be considered "normal" and accepted as such by markets. Other types of adjustments—and in particular adjustments through absorption—would have, whether it is a positive or a negative shock, some costly effects on the expectations of economic agents and/or on the credibility of government policy. The main risk associated with such a policy corresponds to a case of misrepresentation, in which a durable shock is interpreted as a short-term event (remember the debates after each of the oil shocks). That is why we should avoid benign neglect: careful and permanent monitoring is needed, because if an adverse shock is misread, it may be very costly to not react in due time (generally, as soon as possible). If this analysis is correct, it implies that a small country must have sufficient official foreign currency reserves to absorb a shock. It is a prerequisite for making government policy, focused on permanent or durable changes, more legible and understandable.

The discussion of the optimal allocation of resources in the case of a permanent shock calls for some criteria on which to base inter-temporal choices. I assume that prior to the shock, the society could arrive at a consensus on a satisfactory and sustainable level of investment.

I assume that the shock is adverse and permanent. In the long run a hands-off policy that would lead to a permanent trade deficit and, as a consequence, increased cumulative indebtedness is generally neither sustainable nor credible. The answer "work harder" in this situation makes sense if the economy wants to maintain the same level of internal absorption. But in many countries the government does not have at its disposal the means to regulate labour supply. That is why the main concern in such a case is to reduce internal absorption. At this stage it is essential to make a distinction between the two main parts of absorption: current expenditures and capital formation. In a world in which arbitrage is left completely to private initiative, there could be strong temptation to sacrifice future bene-fits for immediate satisfaction. In such a case, however, the problem is to reduce internal absorption without jeopardizing the welfare of future generations—meaning that the best policy is to reduce current expenditures and maintain the previous level of capital formation.

This reasoning assumes that the permanent shock does not change the balance between investment and current expenditure. But with the new structure of prices, the set of profitable production processes may be modified. For instance, if the price of oil increases, it may not pay to produce flowers or vegetables in France's greenhouses in the winter. At the same time, it may become profitable to exploit oil fields that would not have been profitable before the shock (for example, North Sea oil). In such a case, because there is no hope for an increase in internal saving, it makes sense to accept a temporary increase in external indebtedness that is clearly devoted to a specific investment effort so that the economy can adjust to the new environ-ment. It is essential for external credibility that the policy emphasize that the extra indebtedness created is temporary, not the result of non-adjustment, and that it corresponds to well-identified investment programmes that are profitable enough to repay the borrowed money.

When confronted with a permanent, favourable shock, a country may use the corresponding room for manoeuvre to reduce indebtedness, external debt and public debt in some cases. This is what happened in many countries with the peace dividend generated by the end of the Cold War (see United Nations, 1995). Certainly, if in the past government went too far and created large deficits—perhaps because of military expenditures—such a windfall gain could be an excellent opportunity to adjust. One good reason to do so is to improve the economy's ability to react to future shocks or to benefit fully from future positive shocks. But it is not the only possible strategy: a significant, favourable, permanent shock should also be an opportunity for society to make a lucid decision about the best allocation of the emerging gain. It could be increasing leisure, saving more national resources for future generations or increasing internal absorption with a judicious balance between current expenditures and capital formation. Unfortunately, the proper forums for such a debate rarely exist. Governments, even in countries that have a tradition of some form of planning, sometimes prefer to leave the gain to current consumption, avoiding the debate that could lead to more courageous (from a political point of view) decisions (see Malinvaud and Nabli, 1997).

One might be astonished by the fact that I have not used the word "devaluation". Most people think that a devaluation worsens the terms of trade. Here, we must consider the currency in which the price of trade flows is defined. Germany exports cars, the prices of which are generally quoted in deutsch marks, and imports oil, the price of which is quoted in dollars. It is true in such a case that a devaluation of the deutsch mark can be analyzed, at least in the short term, as a decrease in the terms of trade, since the price of exports in deutsch marks is unchanged and the price of imports in deutsch marks increases. The same demonstration, however, would not hold for a developing country that produces a commodity, the price of which is determined in dollars in an international market, and imports (consumption or equipment) goods with prices quoted in foreign currencies—often dollars. Thus for a small country that is a price taker—in the sense that prices are fully given, particularly because all of the country's external transactions are defined with reference to foreign currencies—a devaluation does *not* change the terms of trade. This statement is, however, tautological because there is no change in terms of trade in foreign prices.

Obviously, this does not mean that a devaluation is neutral for a country trading in dollars. Keeping in mind our simple model (presented in the annex), a devaluation in such a country results in cheaper non-traded goods (with respect to traded goods). Such a mechanism corresponds to what some economists (see, for instance, Fischer, 1988) call "expenditure switching": a devaluation that succeeds is one that creates a new price structure, so that economic agents demand less traded commodities and more domestically produced commodities. Obviously, in such a case complex dynamics can occur—inflation in particular—the control of which is especially delicate (and is analyzed in the literature on devaluations). At this stage specification of demand functions is necessary, an exercise that we will not undertake (noticing, however, how remarkable it is that we could reach this point without such a specification).

A bias towards deflation?

Adaptation to an external shock is a complex game whose result depends not only on the strategy of one player, but on the strategies of all players. Let us imagine that an adverse external shock affects the G–7 countries. Each country must make a judgement about the durability or transitory nature of the shock. In the case of an adverse durable shock, making a wrong judgement unilaterally may be very costly, especially in terms of the external deficit (for example, France in 1981).

Given a large set of preferences, a player will prefer the strategy of always adjusting. If such a representation is correct, there may be a temptation for decision-makers to react to external shocks through excessively prudent policies, causing a global deflation.

A general question, often mentioned in planning theory, is whether it makes sense to create a forum in which, without necessarily coordinating their decisions, actors can exchange information and become more aware of the beliefs of their fellow players. The G–7 meetings, as they are organized today, could be considered a forum of this kind.

The role of government in adjusting to changes in the international environment

This book focuses especially on the right blend of public and private action in managing a market economy. What, then, should be kept in mind concerning the correct response to external shocks? Public policy-makers must play an important role in two domains: information and macroeconomic policy. Information is crucial, first in the simple sense of good monitoring. For the government this means receiving the right external and internal information at the right time—as soon as possible in most cases—which does not always occur without difficulties. For instance, there might be a temptation for those who produce information to minimize bad news because of a fear of "killing the messenger" when he does not bring the news the king is expecting. Getting internal information also means devoting sufficient resources to data collection and processing—a prerequisite for sound policy-making and policy analysis.

But the most difficult step is to interpret that information. I emphasized the importance of determining whether an external shock is temporary or permanent. Such a judgement often calls for the cooperation of many economic and social actors in order to get to a better understanding of various beliefs and points of view. It also calls for sufficient international openness, because information must be shared and because it may be useful to discuss the policy orientations that must be implemented.

The most delicate case is that of an adverse permanent shock. It is essential in such a case to present to the general public a clear analysis and to explain the policy that must be implemented. In particular, the government will have to repeat that there are no miracle solutions. In the case of financial volatility it is essential to show that the government is aware of the seriousness of the situation and that it is fully determined to apply a tough line.

In the case of a real, adverse, permanent shock the main tool at the disposal of government is fiscal policy. The shock may call for a sharp reduction in current expenditures (including the wage bill);

some tax increases, particularly on households; and a careful review of the investment expenditures in the public sector in order to ensure that the programmes are well adapted to the new situation. Certainly, proper equity considerations must be taken into account at this stage to avoid imposing most of the burden on the worst-off taxpayers.

From a political point of view the government of a country facing an external shock must balance its public statements in order to keep the internal situation under control—in this sense the adjustment must be politically and socially feasible—and to maintain sufficient external credibility with regard to markets, international organizations and, more broadly, the general public.

MAKING AN INTERNATIONAL ENVIRONMENT

Government's role in helping the overall economy make the right decisions when confronted with an external shock is just one part of the story. Beyond what I called environment-taking policy, there is room for environment-making cooperative actions that are the everyday product of economic diplomacy.

The types of cooperative actions envisaged must be understood as a continuous spectrum covering a broad range of possible arrangements—from autonomy to federalization (box 7.1). The deeper one digs in terms of real cooperation, the more institutions appear crucial.

Without aiming to cover all the aspects of environment-making, I will propose some illustrations in the field of trade, the provision of global public goods, the issue of international redistribution and the coordination of macroeconomic policies.

Trade

Ensuring the preconditions for the proper working of markets is an important part of environment design. The question of trade is central at this stage. The recent completion of the Uruguay Round is the best answer to today's global pessimism. The negotiations covered highly complex and protected sectors, like textiles and agriculture. They addressed new issues, such as trade in services and some aspects of investment and intellectual property. They represent an essential step

---

Box 7.1: A Glossary for the Environment-Maker

National autonomy: Governments make decentralized decisions with little or no consultation and no explicit cooperation.

Identification of collective concerns: Participants acknowledge the problem, cooperate in information gathering and orient, in a non-binding spirit, their policies to the concern in mind (for example, the convention on climate change).

Mutual recognition: Each member nation explicitly accepts the regulations, standards and certification procedures of other members (for example, medical doctors in France and Germany).

Monitored decentralization: Governments agree on rules that restrict their freedom to set policies or that promote gradual convergence in the structure of their policies (for example, G–7 macroeconomic policies and IMF surveillance).

Coordination: Governments jointly adjust national policies (for example, the control of communicable disease through World Health Organization procedures).

Explicit harmonization: Governments agree on regional or world standards (for example, road signalling, national accounts, some banking regulations).

Federalist mutual governance: Supranational institutions enable member states to proceed through continuous bargaining towards joint, centralized decision-making (for example, the European Union).

Source: These definitions rely in particular on Aaron, Bryant, Collins and Lawrence (1994).

---

in the the building of multilateral institutions. Remembering that in 1948 the United States failed to ratify the Havana Charter, which would have established an international trade organization, the creation of the new World Trade Organization (WTO) is an important endeavour towards more transparency and enforceability of GATT rules. (For an assessment of the Uruguay Round, see Kahler, 1995 and Goldin, Knudsen and van der Mensbrugghe, 1993.)

Here, I focus on national policies in an attempt to present a list of main questions that must be addressed by a country that tries to be an environment maker. First, it is essential to avoid ambiguity: the global logic of openness must be recognized as essential and made central in political choices. In industrial countries in particular, it is important to overcome the old fear that developing countries (especially low wages in developing countries) are a menace to their industries (see Krugman, 1994). Certainly, openness may call for the solution of some sectoral problems, but it is essential to remember that increased openness implies a larger overall cake and, in general, an improvement in the share for each player. Cases of deterioration in individual situations are rare and should be clearly identified. The literature reports a lot of developments on bilateral and regional agreements, the main question being possible damage to third countries (see in particular Haggard, 1995). There is no definite answer to such a problem, but often the size of the effects, if they exist, is modest. As a consequence it would be unwise to rule out such agreements, especially if they are elaborated in a perfectly transparent way. This last assertion makes me much more comfortable in clearly ruling out unilateralism as incompatible with the spirit of a normal international cooperative game.

A second issue now emerging, which is deeply related to trade, particularly trade in services, is that of international labour migration (see, in particular, Razin and Sadka, 1994; Stalker, 1994; and Stark, 1991). There will be more and more pressure towards further migration because of huge inequalities between countries and because of cheaper transportation services. Behind these issues are concerns about social and human rights (family reunification, for example) that call for a broad approach at the international level. Unfortunately, there is no political agreement for a general debate on international migration. Today, the correct response might be to pave the way for future international negotiations, trying to improve our knowledge and understanding of these phenonema. Such an endeavour calls for active participation of concerned states in collecting data and analyzing the rationale behind migration. There is little doubt that international migration will have to be managed to ensure its sustainability. It may become one of the main aspects of managing the world economy in the next century.

A third set of issues relates to exploring new dimensions for international negotiation, including trade and other issues on the international agenda. Leaving aside the special case of international sanctions (see Cortright and Lopez, 1995), we may, for instance, raise the question of integrating human rights aspects (such as child labour) into trade negotiations. One possible economic approach to such a question consists of noticing that such concerns are akin to "merit wants"[1] in the sense of Musgrave (1959). As a consequence proper regulations must be invented at the international level in order to prevent abuses. Fortunately, because these problems concern only a few countries in the world, it is probably not a good method to combine negotiations on trade and human rights abuses. But the question remains of possibly using embargoes as a sanction for failure to apply a well-defined international regulation. The answer is more nuanced if one considers questions related to the environment or to labour law. However, one should remember that, instead of taking the risk of jeopardizing the liberalization of trade itself, alternatives should be considered in which one tries to inform the "consumer-trader-citizen of the world" about the production process itself (possibly harmful to the environment or to the labour force), leaving the decision of buying or not buying to households and (or) to retailers.

Global commons and international public goods

Up to now we have been talking about cases in which most of the inter-dependence among actors passes through the markets. Let us now consider other issues, like externalities and public goods, in which inter-dependence passes through other channels.

A basic principle of international law is the sovereignty of states over their respective territories. But the largest part of our planet is "global commons". These areas are not subject to any jurisdiction: the ocean, the Antarctic continent and outer space are examples. Because of the absence of property rights, no particular nation feels responsible for avoiding degradation, whether by overexploitation (whales, fish, and so on) or pollution (tankers, ozone depletion, and so on). In the absence of a price associated with the use of global commons, the likelihood of overexploitation is very high. Many characteristics of these global commons may be considered global public goods.

An international public good is defined by two properties: *collective international concern,* as opposed to national concern, collective international meaning directly relevant for actors in at least two different countries, and *non-excludability*, meaning that it is impossible to exclude residents of other countries from enjoying the international public good. Examples of international public goods include regional or global defense services or fundamental, non-patentable research.[2] These public goods are characterized by free riding—nations may benefit from the goods without contributing to the cost of their production (whether paying for defense or applying international regulations to combat pollution). Part of these goods are financed through international voluntary contributions, which are certainly better than nothing, but which lead to a level of production that is less than optimal.

For most international public goods, in the absence of institutions endowed with a supranational decision-making power, international cooperation remains low, just at the level of the "identification of collective concerns" (see box 7.1). This is particularly true for many of the international agreements concerning the global environment. For an analysis of these agreements, see Cooper (1994).

If one is interested in digging further in box 7.1—that is, accepting more compelling coordination—the question of global taxes must be considered. Until now multilateral financing has been based on two types of resources: at a very low level some budgetary contributions generally linked to the economic size (GDP) of contributors, and voluntary contributions. Raising global taxes would be an essential step in recognizing some global concerns. Most of the literature on global taxation tries to kill two birds with one stone—levying resources for the provision of international public goods or some international redistribution and improving the allocation of resources (through various forms of Pigouvian taxes) or attempting to stabilize some markets (see the discussion of the Tobin tax later in this section). There are many interesting debates behind this literature. The main difficulties, however, are not economic, they are legal and institutional.

In the United Nations, for instance, the only way to "raise taxes" is through the budget, with a system that looks like the poll tax levied against each citizen in the early Roman Republic. More precisely, according to article 17b of the United Nations Charter, "The expenses of the organization shall be borne by the Members as apportioned by the General Assembly", which states that there is a political authority (the United Nations General Assembly) endowed with a taxation power that must be implemented through apportionment. As soon as one talks about taxation, a radical change in terms of political power must take place. And for such a global tax to be implemented, member states would have to give up a little of their sovereign (and exclusive) right to raise taxes.[3]

The other difficult point is related to tax collection. The existence of a national tax administration is a prerequisite for the enforcement of any modern tax system. Today, in most countries people can be prosecuted and jailed if they do not pay their personal income tax. At the same time a member state may decide to postpone, without justification, its payment to an international organization without incurring serious sanctions. Thus if one thinks that the issue of global taxes is worthwhile, it is crucial to remember the institutional problems when refining the definition of the tax base.

Equity, distribution and redistribution

Adding an international dimension to the debate on equity, distribution and redistribution demands more than simply transposing the terms of reference of the national debate. At the national level solidarity may require various transfers akin to negative income taxes. Indeed, a political and economic controversy often erupts over the effectiveness of such a redistribution—the main idea being that the size of the cake is not independent of the way it is divided up. Consequently, it may not be a good idea to transfer too much—even to help the poorest people—because massive transfers may worsen a situation by shrinking the pie.

It is hardly an exaggeration to say that, at the international level, this logic is not directly relevant. In fact, it might have to be reversed. Because of the small size of the transfers we are considering (official development assistance today represents less than 0.3 per cent of donors' GDP), the question of distorting the allocation of resources is a minor one. The main issue, then, is how to take advantage of market mechanisms in the redistributive effort and how to change the primary distribution of income, even if it is a long-term process. Simplifying a lot, I would say that international redistribution must be deeply rooted in the allocation of resources, using it as a kind of lever to redistribute efficiently. Suppose that in each country each citizen gets an equal part of national income, often approximated by GDP. With such an approach one may examine the changes through time in the distribution of world resources among countries. In 1992 some experts (UNDP, 1992) revealed that the income disparities between the rich and the poor was growing steadily in the long run (between 1960 and 1990). A second glance at the data (including or excluding China, for instance), making reference to purchasing power parities (PPPs) instead of exchange rates, has shown that such a result is not robust (see United Nations, 1994 and Tabatabai, 1995).

Few data are available to characterize the distribution of income within countries, particularly in least developed countries. However, our knowledge of income distribution has improved a lot in the past 30 years (see Lecaillon, Paukert, Morrisson and Germidis, 1984 and Chen, Datt and Ravallion, 1994). The data presented each year in the World Bank's *World Development Report* are rightly accompanied by a serious warning about the fragility of that data. Within countries the most common data do not refer to distribution, but to a poverty line (generally $1 per day), providing the estimate of an index of "poverty incidence", which is the percentage of individuals (or households in some cases) below the poverty line. The consensus today is as follows: there has been a steady improvement in Asia (incidence is approximately 15 per cent in east Asia but remains very high, around than 60 per cent, in south Asia); a deterioration of past improvements in Latin America during the "lost decade" of the 1980s; and a worsening of mass poverty in Africa, mainly in sub-Saharan Africa. Looking carefully at the data from developing countries as a whole in the last two decades, it is probably correct to say that the incidence of poverty has declined, although the number of poor has risen steadily.

Do these data raise global issues? The answer is yes from many points of view. They show an important market failure: in any general equilibrium model (for instance, Debreu, 1956) there is a "survival" condition, which holds that for an equilibrium to exist, a vector of endowments must belong to some "consumption set". If it does not, and if, as Sen (1991) and Nussbaum and Sen (1993) write, there is an entitlement failure, then both emergency answers and long-term approaches must be envisaged.

Emergency answers make up a large part of humanitarian assistance. There is no doubt that generally shared values of international solidarity must prevail when faced with droughts, natural disasters, sudden epidemics and so on. The debate concerns the various means to provide assistance, including the respective role of international specialized agencies and non-governmental organizations (NGOs), the provision of goods or direct monetary transfers enabling the country to purchase needed goods on the markets (Drèze and Sen, 1994), and transition from immediate relief to normal market conditions (including, hopefully, labour markets). One orientation is clear today: relief, assistance and peace-building following a conflict are difficult subjects that call for professional competencies. These competencies may be found in specialized agencies or offices and in many NGOs, whose role may become crucial. It means that, in general, a benevolent government facing such a situation should focus on raising funds to be oriented towards professional channels and, hopefully, used efficiently.

In the long run there is more and more scepticism of the idea of helping the worst off through permanent transfers comparable to a global welfare system. An alternative to redistribution consists of promoting long-term policies that change the distribution of primary income itself. As nicely put in World Bank (1995), the problem is "reaching the next generation".

Two main paths are broadly accepted for helping those left behind. The first priority is investment in people. The major concern is obviously children, keeping in mind that good nutrition and health contributes to good learning capacity. Also, training must be encouraged—targeted training programmes for women appearing today are especially effective in many developing countries. Secondly, the importance of physical and social infrastructures must be recognized. This priority often concerns both investment and some current spending in the state or local budgets. It is relevant to the development of health services and school facilities in poor communities, roads in rural areas and sewerage in large cities. These conditions, though necessary, are generally not sufficient, and it would be a mistake to switch without any precaution from one type of assistance to another.

Coordination of macroeconomic policies

There is much controversy over coordinating macroeconomic policies. The debate in the 1970s was based on an implicit Keynesian paradigm with a kind of "trade multiplier". The idea was simply that if there is an increase in internal demand (for instance, because of fiscal policies) in two countries that have a trade relationship, global output will increase more if these increases are synchronized. In the language of international meetings it used to be expected that a few countries would play the role of "locomotive", leading the train of growing economies. Sometimes, however, the deal was more complex. For instance, in 1978 a deal concerning growth in Europe (France and Germany) was accompanied in an OECD package by some conditions concerning US deficits. With increasing scepticism concerning the efficiency of "fine tuning", more attention was paid to long-term effects of fiscal (and monetary) policies. As a consequence this implicit reference disappeared in the international policy debate in the early 1980s.

A second dimension appears at this stage with the ideas developed in particular by Martin Feldstein, former chairman of the US Council of Economic Advisers, who participated, as a member and chairperson, in the work of the Economic Policy Committee at OECD. Feldstein (1987b) emphasized the risk of a kind of alibi that the "non-adjusting countries" can present. In a crisis situation the governments of such countries—this was probably part of the story in the 1980s—said that they did not (or could not) adjust because of the poor environment they were facing. If coordination had taken place, their own performance would have been much better. As Feldstein (1987a) said in a rather provocative article: "An emphasis on international interdependence instead of sound domestic policies makes foreign governments the natural scapegoats for any poor economic performance".

Any person who participates in international meetings like the OECD (or European Union) Economic Policy Committee knows the trick. When you are under attack because your government did not make the courageous decisions required, a possible defense is a counter-attack: "If our colleagues had provided us with a better environment, we would have been happy to make such an adjustment". It seems to me that this argument refers more to tactics than to strategies. But if the risk of deflation could be an incentive for more coordination, it is also important to evaluate the danger of some governments permanently postponing painful adjustment because they expect (or hope) that international coordination will create ideal conditions to get their house in order.

The literature on coordination is often too general. The concept becomes clearer when applied to some specific issues. For instance, recently, many discussions about coordination focused on stabilizing exchange rates. A very interesting case is the ex-post assessment of the coordination policy implemented (in a rather loose form) by the members of the G–7 in September 1985. At that time, with an overvalued dollar and a large US budget deficit, the fear was of a "hard landing" in which the necessary adjustments in the United States would cause both recession and inflation in the United States and have severe consequences for the rest of the world. At the end of 1985 Stephen Marris, who had been in the OECD for a long time, published a book entitled *Deficits and the Dollar: The World Economy at Risk*. In this book he argued convincingly that a crash landing could take place absent sufficient coordination among the major OECD members. In an interesting post-mortem Marris (1991) argued that the scenario he had in mind did not take place because there was some policy coordination.

This example is interesting from a methodological point of view for at least two reasons. First, it is difficult for such an assessment to take the exogenous events that occurred in the interim into account—a major one was a sharp decrease in the price of oil in 1986. Second, it raises the question as to whether, ex-post, the determinants of policy-making—for instance, monetary policy by the Federal Reserve—are internal or derive from an explicit willingness to enter a cooperative game. In this field an objective evaluation is especially delicate because a large part of the story may pass through some telephone calls between governors that, for obvious reasons, have to be kept discreet. As is now well known, the Plaza

Agreement may have contributed to the relative stabilization of exchange rates until the end of the 1980s. But the later drop of the dollar reinforced the scepticism of those who think that such coordination does not work.

The question of coordinating macroeconomic policies comes back today with the emergence of situations in which financial resources have become extremely volatile in some countries or regions. One should not be astonished by the existence of such volatility. The widespread securitization of credit and the increased sophistication of financial products (derivatives) contribute to "bang-bang" reactions through various leverage effects. But the question of expectations is a central one. Indeed, it is not the market that makes judgements on government policies, it is the people who intervene in the market. These people have beliefs of their own, and there is a non-negligible risk of overreaction, especially if people do not have correct information. Moreover, the rise of high performance computer programming increases considerably the speed of reaction of financial operations. And because most of these programmes have the same type of structure, the possibility of general sheeplike reactions is a risk for the market itself.

A new type of international policy coordination is now being discussed. Among these actions is an authoritarian limitation of capital inflows, which may be useful in some situations (Chile, for instance). But it should certainly not appear as a permanent measure, and it has to be clearly defined for a transitional period. Some economists (Tobin, 1978) have proposed interesting ways to throw sand in the wheels of international finance. The Tobin tax proposal aims at reducing volatility by levying a small tax on some financial operations (exchange operations, for instance). But such a tax would be very difficult to implement, and many economists doubt that it would slow down speculation in tense situations.

The issue of the speed of reaction is a difficult one. There is no good way to prevent operators from using sophisticated computer programs, enabling them to react quickly at any moment. Some countries defined certain prohibitions on quick liquidations, which indirectly reduced large capital inflows. Obviously, such techniques are not applicable to countries that want to attract foreign capital.

Expectations are based on information and judgement. The reassessment of a country's policy may depend on the reputation of the policy-makers inside and outside of the country. Thus expectations, to the extent that they are related to political judgement, may be highly volatile (as in Mexico in 1994), and little can be done in response. The issue of information is crucial at this stage. A good way to avoid sheeplike reactions that may take place when operators realize something significant happened that they were not aware of, is to disseminate timely and reliable economic information, providing a kind of continuous monitoring.

Finally, the debate over the coordination of macroeconomic policies looks like some of the controversies over the merits of long-term planning. We can discuss the best modalities of coordination. But the truth is that governments must address difficult questions, the answers to which are certainly not autarkical approaches. The most recent developments in international concertation (the Halifax Summit) call for clearly reinforced surveillance of macroeconomic policies and for improved information systems as an input to better monitoring.

An enabling environment

Let us keep in mind the three functions of public finance developed by Musgrave (1959): stabilization, allocation and distribution. It may be correct to say that there is more scepticism today than there was 20 years ago on the merits of coordinating macroeconomic policies. At the same time in the field of stabilization information issues have become more important, as has the concern over the volatility of international capital movements. As far as allocation of resources is concerned, significant progress should be made for the optimal provision of global public goods. Such an endeavour calls for coordination that does not exist today. Financing global public goods through voluntary contributions is certainly a suboptimal solution. At the international level distribution is motivated more and more by efficiency considerations, rendering questionable the transfer approach. This should result in more long-term and well-targeted policies.

For the first time, the world is endowed with multilateral institutions that are comprehensive from two points of view: their constituencies cover most of the world and they may address, at least in principle, all of the issues discussed in this chapter.

I emphasized the importance of the recent creation of the World Trade Organization (WTO). Most trade issues involve technicalities that call for assistance to member states, particularly developing countries. From this point of view, the reinforcement of the responsibility of the United Nations Conference on Trade and Development (UNCTAD) to support the poorest countries and the increasing role of OECD, especially on issues of investment, competition and labour standards, will contri-bute to a more balanced trade pole.

Managing the global commons and providing international public goods constitute a huge field for international cooperation, in which the United Nations system has clear leadership. The subject areas include peace and security (traditionally seen as a responsibility of the United Nations), but also a large range of issues with an international dimension, from environment to brain drain problems to the prevention of pandemics in some parts of the world. A subsidiarity principle[4] must be applied to these international public goods, when possible, in order to avoid overwhelming headquarters with issues that might be better tackled at the regional level. Towards this end, a more precise role for the regional organizations is still to be defined.

The idea prevails that more should be done to assist the worst-off and that such an endeavour calls for the creation of an enabling environment. The titles of the last three issues of the World Bank *World Development Report* are significant from this point of view: *Investing in Health* (1993), *Infrastructure for Development* (1994) and *Workers in an Integrating World* (1995). Other agencies and NGOs also undertake a large variety of initiatives. It means, then, that many long-term issues must be addressed and that this is primarily a responsibility of countries themselves. The long-term horizon is probably closer to a generation than a decade. The analysis and coordination of long-term issues at the field level remains weak, although significant efforts by the resident coordinators of the United Nations Development Programme and other field representatives of the various agencies have been made.

The question of coordinating macroeconomic and financial policies has changed in nature, because the understanding of these
policies has evolved from very short-term to medium-and long-term
concerns. The International Monetary Fund (IMF) plays a central
role, providing the main forum in which the ministers of finance of
the world may exchange information and confront views on the
policies they implement. The explicit recognition of the global
character of international finance is certainly an important step. One
of the new dimensions to be added to the picture would be a better
integration between this increasing long-term concern in the elaboration of macroeconomic policies and the stakes of the three other
clusters. That is why it is important to keep the UN, the World Bank,
the WTO and the main regional organizations as members of the
IMF Interim Committee, at least in the role of observers.

For the countries of the world an enabling environment must be
founded on the four pillars I have tried to define along the lines
sketched by Camdessus (1993). This design is now broadly accepted
by the overall international community. This is significant progress.

ANNEX. A SIMPLIFIED GENERAL EQUILIBRIUM MODEL

Assume there are four goods: goods 1 and 2 are non-producible resources—say, labour and energy—that are used to produce two more goods, 3 and 4.

The technical constraints are represented by the following production functions:

(1) $\quad y_3 = f(y_1^3, y_2^3)$ and

(2) $\quad y_4 = g(y_1^4, y_2^4)$,

where y_3, y_4 are the outputs of goods 3 and 4, respectively, and y_j^k denotes the input of commodity j used to produce good k ($j = 1, 2; k = 3, 4$). These production functions satisfy the standard continuity and concavity assumptions.

For a given period the economy has a given (exogeneous for the moment) supply of labour and energy, which are denoted ω_1 and ω_2. Let us suppose that the country is an energy importer. It imports a volume i_2 of energy at a given (exogeneous) international price π_2. To pay for these imports, the country exports one of its produced goods, say, good 4. The volume of its exports is thus e_4, at a given international price π_4.[5]

The external balance of trade is thus represented by:

(3) $\quad \delta = i_2\pi_2 - e_4\pi_4$,

where a positive δ indicates a trade deficit.

Let us call x_3 and x_4 the internal absorption of goods 3 and 4 within the country. The equations that characterize the equilibrium in each of the four markets may be written:

(4) $\quad \omega_1 = y_1^3 + y_1^4$

(5) $\quad i_2 + \omega_2 = y_2^3 + y_2^4$

(6) $\quad y_3 = x_3$

(7) $\quad y_4 = x_4 + e_4$.

For each of these markets, one may define internal prices p_1, p_2, p_3, p_4.

At this stage, I make two more assumptions. These are highly simplifying and could be relaxed to generalize the results.

Assumption 1: π_2 is c.i.f. and π_4 is f.o.b., and standard assumptions of free trade prevail fully, so that:

(8) $\quad p_2 = \pi_2$

(9) $p_4 = \pi_4$.

Assumption 2: Production is efficient so that the marginal productivities are proportional to factor prices. More precisely, the standard equations hold:

(10) $$\frac{\frac{\partial f}{\partial y_1^3}}{p_1} = \frac{\frac{\partial f}{\partial y_2^3}}{p_2} = \frac{1}{p_3}$$

(11) $$\frac{\frac{\partial g}{\partial y_1^4}}{p_1} = \frac{\frac{\partial g}{\partial y_2^4}}{p_2} = \frac{1}{p_4}$$

The problem can be now formulated simply. Let us suppose that there are changes $d\pi_2$ and $d\pi_4$ in the prices of imports and exports. Given such a shock, let us say an adverse shock, the reaction might be: working more ($d\omega_1 > 0$), drawing more national resources ($d\omega_2 > 0$) or increasing the trade deficit ($d\delta_1 > 0$). All of the variables will change as a consequence. So, a priori, the solution could appear inextricable. However, the final result is rather simple.

What kind of result are we interested in? As a consequence of the change in exogenous variables, the internal absorption of the economy will change. This change is the crucial part of the story, and it plays a central role in the shock absorption. Let us try to calculate its size.

With the price of the reference situation p_3 and p_4, the change in the volume of internal absorption will be:

(12) $dA = p_3 dx_3 + p_4 dx_4$.

Let us now proceed and make the calculation under assumptions 1 and 2. From equations 4–7 we get:

(4') $d\omega_1 = dy_1^3 + dy_1^4$

(5') $di_2 + d\omega_2 = dy_2^3 + dy_2^4$

(6') $dy_3 = dx_3$

(7') $dy_4 = dx_4 + de_4$.

Equation 12 may thus be rewritten:

$dA = p_3 dy_3 + p_4 (dy_4 - de_4)$.

From equations 1 and 2 we get:

$$dA = p_3\left(\frac{\partial f}{\partial y_1^3}\,dy_1^3 + \frac{\partial f}{\partial y_2^3}\,dy_2^3\right) + p_4\left(\frac{\partial g}{\partial y_1^4}\,dy_1^4 + \frac{\partial g}{\partial y_2^4}\,dy_2^4 - de_4\right).$$

Taking equations 10 and 11 into account:

$$dA = p_3\left(\frac{p_1}{p_3}\,dy_1^3 + \frac{p_2}{p_3}\,dy_2^3\right) + p_4\left(\frac{p_1}{p_4}\,dy_1^4 + \frac{p_2}{p_4}\,dy_2^4 - de_4\right).$$

From equation 4' and 5' we get:

(12*) $dA = p_1 d\omega_1 + p_2(d\omega_2 + di_2) - p_4 de_4,$

and from equation 3:

(3*) $d\delta = \pi_2 di_2 + i_2 d\pi_2 - \pi_4 de_4 - e_4 d\pi_4.$

Combining equations 12*, 3*, 8 and 9:

(12**) $dA = p_1 d\omega_1 + p_2 d\omega_2 + d\delta - i_2 d\pi_2 + e_4 d\pi_4.$

It is convenient to define the "size" of trade τ by the formula:

(13) $2\tau = i_2\pi_2 + e_4\pi_4.$

By elementary calculations, we get from 12**:

$$(14) \qquad dA = p_1 d\omega_1 + p_2 d\omega_2 + \tau\left(\frac{d\pi_4}{\pi_4} - \frac{d\pi_2}{\pi_2}\right) + \delta\left[\frac{d\delta}{\delta} - \frac{1}{2}\left(\frac{d\pi_4}{\pi_4} + \frac{d\pi_2}{\pi_2}\right)\right].$$

Or, reordering the terms, we get the fundamental equation of the allocation of the gain (or loss) related to a change in terms of trade:

$$(15) \qquad \tau\left(\frac{d\pi_4}{\pi_4} - \frac{d\pi_2}{\pi_2}\right) = dA - p_1 d\omega_1 - p_2 d\omega_2 - \delta\left[\frac{d\delta}{\delta} - \frac{1}{2}\left(\frac{d\pi_4}{\pi_4} + \frac{d\pi_2}{\pi_2}\right)\right].$$

NOTES

1. Merit wants are those whose satisfaction is considered intrinsically desirable or undesirable. The concept has been criticized because of its paternalistic aspects.
2. I deliberately left aside the concept of "non-rivalry" and the difficult question of crowding that could possibly change the public good nature of infrastructure. They seem to me more relevant concepts at the national or local level. (For a discussion the difference between "non-rival" and "non-excludable", see Mendez, (1992).
3. An interesting analogy: the United Nations today is in a situation that could be compared with that of the US federal authority before the vote on the sixteenth amendment of the constitution, according to which "the Congress shall have power to lay and collect taxes on incomes from whatever source derived, without apportionment among the several States, and without regard to any census of enumeration."
4. The principle according to which political authority rests in the most local jurisdiction possible.
5. There is no assumption about the sign of i_2 and e_4. As a consequence, one could interpret them as negative, a situation in which a country exports commodity 2 to buy good 4, which might be, for instance, an investment good.

REFERENCES

Aaron, Henry J., Ralph C. Bryant, Susan M. Collins and Robert Z. Lawrence. 1994. "Preface." In *Studies on Integrating National Economies*. Washington, D.C.: The Brookings Institution.

Camdessus, Michel. 1993. "Statement at the U.N. Economic and Social Council." International Monetary Fund, Washington, D.C.

Chen, Shaochua, Gaurav Datt and Martin Ravallion. 1994. "Is Poverty Increasing in the Developing World?" *The Review of Income and Wealth* 40(4):359–76.

Cooper, Richard N. 1994. *Environment and Resource Policies for the World Economy*. Washington, D.C.: The Brookings Institution.

Cortright, David and George A. Lopez., eds. 1995. *Economic Sanctions*. Boulder: Westview Press.

Debreu, Gerard. 1956. *The Theory of Value*. New York: Wiley.

Drèze, Jean P. and Amartya K. Sen, eds. 1989. *Hunger and Public Action*. Oxford: Clarendon Press.

____. 1990. *The Political Economy of Hunger*. Oxford: Oxford University Press.

Feldstein, Martin. 1987a. "The End of Policy Coordination." *The Wall Street Journal*, November 9.

____. 1987b. *International Economic Cooperation*. Chicago: University of Chicago Press.

Fischer, Stanley. 1988. "Devaluation and Inflation." In Rudiger Dornbusch and F. Leslie C.H. Helmers, eds., *The Open Economy: Tools for Policy Makers in Developing Countries*. Oxford: Oxford University Press.

Gavin, Michael. 1988. "Adjusting to a Terms of Trade Shock: Nigeria 1972–1988." In Rudiger Dornbusch and F. Leslie C.H. Helmers, eds., *The Open Economy: Tools for Policy Makers in Developing Countries*. Oxford: Oxford University Press.

Goldin, Ian, Odin Knudsen and Dominique van der Mensbrugghe. 1993. *Trade Liberalization: Global Economic Implications*. Washington, D.C.: World Bank and Paris: OECD.

Haggard, Stephen. 1995. *Developing Nations and the Politics of Global Integration*. Washington, D.C.: The Brookings Institution.

Kahler, Miles. 1995. *International Institutions and the Political Economy of Integration*. Washington, D.C.: The Brookings Institution.

Krugman, Paul. 1988. "External Shocks and Domestic Policy Responses." In Rudiger Dornbusch and F. Leslie C.H. Helmers, eds., *The Open Economy: Tools for Policy Makers in Developing Countries*. Oxford: Oxford University Press.

____. 1994. "Does Third World Growth Hurt First World Prosperity." In Kenichi Ohmae, ed., *The Evolving Global Economy*. Cambridge, Mass.: Harvard Business Review.

Lecaillon, Jacques, Felix Paukert, Christian Morrisson and Dimitri Germidis, eds. 1984. *Income Distribution and Economic Development*. Geneva: International Labour Organization.

Malinvaud, Edmond and Mustapha K. Nabli. 1997. "The Future of Planning in Market Economies." In Edmond Malinvaud et al., eds., *Development Strategy and Management of the Market Economy*, Volume I. Oxford: Clarendon Press.

Marris, Stephen. 1985. *Deficits and the Dollar: the World Economy at Risk*. Washington, D.C.: Institute for International Economics.

____. 1991. "Why No Hard Landing?" In F. Bergsten, ed., *International Adjustment and Financing: The Lessons of 1985–1991*. Washington, D.C.: Institute for International Economics.

Mendez, Ruben P. 1992. *International Public Finance*. New York: Oxford University Press.

Musgrave, Richard A. 1959. *The Theory of Public Finance*. New York: McGraw-Hill.

Nussbaum, Martha C. and Amartya K. Sen. 1993. *The Quality of Life*. Oxford: Clarendon Press.

Razin, Assaf and Efraim Sadka. 1994. "Interaction Between International Migration and International Trade: Positive and Normative Aspects." In Centre of Economic Policy Research, *The Location of Economic Activity: New Theories and Evidence*. London: Centre for Economic Policy Research.

Sen, Amartya K. 1991. *Poverty and Famines: An Essay on Entitlement and Deprivation*. Oxford: Clarendon Press.

Stalker, Peter. 1994. *The Work of Strangers: A Survey of International Labour Migrations*. Geneva: International Labour Organization.

Stark, Oded. 1991. *The Migration of Labour*. Oxford: Basil Blackwell.

Suzumura, Kotaro. 1997. "Industrial Policy in Developing Market Economies." In Edmond Malinvaud et al., eds., *Development Strategy and Management of the Market Economy*, Volume I. Oxford: Clarendon Press.

Tabatabai, Hamid. 1995. "Poverty and Inequality in Developing Countries: A Review of Evidence." In G. Rodgers and Rolph van der Hoeven, eds., *The Poverty Agenda: Trends and Policy Options.* Geneva: International Institute for Labour Studies.

Tobin, James. 1978. "A Proposal for International Monetary Reform." *Eastern Economic Journal* 3–4:153–59.

United Nations. 1994. *World Economic and Social Survey.* New York: United Nations.

____. 1995. *World Economic and Social Survey.* New York: United Nations.

United Nations Development Programme. 1992. *Human Development Report.* New York: Oxford University Press.

World Bank. 1993. *World Development Report 1993.* New York: Oxford University Press.

____. 1994. *World Development Report 1994.* New York: Oxford University Press.

____. 1995. *World Development Report 1995.* New York: Oxford University Press.

8

A Framework for a Development Strategy in a Market Economy

NICHOLAS STERN AND JOSEPH E. STIGLITZ

A well-functioning economy requires a mix of government and markets. The balance, structure and functioning of that mix is at the heart of a development strategy. The mix is not simply assigning certain areas to one or the other domain. The more appropriate analogy is that of a partnership, in which each partner is given certain areas of responsibility. The political process makes the assignments. The task of this book is to provide an analytic basis to help examine how those assignments should be made.

The first ingredients of a development strategy are its basic objectives, together with an analysis of the long-term assignments in light of those objectives. The nature of those assignments is altered by changes in the world economic environment and country circumstances, as well as with changes in, and emphasis among, the objectives that government sees as falling within its purview. These are the issues to which we turn in the first section. The second section then focuses on institutions and instruments. The details of these institutions and the precise nature of the instruments employed by government are as crucial a part of the development strategy—determining how the partnerships actually function—as the assignments themselves.[1]

OBJECTIVES AND SCOPE

This book presents a broad set of objectives that should underlie development strategies. While all of these may be summarized within the rubric of "raising living standards", they go far beyond the standard objective of increasing GDP per capita. They include promoting education and health, maintaining and improving the environment, and enhancing and protecting opportunities for all citizens to participate in, and benefit from, the economy and society. Some of these objectives are also important instruments—means to obtain other objectives. Nonetheless, we should not forget that they have value in their own right: improved education may lead to higher incomes, but it also enriches directly the lives of individuals; improved medical care may lead to enhanced productivity, but it also improves directly the quality of life.

A focus on living standards involves a focus on individuals—and therefore on distributions, as well as aggregates. Again, reducing inequality and poverty may be viewed as objectives or as instruments: societies with less inequality may perform better, because they avoid some of the political tensions associated with huge disparities in income and wealth and because egalitarian policies result in more of a society's human resources being used closer to their full potential. Still, within this broad mandate, different economies, societies or political movements may emphasize different aspects of an egalitarian agenda. Some may attach priority to ensuring equality of educational opportunities and access to health care, regardless of the short-run impact that this might have on measured inequality, while others might focus more directly on measured outcomes, for example, through a safety net so that no one's access to basic needs, like food and shelter, falls below a certain threshold.[2]

We have defined the objectives of a development strategy fairly broadly in terms of standards of living and examined the major elements determining those standards. But development strategies will have more specific objectives (what may be viewed as intermediate goals), depending on where the country finds itself. Thus, for example, while women's literacy may, or should, constitute a high operational priority in some circumstances, this objective is less pressing where the population is already broadly literate.

We must, however, ask deeper questions concerning the origins of objectives for a community. If everyone agreed on the objectives—and on the weights to be assigned to each—of a development strategy, matters would be simple. But there is never such unanimity. Objectives and the strategy that supports them will emerge from a political process. If there is a broadly shared commitment to the objectives and strategy, then the strategy is likely to function much more effectively than it would absent such a commitment. But that broad commitment may not be present. If it is not, then the government faces difficult dilemmas. It could try to confine itself to introducing only those policies on which there is neat unanimity. This will represent only a narrow range of options. Or, a government could try to build a consensus. Some methods of consensus building may be deeply unattractive, such as starting external wars or promoting heavy propaganda. Other examples are more positive and involve a process of discussion among different groups. In some circumstances a broad consensus can come from shared values, traditions and cultures. It can also come from solidarity. There is no magic formula for producing consensus and cohesion. Attempts to enforce such an approach would be deeply worrying and unacceptable from some political perspectives.[3]

We cannot resolve these issues here. We simply draw attention to their importance for building and implementing a strategy. We can say, however, that realism as to what can be achieved and a track record of honesty and achievement—particularly achievement that is in accord with expectations or government promises—are likely to make the development of a strategy easier.

The institutions that support strategies and the strategies themselves must take account of uncertainty and lack of information, and the limitations on what organizations can expect to achieve. Thus any attempt at finely tuned optimization runs the risk of going badly wrong—which is not, of course, a counsel to do worse rather than better if the option is there. It is simply to recognize that information and capacities are limited, and that it is thus important to build strategies and institutions that will function well in a range of circumstances. In this sense we should be looking for robustness as an important feature of strategies and institutions.

The issues of robustness and the formation of objectives are linked to a changing perception of the role of planning and strategies. Early planning models embodied optimization under (pressured) direct control and full information. They then moved to principal-agent models, which took account of incentive compatibility issues. At this later stage it was still assumed, if only implicitly, that the planner had full information but limited ability to control households and firms. Models of planning remained constrained optimization problems, but with the important extra constraint that planners could use only the limited instruments under their control (such as indirect and direct taxes) to induce firms and households to act in a preferred manner. These models are useful for understanding important features of planning problems, but they capture only one aspect of a fuller story.

A broader perspective puts much more emphasis on the lack of knowledge, both about the structure of the economy and the relevant parameters. While it is still possible to formulate an optimal Bayesian plan, formally taking into account limitations on information and changes in information over time, the difficulty of solving such problems in any practically usable way has led to a switch in emphasis—to robust development strategies and institutions that perform well under a wide set of relevant environments.

The formal modeling described above depicted the planner working outside of the political framework. The planner solved the optimization problem. If the model is taken literally, and everyone agrees that we should do what is optimal, there is seemingly no reason that the optimal strategy not be adopted. The broader perspective recognizes that planning and, more generally, all aspects of economic decision-making are highly political: there are winners and losers, or at least some who gain more than others. Although there are no formal political constraints—governments repeatedly undertake policies that only a short time earlier were judged to be politically unfeasible—political pressures do affect the ease with which different strategies can be undertaken or the likelihood that particular processes will be adopted. In some cases the political process may even reject a proposal that appears, from a static perspective, to be a Pareto improvement, because that decision will affect future options or decisions in ways that will adversely affect a particular group. For example, in the United States recent proposals to auction off rights for further development of hydroelectric sites have been criticized by those currently receiving "below-market" electricity, not because they would be hurt directly, but because they worry that it would make more transparent the hidden subsidy they currently receive (electricity priced below the opportunity cost, though at or above the production cost) and in the long run increase the likelihood that their subsidy would be eliminated.[4]

The basic elements of a partnership

The basic elements of a partnership are the allocation of responsibilities and frameworks for finance and decision-making. In both areas there are a variety of sharing arrangements. It has long been recognized that finance and production are not the same issue—the government may provide finance, leaving production to private entities (as in the case of health care for the aged in the United States), or it may engage in production, relying on conventional pricing mechanisms to raise revenue (as in the case of public utilities). Arrangements for sharing in finance can be fairly transparent (although the ultimate incidence/destination of expenditures is not always straightforward). In education, for instance, most governments assume a large financial responsibility for elementary education, but put some of the financial burden for higher education on students and their families (though they often provide loans, sometimes at subsidized rates).[5] But sharing decision-making is often more complex. In many sectors there are complex regulations governing the decisions of private actors.

There is an emerging consensus, based on both theory and experience, on certain elements of how sharing can be most effectively conducted. Markets have primacy in the production and allocation of goods and services. But markets on their own often fail to produce socially desirable outcomes. Government has the central responsibility to provide an institutional infrastructure in which markets can function; defence and law and order; macroeconomic stability; an environment to preserve public health; access to education and health care that allow, protect or enhance effective participation in the market economy; and a safety net. There is shared responsibility—the terms of which differ across countries—to provide education and health, establish the physical infrastructure and develop technology.

Areas in which government is the major partner

Placing the private sector at the centre of production means that there is a presumption against government production and in favour of privatization. But there are several important caveats: there must, for example, be ways of ensuring that markets are competitive. And when government does privatize, it must ensure that it receives fair value—receiving less is not only an invitation for corruption, but also imposes a heavier burden on distortionary taxation in the future.

Institutional infrastructure

Governments must provide the institutional infrastructure in which markets function. This institutional infrastructure goes beyond the legal framework (contract, tort, bankruptcy and competition law). It includes the regulatory structure affecting key industries, such as telecommunications, and the financial services sector. Ensuring the safety and soundness of the financial system is necessary, not only because this sector has a vital role to play in allocating capital efficiently[6] (without confidence in the stability of the financial structure, savers will not entrust their savings to it, and it thus cannot perform its role of intermediation), but also because instability in this sector can be a source of macroeconomic instability.

Ensuring macroeconomic stability must itself be recognized as one of the central responsibilities of government (see chapter 5 of this volume).[7] This basic and fundamental function must be discharged by government. Given its extensive discussion elsewhere in the book, we do not dwell on it here. Nor do we discuss defence and law and order. Again, this is not in anyway intended to underestimate their importance. Stability and effectiveness in these areas is crucial. Indeed, many of the disasters of economic development are associated with a breakdown of order, particularly internal and external wars.

We examine health and education issues under shared responsibilities and develop the discussion further in the second section. At this point we simply emphasize that it is a government responsibility to provide public health and to ensure access, and regulate private activity.

The provision of a safety net is an area in which government activity may be viewed as directly pursuing objectives—here, these include a sense of equity and community—and as instrumental for other objectives. Without an adequate safety net there is often resistance to changes that are essential for economic progress and development. What constitutes an adequate safety net and how can or should it be provided will clearly vary with circumstances in each country. Poorer countries—with limited abilities to raise taxes—may have to rely heavily on families and local communities to provide the safety net. But even in more developed countries increasing attention is being paid to the adverse incentive effects of poorly designed safety nets and to the, often very heavy, costs of their provision. In these countries there is increased emphasis on individual responsibility. This arises not only from considerations of efficiency or cost—for many commentators it is itself a moral imperative (or, more loosely, an objective of government policy). Policies are then evaluated not only in terms of their direct impact on outcomes (in particular, on individual incomes), but also in terms of their impact on opportunities[8] and the extent to which individuals take charge of their own lives. There is nevertheless some agreement on the proposition that a civilized society should provide some protection from extreme deprivation.

Environmental issues

We emphasized earlier that the objective of a development strategy must be to increase standards of living. An important ingredient in living standards is the quality of the environment. Development strategies that accept the sacrifice of a clean environment today for larger growth rates in GDP are generally being misled by, or deliberately overlook, the limitations on our measures of standards of living. Such policies are likely to be worse than "penny wise and pound foolish". Society can lose today *and* lose tomorrow, especially as the costs of clean-up are often a multiple of the costs of avoiding pollution (air, water, toxic waste) in the first place.[9] Government must enforce regulations, taxes and other mechanisms that impel private actors to take account of environmental consequences. And government must carry out those investments that cannot be promoted by market incentives but that are productive from a broader environmental perspective.

Depletion of natural resources represents a different type of problem. Growth can be sustainable as long as there is a more-than-compensating increase in the stock of other capital. But growth strategies must explicitly recognize this necessity—and provide for increases in capital stock that are larger than they otherwise would have been to offset resource depletion.[10]

Areas of shared responsibility

Standard analyses of economic growth present three sources of that growth: the accumulation of physical capital, increased human capital and improvements in the efficiency with which resources are used (growth in total factor productivity). Although there has been some debate in recent years about the relative importance of the various components,[11] a comprehensive growth strategy must address all of the components. The terms of the partnerships in each area differ, and we discuss them, not in the order of their relative importance in an overall growth strategy, but in the order of the significance of the government role within the partnership.

Education

Although education has long been an area in which the private and public sectors have shared responsibility whatever the institutional arrangement, governments of countries that have had successful development strategies have ensured that there is universal primary education—including the education of women—and that there is widespread access to further education. Education, as we have noted, is not only an end in itself, enriching individuals' lives, but it ensures opportunity and enhances productivity. It is necessary if developing countries are to absorb and adopt advanced technologies and methods of organization that will enable them to close the gap between their standards of living and those of the more developed countries.

Technology

Active policies promoting the transfer and development of technology have been an ingredient in most successful development strategies. The nature of these industrial policies remains one of the more controversial aspects of development strategy. Although the United States, Japan, Taiwan (province of China) and many European countries had selective and effective policies promoting technology,[12] economists remain skeptical about their benefit.[13] It must be recognized that central to industrial policy should be the provision of competition and openness—which are crucial to the process of technological change.

But although there is a debate about the appropriate extent and nature of active policies promoting technology, there is little disagreement that government must put in place the institutional infrastructure that is required for the rapid and effective transfer and development of technology. This includes a strong, broad-based education system, with a high (and well-structured) science and engineering content. Education must provide the skills to learn new ideas and the flexibility to adapt to them. There will also be requirements for setting standards and quality control, and for a system of intellectual property protection.

Saving and investment

Most of the successful countries of east Asia had active policies promoting saving and investment—and avoided policies that discouraged saving and investment. We have referred to several of these previously—they clearly fall within the responsibility of government in this economic partnership: maintaining macroeconomic stability, with low deficits (or possibly surpluses), and providing the solid prudential regulation necessary for a safe, sound financial system. But governments have done more: they have helped create markets, for instance, debt and equity markets, by ensuring that there were regulatory mechanisms that would give investors confidence in these markets and by helping to create a demand for the instruments provided by these markets. The development banks provided long-term financing and, arguably, through a variety of risk-sharing and signaling mechanisms, helped catalyze private investment in certain vital areas.[14] By the same token, the postal saving banks, prudential regulation of other banks and provident funds all helped stimulate saving, both by increasing access to financial intermediaries and by enhancing depositors confidence in their safety.[15] There is much to learn from these experiences.

Changing roles

There are many areas in which the scope for government activity is now seen to be smaller than in earlier discussions of development strategy.

Information services

While the government must still make plans for its own activities (indeed, an essential ingredient of a development strategy is the formulation of these plans for the public sector), the role of government planning (or more broadly, information services relating to the future evolution of the economy) for private sector activities will vary from country to country. In some countries private information services providing, for instance, short- and medium-term forecasts, are sufficiently developed that there may be little value to be added by additional public provision. But in other economies the government can provide important information services that extend well beyond the collection and dissemination of statistics. Whether they go far enough to be labelled a "plan" for the economy may be a matter of semantics, but they may provide guideposts for the economy, an issue to which we shall turn shortly. Indeed, whether or not there are private services, the private sector should be interested in, and informed of, the government's perspectives.

Provision of physical infrastructure

Another area in which the scope for government has changed dramatically is the provision of physical infrastructure (see, for example, World Bank, 1994). Fifty years ago it was simply assumed by many that the government should provide infrastructure. But this view overlooked the lessons of historical experience: in the United States, as well as in many other countries, roads and canals were privately provided throughout the nineteenth century. A key argument for government ownership in that context was that some government involvement was required to establish a right-of-way.

It was also recognized that the potential for abuse of private monopolies was great and that regulation was an inadequate safeguard. Although these arguments had considerable validity, there is now an increased recognition and understanding of the disadvantages inherent in government monopoly—both in terms of efficiency and rent diversion. At the same time it has become apparent that for many types of infrastructure—including electricity generation[16] and virtually all parts of the telecommunications sector, except the "local loop"[17]—competition is, in fact, viable. The limited budgets of most developing countries, the requirement to finance investment and the tendency of government enterprises to produce losses imply that there is an obvious advantage—beyond enhanced efficiency—to providing infrastructure privately. International competition among providers, in turn, may have changed the terms of trade: developing countries may be able to obtain foreign capital and technology at favourable terms, with a risk of exploitation limited by competition and by international experience in regulation.

Assignment of responsibilities

Strategies of development and the assignment of responsibilities may have to change with changes in technology (as the example of telecommunications illustrates), changes in the world economy (globalization and reduced transportation costs have facilitated export-oriented strategies and the transfer of technologies between industrial and developing countries, and rising real interest rates have put added pressure on government finances) and changes in the state of development of the economy. Markets are less developed in poorer economies but so, too, are public institutions. Thus while the need or scope for government intervention may be greater, the capacity of the government to intervene in ways that enhance growth and welfare may be more limited. Development entails the advancement of public and private institutions, and on a priori grounds it is not obvious at any particular stage whether relatively more or less reliance should be placed on the public sector. For instance, poor governments' relative difficulties with taxing could suggest a smaller role in the provision of infrastructure than in some developed economies—or at least point to pricing services in a way that would not only cover costs but also provide net contributions to government revenue.

The areas of government activity that we have described go well beyond the "night-watchman" state of defence and law and order plus the institutional infrastructure for markets. But it must be recognized that ambitions for the state's role must be limited by financial and institutional constraints. Notice, further, that the suggested activities do not involve direct government responsibility for the overall level and allocation of investment. In contrast, in older theories of development planning, for instance, emphasis was placed on rapid capital accumulation and investment in basic industries, with the government given a strong role.[18] Further, pessimism about opportunities for export contributed to an emphasis on import-substitution strategies (implicitly, it was assumed that given these limitations, the marginal returns to developing import substitutes exceeded those to developing exports). The success of the countries of east Asia and the phenomena summarized under "globalization" in earlier chapters have not only ended export pessimism, but have shown that the promotion of exports can be an effective strategy for transferring technology and enhancing the competitiveness of domestic industries.

It should be recognized that the central components of the development strategy described here follow directly from the problems a development strategy is designed to overcome. Developing countries are characterized by low standards of living, in particular, low income per capita. Income per capita is low in part because workers lack training, capital and technology. But it is also often the case that the given skills, technology and capital are used inefficiently, making output per worker low. Competition and openness in markets are the greatest forces for increasing efficiency and promoting technological change. But there is much that government can and should do. Government can promote saving and can develop financial institutions that increase the efficiency with which scarce capital is allocated. Government can promote education, which not only directly raises the standard of living, but which is also necessary for the transfer of technology and which improves the productivity of the labour force. Government can promote the development and transfer of technology directly. Finally, infrastructure is an essential complement to private investment and contributes directly to the standard of living. While government need not provide the infrastructure itself, it must ensure that it is provided in a sound manner.

There is some, though not universal, consensus concerning the elements of the development strategy sketched above. But elements of controversy remain about what further role government should play in formulating and executing a development strategy, and what that strategy should look like. In most of the countries of east Asia government did far more: it helped establish market institutions (like development banks), helped create markets (such as bond and equity markets), and made decisions about which industries to promote (sometimes at a fairly detailed level—steel, plastics, chemicals; sometimes at a broad level—exports) and which sectors to discourage (speculative real estate). It acted as a catalyst, outlining future directions, as well as marshalling resources.[19]

In this more comprehensive view national strategies have some similarities to corporate strategies: they identify problems and opportunities, and possible approaches to addressing those problems and opportunities. They are partly for information gathering and dissemination and partly for national consensus building. Thus as Singapore's per capita output and income increased, the government recognized that if its growth was to continue, it would have to shift into high value-added sectors. While many smart business people had probably already recognized this, public discussion disseminated this idea more widely and, given the complementarity between public investment (in infrastructure, education and technology) and private investment, the discussion provided the basis for coordination.

Still, it must be recognized that nations are not corporations. Their objectives are not unique, not necessarily shared and much less well-defined. Individual agents can, and should, have much greater freedom to pursue their own lines of activity and interests in their lives than employees of a corporation.

North-South relations and development strategy

Earlier discussions of development focused particularly on two aspects of North-South relations: capital and technology. Developing countries were viewed as lacking both capital and know-how, and therefore needed a transfer of capital and technical assistance. The east Asian experience has shown that developing countries can make major strides in generating capital and establishing the conditions (industry, development of human capital, competition and openness) for the transfer of technology. Although the main responsibility lies with developing countries themselves, wealthier countries can make real contributions in these directions. But, perhaps more importantly, they can help generate the conditions in which development strategies can succeed.

Industrial economies have, with a fairly unified voice, recited the mantra of markets and competition for more than a decade. As they too have faced budgetary stringencies, they have promoted "trade not aid". They have encouraged developing countries to open their markets to investment. For the most part they have made good on their promises: they have often granted developing countries preferential access and have not always asked for fully reciprocal treatment.

But in a few instances there has been some duplicity. For example, as some of the transition economies have attempted to enter the world market, they have found the door shut, by quotas on textiles or through threats of anti-dumping actions and countervailing duties. While insisting that developing countries and economies in transition face competition from developed countries, the latter have resorted to protection when confronted with market surges and changing comparative advantage that disadvantaged some of their own industries.

While insisting on the protection of intellectual property rights, industrial countries have been less enthusiastic in insisting that owners of intellectual property refrain from discriminating against poor countries. In some cases pharmaceutical companies have charged poor countries far more for the same drugs than the prices charged to others.

Other issues, the most difficult from an international perspective, are associated with international environmental public goods, such as the production of greenhouse gasses associated with global warming. Many developing countries are among those most likely to be affected adversely by the degradation of these environmental public goods, yet each country has an incentive to try to induce others to cut back on their pollution without doing so themselves. There is growing international understanding that without cooperation from at least the major developing countries, who are likely to rely more heavily on coal as a source of energy than richer countries, greenhouse gas concentrations are likely to increase to potentially dangerous levels by the middle of the next century. There is a growing international consensus (reflected in the Rio Convention) that the increases in greenhouse gasses represent a global problem. The cost of reducing greenhouse gas emissions can be lowered if it is done efficiently. The way that this issue is addressed—including the transfer of environmentally sound technologies to developing countries—will play an important role in the design of development strategies in coming years, particularly in vital areas of energy policy.

Multilateral development banks and development assistance

The development strategy of a poor country must depend on its opportunities for trade and the availability of other forms of support from other sources. As an outside player in repeated and long-term relationships with developing countries, a multilateral development bank can build trust and understanding and make a contribution far beyond the value of the resources provided.[20] From the host-country perspective, there is a greater willingness to accept, and greater recognition of the potential contribution of, a multilateral development bank relative to a private investor or a single-country partner, since it is a party whose interest in a transaction extends beyond narrow self-interest. Moreover, because multilateral development banks are involved in multiple lending projects, they have an incentive to be worried about macroeconomic performance, and they have the ability to enforce, as part of their lending programmes, "conditionality", ensuring that a sound policy environment is maintained. Of course, that conditionality derives primarily from their analysis of good policy and their objective to promote development. Thus a major argument for multilateral development bank involvement is their direct role in improving policies and the conditions for investment and growth.

Multilateral development banks' long-term involvement in development issues has a further advantage: they have developed a collective memory, which can be used to evaluate and design projects and programmes. At their best they have become repositories of information about what does and does not work. This knowledge is particularly important, because many programmes and projects, such as privatization of the telecommunications sector or construction of a major dam, are likely to be undertaken only once by a particular country.

The role of multilateral development banks, however, goes far beyond that of promoting good policies or public investments. In a world of rising international private capital flows, they have a central part to play as participant investors who can unlock, expand and improve the quality and impact of these flows. The fact that multilateral development banks are active partners may comfort other partners, including private investors, who recognize that involvement of multilaterals enhances the strength and reliability of relationships with the host government. In turn, the host government will have more confidence in the private investor if multilaterals are involved, because private investors have valued long-term relationships with multilateral development banks. They also value their own reputation. As a result of this greater comfort a variety of private projects may materialize that otherwise would fail to get off the ground, and will function much better.

The recent market-oriented philosophies of multilateral development banks point to a very important area of activity. Their task is not only to promote the policies, institutions and infrastructure for a market economy. By directly participating in the process of private investment, they can open up new areas of activity for private investment itself. This is a further example of partnership between a public institution and the market that does not involve the displacement of the market by the public institution.

INSTITUTIONS AND INSTRUMENTS

A coherent development strategy will also require a description of the institutions and instruments that will carry out or steer the tasks assigned to government or shared with the private sector. The details of the functioning of the institutions and of the way in which the instruments are constructed are so central to the chances of success of any strategy that it is sensible to see their design as part of the strategy itself.

Why institutions matter

Our emphasis on institutions requires that we offer an interpretation of the term. Dictionary definitions would normally include "an established custom, law or relationship in an economy or society" and "an organization with a specific purpose" among the possible meanings. A focus on institutions, then, is a focus on relationships, organizations and ways of doing things.

Traditional microeconomic theory paid minimal attention to institutions. It centred on technology, endowments and individual agents (and their preferences). The hypothesis held that the outcome was determined by these underlying factors; one did not need to look at the superficial arrangements through which transactions were mediated. Institutions, like sharecropping, were conveniences, but they could not have a significant effect on outcomes—if they did, the tension with the underlying economic forces would overwhelm the institutional arrangements, and the latter would ultimately change.

Institutional analysis, by contrast, begins with the hypothesis that institutions do matter, at least in the short and medium term. To be sure, when there are large discrepancies between underlying economic forces and institutional arrangements, there will be pressure for institutions to change. Such changes may, however, occur very slowly, and in some cases not at all. Thus institutions that originally may have been well-suited for dealing with a set of economic problems may become obstacles. Institutions shape change and are shaped by change.

Institutions can be important for economizing on transaction costs. Take the institution of sharecropping, with a particular set of terms (including sharing provisions). Modern economic theory would have predicted or imagined that there would be a complicated state-contingent contract; and even if the only observable variable was output, only under stringent conditions would the contract entail a linear relationship between payments to the landlord (share) and output. But the cost of negotiating a contract that deviated from a simple standard contract, like a 50–50 share, could be large. If the landlord proposed the contract, the renter would worry that the landlord might have differential information and was trying to turn the contract to his favour. Conversely, if the worker proposed a new contract, the landlord might think that in doing so the worker was signaling something potentially adverse about himself, inducing the landlord to turn down the offer of a contract altogether. Indeed, it is often the case that when there is ambiguity in contract law (as there always is), a non-standard contract is interpreted against the writer of the contract. These considerations provide a further rationale for the use of standard contracts—and the slow evolution of contract forms.

Sharecropping is an example of a (fairly) simple institution. In other contexts there is a much wider range of activities in which participants can be engaged and for which institutions specify appropriate behaviour. Whereas in a few cases relationships can be relegated to formal economic terms—for example, a performance-based contract with a limited number of performance measures—in most cases it is difficult to capture all relevant aspects of desired behaviour in one or two variables. Workers, for instance, have to train new hires, and it is difficult to monitor the extent of such training, let alone to find quantifiable measures of its quality. Institutions thus serve to regulate this kind of behaviour.[21]

Broadly speaking, then, institutions provide incentives and regulate behaviour to promote actions that enhance the organizational objectives in complex situations where a simple monetary reward structure will not provide appropriate incentives. One of the central problems in institutional design for such a partnership is to put appropriate incentives in place and, in particular, incentives that ensure cooperative behaviour, which can enhance economic efficiency.

It is also important to deter collusive behaviour, which may be defined as cooperative behaviour among, say, the firms in an industry at the expense of the general interest. Traditional economic theory suggested that self-interested behaviour ensured economic efficiency. Partnerships were simply not required or desirable. (Adam Smith was explicit on this point.) But the limitations of that perspective are now widely recognized. In some cases the desirability of partnerships is obvious: the relationship between workers and firms is typically not mediated simply through an impersonal price system.

Economic institutions also enable the resolution and avoidance of conflict. Thus, for example, parties with possibly conflicting short-run interests may arrange for forums that allow for an exchange of views (for example, unions, government and employees' organizations). They may construct institutions for arbitration between, or for supervision of, different parties in an industry or contract.

Successful and unsuccessful institutions

It is easy to identify institutional arrangements that work well: each partner does what it is supposed to do, there is good coordination, little conflict and the economy grows smoothly and rapidly. We can also recognize ill-functioning institutional arrangements: change is inhibited by bureaucratic requirement; or there is "bandit capitalism" with pervasive corruption and deceit.

It is, however, somewhat more difficult to identify the essential ingredients of good institutional arrangements. As we have argued, they lower transaction costs, provide appropriate incentives and avoid or resolve conflict. They thus enable engagement in socially constructive activities and do not provide incentives to take actions that enrich one partner at the expense of the other. They typically place considerable reliance on trust,[22] rather than explicit contract enforcement, but they do have some method of enforcement (for without that, long-term relationships cannot function effectively).

Incentive compatibility and dynamic consistency

The set of institutions and instruments that are adopted must follow incentive compatibility and dynamic consistency. Thus economic agents should have an incentive to conform with or honor allocations or commitments. What they plan to do today for some future contingency must be consistent with what they would want to do in the event that future contingency arises. For example, one of the crippling defects of the command system in the former Soviet Union was that there was little incentive to work, so that the notional allocation of tasks and effort in the Plan was not incentive-compatible when it came to actually doing the work. Similarly, non-tradeable rationing of goods in general is not incentive-compatible, since, following any rationed allocation, there will be an incentive to trade in rationed goods. It was a system that inevitably generated, on a grand scale, behaviour that went against the rules. This, in turn, generates cynicism, which further corrodes standards of behaviour and acceptance of rules and government.

Institutional rigidities

But just as institutions in the process of simplifying decision-making do not adapt perfectly to their particular circumstances (for example, to the economic circumstances of each pair of individuals engaging in a sharecropping contract), by the same token they may not change quickly in response to changes in economic circumstances. They thus face the risk of, at best, not addressing adequately the current needs of the economy and, at worst, becoming obstacles to change. There are a variety of reasons why institutions adjust slowly, some of which we have already hinted at. Institutions economize on transaction costs. Also, the design and establishment of new institutions is a public good, entailing high transaction costs. Thus investing in designing a new institution is a high-risk, expensive activity with adverse individual incentives.[23] Moreover, the world is sufficiently complex so that typically two parties may not be in a position to fully apprise themselves of the consequences of a proposed change. Again, risk aversion may create a bias for maintaining the status quo or for slow change.

The interdependence of institutions often makes it necessary to change several institutional arrangements at the same time. This gives rise to the possibility of coordination failure: given the institutions within a society, even when it does not pay to change a particular institution, it may pay to change several of them simultaneously. Governments can facilitate institutional change—they can address the coordination failure and the free rider problems. But turning institutional redesign over to the government raises a host of other difficult questions. For almost any institutional redesign has strong equity consequences, and the political process may block changes that have large adverse consequences for any particular group.[24]

Institutions and economic transitions

Problems associated with inadequate or ill-functioning institutional arrangements are likely to become most severe in periods of rapid transformation, when institutions have not yet had the opportunity to adapt to changed circumstances. Indeed, successful transformation may involve at its heart the constraints of new institutions. While in traditional societies social pressure may serve as an effective mechanism for the enforcement of contracts, as a society develops, greater mobility may make social pressure less effective. And yet the long-term relationships that enforce (implicit) contracts may not have developed. Ideally, institutions should both facilitate change and adapt to change. But that is asking a great deal.

While the above examples are far from exhaustive, they do bring out the importance of institutions and rules of behaviour needed if market systems are to yield effective results. Broadly speaking, one can summarize the issues involved by saying that a market economy requires certain kinds of institutional infrastructure if it is going to function well. It is important to understand and analyze institutional design.[25] The building and protection of the institutional infrastructure is a major challenge to which we return briefly at the end of this section.

Basic institutional arrangements for a public-private partnership

We begin our more detailed discussion of institutions and instruments by looking at the general institutional arrangements required for a well-functioning public-private partnership. We group these general institutional arrangements under three broad headings: democracy and openness, governance, and contracts/trust/long-term relationships.

Democracy and openness should be seen as both objectives and institutions/instruments. It is clear that democracy and openness are not necessary conditions for economic growth in the short or medium run. Indeed, there are many historical examples of successful growth and transformation in non-democratic societies, though, typically, not for very long periods. In post-war experience there are clear examples of growth without democracy in Africa, Asia, Europe and Latin America. On the other hand, democratic institutions are a vital end in themselves and should thus form part of the strategy. Further, they have many important advantages for the functioning of a market economy. First, they allow for political acceptance of economic and other structures, and for acceptance of change in these structures. Second, they can provide for some stability in other institutional arrangements, which may facilitate change. Third, they can improve the quality of governance by providing checks and balances on the executive. Fourth, they can quickly bring attention to serious problems. For example, Sen (and see chapter 2 of this volume) has argued that democratic institutions have been very important in preventing serious famine in India since independence in 1947. The political process is such that speedy reaction to the probability of severe famine is demanded.[26]

High standards and competence in public administration provide for an efficient and stable environment in which to make economic decisions. Many studies of comparative economic growth have concluded that the quality of governance is a crucial determinant of economic performance. Such results are not surprising, since intelligent and reliable governance, as we have discussed, is important for the functioning of markets and, particularly, for investment decisions. Further, in understanding the determinants of good governance, it should be recognized that in democracies there is at least some alignment of interests between the governed and the governing, since the governing must from time to time persuade those who are governed that they are acting in their best interests. Thus, while no form of government has a monopoly on either good or incompetent governance, democracy has a fundamental check: bad governments can be thrown out. And thus the nadirs that non-democratic governments can attain are seldom reached in democracies.

Governance is not only a concern of governments but also of enterprises. Indeed, high standards of corporate governance are central to the performance of firms. In the case of corporate governance the issue of objectives would seem to play a less important role:

are not managers supposed to simply to maximize the value of shares on behalf of shareholders? Yet information asymmetries, the limited incentives of shareholders to vote (and to acquire the information required to vote intelligently) and the limited ability to displace existing management give incumbent management enormous discretion. And there is considerable evidence that they frequently use that discretion not only to entrench their power, but to enrich themselves at the expense of shareholders.

Investors from outside a firm can play a crucial role in establishing good corporate governance. Investors are not prepared to provide resources to a firm, be it through loans or equity, unless they have a clear idea of how those resources will be used. High standards of business conduct will not, however, arise from strong corporate governance alone. There must be in business affairs standards of transparency, information and behaviour that are enforced by both the state and effective corporate governance. Without such standards a system of external finance (loans, equity or other instruments) will not function effectively. That is why strong legal and accounting systems with effective protection from fraud are so essential to the development of modern capital markets. Thus institutions—laws, regulations, and customs, including accounting systems, fraud laws, and securities and exchange commissions—both constitute the financial market and determine how well it function, that is, whether investors have confidence to trust their money to certain institutions within the financial market and whether the market brings about an efficient allocation of resources.

We have emphasized incentives and long-term contracts in institutional relationships. These will form part of, and be underpinned by, definitions of property rights. In many cases these rights will be supported by the law. But one should not take an excessively legalistic approach. The key issue is one of confidence—that commitments and obligations will be met.[27] And confidence arises from social relationships, as well as from legal underpinnings. For example, in a number of east Asian (and other) societies formal legal structures for contracts and their enforcement are weak, but enforcement is, nevertheless, made strong through social and other sanctions.

Specific examples: public responsibility

We turn now to some specific examples of the importance of the ways in which institutions operate. Following the pattern of the preceding section we focus first on areas of government responsibility and then on those of shared government-private responsibility. As has been argued in a number of chapters in this volume, macroeconomic issues are clearly matters for government responsibility. We give two examples to emphasize the importance of institutional arrangements and associated instruments: tax policy and administration, and the workings of a central bank.

Tax policy is a classic example in which the instruments (tax bases and rates) should be designed both to reflect the objectives of government and to be incentive-compatible. In a market economy resources must be raised by government from tax payers. In contrast, in a command economy the government, at least in theory, has first call on resources[28], and residuals are then provided to consumers. The collapse of tax revenues in many transition economies has highlighted these issues in a dramatic fashion.

It is not enough to simply design tax policy in a way that makes individual responses incentive-compatible. Taxes must be collected. This requires commitment and administrative capacity. It also requires that tax payers accept taxation. These requirements are much more easily satisfied if tax systems are transparent and simple, and the resources raised by taxation are used effectively. The institutional arrangements for collection and enforcement will be crucial to the effective functioning of an economy. Without effective collection arrangements a cynicism will develop that devalues the legitimacy of the state and destroys good governance. A tax system that is not enforced effectively leaves great and arbitrary power in the hands of officials. It can lead to macroeconomic instability and the inability of the state to discharge its basic functions. Thus an effectively designed and administered tax system is at the heart of a well-functioning economy. Indeed, one could go as far as to say that one key measure of the extent of good governance is the ability of a government to collect the taxes it has set.

Economic development can enhance the ability of the tax authorities to collect taxes. More sophisticated technology allows the government to monitor transactions that it otherwise could not monitor. But these advances in technology may also allow the private sector to find new ways to avoid taxes. Developments in financial markets provide an illustration. It is impossible for the government to monitor every loan between two parties in a village. But the government can monitor transactions that occur in sophisticated financial markets. On the other hand, sophisticated financial markets have the ability to reorganize transactions to avoid taxation. If, for instance, a government taxes loans made within its country, the location of the transaction can easily move.

A second example of the importance of strong institutions in a market economy is the functioning of a central bank. The central bank must have sufficient strength as an institution to be able to say "no" to a government that seeks to expand credit in an irresponsible way. It must also have the ability to enforce standards in financial institutions. Without such enforcement the confidence of transactors, which is vital for the functioning of a market economy, will be absent. Again, the design of its institutional structure—the powers, responsibilities, accountabilities and incentives—will be crucial if the market economy is to work well.

The degree of independence of the central bank is an issue of the balance of power in a democratic society. The variables controlled by the central bank are of great importance and thus require democratic accountability. At the same time the central bank can act as a check on government irresponsibility. The most successful economies have developed institutional arrangements that afford the central bank considerable autonomy, but in which there is a check provided by public oversight, an oversight that ensures the broader national interest is taken into account in final decisions.[29]

These two examples underline the general principle that good governance involves actions and policies that show credibility, competence and probity. These should be supported by the right kind of checks and balances, training, rewards and punishments. The systems that provide this support will be crucial. They are also greatly influenced by culture and history. For this reason good governance may be difficult to reconstruct, or create. But it can be created, and good system design and vigilance by the population through democratic procedures, including a free press, will be basic ingredients in the process.

Specific examples: shared responsibility

We turn now to examples of the importance of the institutions and instruments surrounding shared public-private responsibilities. We focus briefly on four examples that are vital to both the functioning of the economy and the standard of living of its participants: infrastructure, health, education and industrial policy.

Infrastructure

As we argued in the first section, infrastructure is no longer seen as the exclusive reserve of government. The change in perception is partly due to experiences in which government monopolies have performed badly, pressures on public finances together with the fact that public infrastructure has often made huge losses, a general view that the role of government should be limited and changes in technology making many activities no longer natural monopolies. If the private sector is involved in the provision of infrastructure services, its activities are regulated. Regulation can apply to prices, rates of return, requirements and allowances for capital expenditures, access of suppliers and consumers to parts of the market, quality, environmental obligations and so on.

The institutional arrangements for the regulator and the way they work will have strong influences on the performance of the industry. Many economists have argued that the most important feature of regulation is to ensure competition in an industry, where this is feasible. And, increasingly, changing technology and unbundling (for example, separating electric power generation from the grid and from distribution to consumers) makes real competition possible in parts of sectors, where the sector as a whole might previously have been a natural monopoly. In other areas, such as water supply, allowing competition and free access will be technologically more difficult. In these cases it will be important to promote competition for the market (that is, a monopoly concession for some time period) in place of competition within the market, and then to regulate closely prices and services after concessions have been granted. In a sense the regulator has to step in where competition is not able to control suppliers and stimulate them to perform well.

When the right to provide a service is to be auctioned off, delicate issues of control arise: maximizing the auction price might entail committing to not impose new restraints, but then social welfare will not be maximized. The outcome is analogous to what would have happened if the government had run the enterprise as a monopolist. Hence, there must be some price and service regulation.

It might appear desirable to auction off a "temporary" monopoly—only if the firm performs well (in the social interest) will the right be renewed. But this, too, has its problems: the initial winner would either underinvest in long-term assets and/or overinvest in firm-specific assets that give it an advantage in the next round of bidding (regardless of how they contribute to social welfare).

Substantial areas of infrastructure will remain in the public domain, as decided by technology, history and politics. It is likely, for example, that roads and railways will remain largely in the public sector in most countries for some time. Telecommunications, on the other hand, is becoming increasingly a private sector activity. But there are important examples involving both public and private activity in virtually all areas of infrastructure. The best prognosis is for a continuing mixture between the two, with private activity increasing, and where the mix depends on, and changes with, technology.

As with other aspects of policy and strategy, the credibility, competence and probity of the regulator of an infrastructure sector are crucial to performance. Investors will not make long-term commitments to markets if the rules of the game are not clear and reasonable profits are not available. Consumers will not, or should not, accept private monopolies that can exploit rents and abuse privilege, or for which political and democratic supervision is inadequate. But all too often the choice facing a country is between a private monopoly, checked with government regulators of limited competence, and a public monopoly, which has most of the vices of a private monopoly plus unfettered access to the treasury to finance any losses.

Where privatization of infrastructure works well, improved incentives enhance economic efficiency. And although the infrastructure will always be part of the political process, whether public or private, its movement to the private sector may reduce the temptation to use productive activity as a form of rent seeking (which can take on a variety of forms, for example, locating or not closing activities in politically critical districts, regardless of economic merits). These challenges in providing for infrastructure are tasks for government—the institutions created, how they function and the instruments they use are fundamental to the quality and cost of services that influence both the standard of living of consumers and the effectiveness of production. Details matter.

Health

A second area of shared responsibility is health. Most countries have active public and private health sectors. The issues for public policy concerning health are in many respects deeper than those for, say, telephony. First, health is in itself a vital element in an individual's standard of living. It is a key determinant of an individual's ability to enjoy other aspects of life and to participate in the society and economy. It is therefore universally recognized as a central issue for public policy in all countries. Further, there can be strong external diseconomies to bad health. Individuals are believed to have rights to both protection (good public health) and health care. Correspondingly, governments have a responsibility to ensure certain basics. The nature of these rights is, however, much less clear, and agreement on what they are, or should be, is far from universal. Second, the determinants of good health have much more to do with public health and lifestyle (which are, in part, determined by income, but also by education, culture and other social forces) than with medical care. Third, information is central to any form of health care provision. Individuals have information about themselves that others may not have but are typically ignorant of medical science and practice.

We cannot do justice to the importance and complexity of these issues in a few short paragraphs. We will focus on health care, though without denying the relative importance of public health, including clean water supplies, disposal of sewage, immunization, air pollution and so on, in determining health status. Also, influencing lifestyles and eating, smoking, drinking and other habits may be much more cost-effective ways to improve health status than the provision of health care. Nevertheless, health care takes a very large fraction of government budgets and national income in most countries. The institutions surrounding its delivery play a very important role in determining quality and coverage of supply and, thus, the lives and anxieties of the population.

Health care generates three related and difficult challenges: how to organize its provision, how to finance its provision and whether to ration access and, if so, how. The response to these questions affects both the efficiency of the health care sector and the degree of inequality in the provision of health care services. For instance, the design of the system is likely to affect the extent to which a two-tier health care system develops. Some take the view that equality in the provision of health care services is desirable in its own right (specific egalitarianism).[30]

The asymmetries of information between consumers and providers (who, after all, are supposed to know what consumers need) combined with the limited ability of consumers to make informed choices because they are not repeat buyers of the treatment or information, has led to various organizational arrangements for screening and initial provision. In many countries, including the United Kingdom, a general practitioner makes a preliminary assessment and usually prescribes treatment. The patient is then passed on, if judged necessary, to a specialist. Transaction costs may be much lower in this organizational form than in fee-for-service systems (especially when fee-for-service is combined with reimbursement through insurance companies, which have to be concerned with fraud and abuse). At the same time, capitation systems may provide incentives for doctors to underprovide services,[31] while fee-for-service systems may provide incentives for excessive provision (especially when a significant fraction of the costs are borne by third parties).

In the United States we see, increasingly, reliance on Health Maintenance Organizations (HMOs). In this system capitation fees are provided to competing health organizations, whose overall performance can be judged on statistical bases. Rather than managing their own care, individuals, in effect, hire doctors to manage their care. A competitive market can then arise among these managing doctors. Such an organizational form (like the fee-for-service) can occur within either the public or the private sector. Capitation schemes tend to provide fairly equal treatment to those within the same plan, but different plans may provide markedly different levels and quality of services—with corresponding differences in prices.[32]

The arrangements for screening and initial provision (primary care) will also vary with the stage of development. For example, paramedics with only modest qualifications may provide a service that is of considerable value if spread broadly throughout the population, notwithstanding the fact that they (possibly) make more mistakes than would a better, but more expensively trained and paid, counterpart. There is some question as to whether the balance between primary and specialist care in some developing countries accurately reflects an assessment of social costs and benefits.

There are two major problems facing private market financing of health: because there is large variability in expenditures, finance will inevitably come through insurance firms, and insurance can raise the problem of adverse selection.[33] Insurance companies react to this problem in part by seeking information on the health status and risks of individuals so that each group pays for its actuarial risk, in part by limiting protection and in part by requiring deductibles. There is no general agreement about the desirability of such reactions, but there are two consequences. First, there is inefficient utilization of resources (for example, insufficient protection), and, second, the premiums facing some groups may be so high that they simply do not buy insurance, thus becoming charges on society as a whole in the event of illness.[34] Many governments have responded by requiring a form of at least minimum compulsory insurance or providing a public sector safety net.[35]

The underlying philosophical rationale for a society's commitment to provide health care to all seems appealing: everyone has a right to live, and this should not be conditioned on income (health as a basic right), and a healthy populace will be a more productive one (an instrumental approach). There is broad acceptance of the principle that social justice requires some help to be provided to those who have poor health.[36] But the demand for medically provided services that are effective in relation to some specified criteria, such as life extension, may be beyond the capacity of the economy. There will have to be rationing and, in a sense, all societies face an "error trade-off" inherent in information problems: denying services to those who need it versus providing services to those who do not. In most cases the form of rationing will be determined within the medical services in an informal way. It is not easy to provide more formal methods that can command broad ethical support.

Education

Education is a further example in which considerations of rights and costs/quality of service will lead to a combination of public and private provision, and in which institutional arrangements will have a profound influence on outcomes. Again, we cannot go into great detail here, and many issues have been covered in earlier chapters. Education allows effective participation in society and can be regarded as a right. It has strong positive externalities. It is also regarded in many countries as a duty of parents or guardians to insist on children's education and of the state to make it available up to a certain age. It can also be argued, as for health, that individuals have a right to buy private education if they wish to.[37]

There are difficult issues, however, of deciding how far rights to education go and how education should be supplied. As with health the assertion of rights does not imply unlimited rights and does not imply state provision. In adulthood (for example, over age 18) it can be argued that individuals and families have a responsibility to provide for themselves. But, again, the relevant markets will have deep imperfections, and institutional arrangements will be important. Borrowing to finance education is not straightforward. Human capital is not easily collateralized. Banks find it very costly to keep track of former students who are indebted to them. This need for tracking provides a further example of where the public sector can be administratively more efficient than the private sector.[38] The state is better positioned to follow individuals over time at low cost than the private sector. This can occur in a number of ways (for example, through the tax or social security system). Again, the institutional arrangements of public-private partnerships depend intimately on the structure of the industry or activity.[39]

Industrial policy

Industrial policy should not be about picking winners. It is not clear that governments are able to do this better than markets. And it should not be about judgements that some production or consumer activities are inherently better than others. The neglect of services and the promotion of heavy goods in the former communist countries was a clear example of ideology and prejudice imposing limitations on choice that were deeply damaging to the quality of life. There are, on the other hand, important issues for industrial policy concerning capital markets and risks, and concerning technological spillovers.

Capital markets do not always provide for finance and risk allocation for investment projects that are risky and that have long time horizons. Governments may be able to help private markets develop by providing appropriate protection or insurance, or facilitating the creation of bond or equity markets. Other alternatives are development banks. (For further discussion see chapter 6 in this volume.)

There are many technological knowledge-based activities for which advance involves investment, but where not all the benefits from the knowledge produced come to only the investors (others share in the benefits). These are areas of spillovers or positive externalities. The government can help in part by providing for intellectual property rights. On the other hand, such institutions have their costs not only in administration, but more fundamentally in that they restrict access to knowledge, the dissemination of which has low (or zero) cost after it has been produced. In these circumstances there are arguments for government subsidization of, or direct involvement in, research and development activities. These are essentially arguments why, to use a popular phrasing, production of computer chips does indeed merit more government support than the production of potato chips.

Changing strategies

For the most part in this chapter we have been describing the content of government strategies for economic development in a market economy. We have not, however, focused on the process of transition or adjustment from one type of strategy to another. To some extent this issue of transition can be embodied in the kind of strategy that we have been describing. Appropriate private-public combinations, as outlined above, are indeed oriented towards investment, growth and improving the standard of living in a dynamic economy. On the other hand, as the importance of market-oriented strategies becomes more widely understood, some countries face the problem of switching away from a strategy that gave the market less emphasis. Indeed, many countries are faced with the industrial and institutional legacy of a system that attached great importance to government control of the details of economic activity, whether through public ownership or strong restrictions on private activity (including biases against trade). The task of changing from one system to another is formidable.[40]

In this process of change competition, hard budget constraints and macroeconomic stability will be crucial in promoting and setting the right context and incentives. These can be achieved fairly quickly. Institution building will, however, take longer and will require close attention. The length and depth of the tasks involved mean that this process cannot be delayed—nor will it happen quickly or automatically. Building legal structures and institutions, financial institutions and restructuring industries takes time. Furthermore, the state will have to play an active role in its own redesign.

The investments in structural adjustment or transition will look less attractive if real interest rates are high. Hence the current era of high real interest rates makes these problems more onerous. This underlines the importance of raising world savings and limiting uncertainties so that real interest rates can be reduced.

When we recognize, however, the difficulty of changing institutions, once put into place, we also understand the importance of getting things right as we go through the adjustment process. We cannot blithely say, "this institutional arrangement will do for now, we will fine tune it later". Property rights and special interests are quickly established, and even temporary arrangements have a way of maintaining themselves. Thus it may be far easier to break up a government monopoly before privatization than to privatize a monopoly and, after anti-trust laws are passed, attempt to implement them to stop restrictive practices.

CONCLUSIONS

Over the last two to three decades there have been major changes in views about the development process, the role of government in general and the role of planning in particular. There is confidence that development is possible. Although markets are at the centre of most successful development, government has played a vital role. It is recognized that the role of government should be, and has been, far more circumscribed than envisaged in the command and control approaches in the early planning literature. We have a better understanding of the limitations—both on resources and on control—facing governments and of the myriad of indirect ways in which government actions can affect economic activity.

In thinking about development strategies, it may be useful to visualize the similarities and differences between national strategies and corporate strategies. In both cases one can think of three pieces to the strategy: the setting and clarification of objectives, the formulation of organizational design and the identification of the substantive agenda. A sensible strategy must, of course, be one that can be implemented. We have argued for seeing the objectives of development strategies in terms of raising living standards (not just increasing GDP), taking into account impacts on the environment, education, health, opportunity (in a broad sense) and political rights. At the same time, we recognize that the objectives of a nation and of a corporation are very different. The democratic process can elect governments to govern, but this does not imply consensus on, or clarity of, objectives. Some governments may see part of their job as building consensus and a sense of shared values, but one should not expect these values to have a coherence that might be seen in the corporation.

The old planning models were essentially models of optimization under full information, certainty and full control. The models became more sophisticated when indirect control was introduced through prices, taxes and rewards as principal-agent models embodying incentive compatibility. But a still different kind of model sees government and private individuals as players in a dynamic game in which rules are to be set and argued over, and government is composed of individuals and groups with their own agenda. In our view the analysis of the role of the state should be enriched by both the principal-agent and the game-theoretic approaches. Institutional design is not merely a matter of optimization, but of building on existing foundations and finding institutions that work fairly well under a variety of circumstances. Development strategies then have to be based on a broad interpretation of objectives, where they come from and the institutions through which, and with which, they have to work.

A central element in institutional or organizational design is to view the various participants/institutions within the economy as forming a partnership. Development strategies focus on the assignment of roles within that partnership, and on establishing the institutional infrastructure that affects each of the participants in the economy (through impacts on incentives, information flows and transaction costs). This institutional infrastructure embraces not only the basic legal structure (which defines property rights, including those pertaining to intellectual property, contract, bankruptcy and liability law), but also ensures competitive markets and the safety and soundness of the financial system. The government must establish a partnership framework that ensures the provision of physical infrastructure (and protects consumers against abuses of monopoly power associated with control of the infrastructure), education and health.

The organizational approach suggested here as part of a development strategy differs markedly from that associated with Gosplan[41] and from that of a standard firm planning its activities. It is crucial to recognize that "central headquarters" can (fortunately) exercise only limited control over participants in the economy, especially within democratic societies—and that it has only limited information about the actions of participants. The institutions established as part of the development strategy do affect behaviour, but they do not control directly the actions of participants in the economy. The government plays a role not only in helping create institutions and the institutional infrastructure that allows them to operate (for example, prudential regulation of banking, securities and exchange commissions for bond and stock markets), but also in establishing pay-offs in ways that are conducive to co-operative actions that are in the national interest.[42] Given uncertainty and limited information, it is important to underline the role of robustness in the sense of finding arrangements that will work fairly well across a range of circumstances.

The final aspect of a development strategy is its substance: the decisions about which sectors to encourage or discourage, and whether and how to spend more on primary or secondary education, basic research or improvements in technology. Here, again, there are similarities and differences between the formulation of corporate and national strategies. Corporate strategies typically begin by identifying the resources and special features of the enterprise, focusing on areas in which those resources can yield a (dynamic) comparative advantage, and looking for niches—areas in which corporate rents will not be eroded quickly as a result of competitive entry. National strategies, too, can begin by identifying underlying special resources. They, too, look at dynamics: both areas in which competence can be developed and in which comparative strengths can be maintained over extended periods of time.

But national strategies focus on the particular role of government relative to what markets will do on their own. They thus focus particularly on market failures, areas in which there are large spillovers or limitations posed by capital market imperfections. And they focus especially on the role of the government in providing the conditions for markets to flourish—not only on the institutional infrastructure, but on macroeconomic stability, which is so essential for long-run economic performance. Competition and openness are crucial to technological advance, which is itself crucial for economic growth. Thus a national strategy differs fundamentally from a corporate strategy in that the central concern of government is, or should be, to allow other parties to benefit from its actions, whereas that of the corporation is to focus on its self-interest. Of course, in looking at the problem in this way we do not assume a benign, all-knowing government. A development strategy should take account of what can be expected of government in terms of behaviour, competence and knowledge.

This leads us directly to implementation—a strategy that does not take account of issues of implementation cannot be a good one.

Ability to implement will depend on the dynamic consistency of the strategy itself. If there are clear incentives to renege on commitments, commitments will not be believed. Procedures, institutions and instruments should be sufficiently simple to match the competence of the participants, be they public or private. They should not assign levels of trust to public servants that are unrealistic. At this stage we can only underline the importance of implementation issues and cannot go into them in any further detail, aside from the following. The implementation of a development strategy (at least as conceived of here) reflects organizational decisions made within the public sector. Part of the development strategy must reorganize the public sector so that it will be likely to execute the development plan. As noted, this requires that the plan exhibit incentive compatibility and dynamic consistency. We know a lot about policies that enhance the likelihood of success in implementation. These include: repeatedly checking and rewarding performance, competence and probity; paying "efficiency wages", that is, not pushing wages down to levels where energy and commitment are lost; making ex post and ex ante evaluations of costs and benefits of projects; and implementing a variety of policies designed to reduce the likelihood of corruption of public officials.

We recognize that consensus on the appropriate role of the state and on government strategy for economic development is unlikely to appear. Fairly universal agreement is probably likely to emerge only on the need for defence and law and order, the basic institutional infrastructure for markets and contracts, and macroeconomic stability. But the arguments presented here go considerably beyond the night-watchman state. The market itself cannot deliver broad-based improvements in the standard of living without an active state that establishes the right conditions, responds to change and, together with the market, delivers health, education, infrastructure and social protection. The way in which the role of the state is defined, and in which its services are delivered, are probably the most important determinants of the standard of living of a community over the long term.

NOTES

The views expressed are the responsibility of the authors, not that of the US Government, the European Bank for Reconstruction and Development, the London School of Economics or Stanford University. The chapter draws on the extensive discussions and writings of the United Nations High Level Group on Development Strategy and Management of the Market Economy. The authors are grateful to all their collaborators in that group and particularly for the helpful comments of Amartya Sen, István Székely and Vanessa Elasmacher at the IBRD.

1. The approach here does not have rigid, compartmentalized assignments to one sector or the other. Nor does it have unique assignments of objectives to particular instruments and institutions. It is concerned with how government and markets can and should function. It thus differs fundamentally from Tinbergen's influential objectives-instruments approach. Implicitly, Tinbergen envisioned the economy as described by a set of N equations, determining the values of the variables designated as "objectives", with a set of N "instruments" or control variables. Tinbergen held that the objectives could be moved to desired levels. In special cases objectives could be "assigned" to instruments.

2. The focus on outcomes versus opportunities reflects in part perspectives on the terms of the partnership between the state and its citizens. Some argue that in this partnership it is the responsibility of the state to ensure that all have opportunities, and it is the responsibility of individuals to take advantage of those opportunities. If some individuals fail to take advantage of the opportunities afforded them—and the consequence is inequality—it is the individuals who carry the responsibility. Others propose a wider role for the state within the partnership, recognizing its roles in either shaping preferences or overcoming "handicaps" that impede certain groups availing themselves of these opportunities.

3. A few countries have been successful in developing some degree of consensus through the public education system. But the political process sometimes works to break down consensus by emphasizing differences/product differentiation.

4. Formally, one can think of this in terms of a dynamic game, in which those involved have differing objectives and limited information and understanding of the pay-offs. The government can be thought of as attempting to change the parameters (or perceptions of the players) of the game and/or as a player in the game itself.

5. Some principles underlie this division; at some age individuals can be made responsible for their own decisions. At this point the individual becomes the "partner" and the state provides the opportunities, which may or may not be taken. In this context distributive consequences should be evaluated forward-looking, rather than backward-looking (that is, in terms of the family from which the individual comes). On the other hand, parents make decisions concerning their children, and the state may feel it has some responsibility to ensure that those decisions are made in ways that advantage the children, particularly in cases where parents behave in ways that are irreparably damaging.

6. The "East Asian Miracle" arose partly because these countries were able to generate so much savings, but also because they were able to invest this huge flow of savings efficiently. Elsewhere, marginal capital-output ratios soared when savings rates increased.

7. Macroeconomic stability, sound fiscal management and a robust and well-regulated financial sector played an important role in delivering the level and efficient allocation of savings that underpinned the "East Asian Miracle".

8. This can be reflected (albeit imperfectly) in the transition probabilities in mobility matrices (that is in the chances that a lower-income individual becomes a middle-income individual, or a middle-income individual becomes an upper-income individual), where the probabilities for an individual are affected by her/his own decisions.

9. In developing countries the greatest immediate environmental threat comes from inadequate water supply and treatment. There are at least three major environmental issues associated with air pollution: that associated with particulate emissions from automobiles and factories in towns, that derived from domestic cooking and that from acid rain (largely from coal burning utilities). There are, of course, many other environmental issues that are threatening to livelihoods in developing countries, including deforestation and pollution from natural resource development and other industrial activities. While the environmental damage associated with each is large, inroads into each of these can be made at relatively low cost.

10. Similarly, non-renewable resources should be considered a further part of the capital portfolio (in addition to conventional capital and renewable resources), and their reduction should be accounted for. Put more generally, the intra- and inter-temporal trade-offs should be set in the context of the whole range of capital stocks, including environmental.

11. The importance of the residual or total factor productivity growth, may have declined, at least within the United States in the past two decades, while, it seems, human capital may have become more important. It is not easy to tell, of course, the extent to which these statements are artifacts of modelling or measurement.

12. For instance, in the United States the government paid for the first telegraph line and developed the Internet. It played a major role in the enormous increases in productivity in agriculture. It engaged in basic research that led to important surges in the biotechnology industry. In many countries the civilian aeronautics industry (including the jet engine) has been heavily influenced by military research. Government-sponsored research (or research in regulated industries) was responsible for the transistor, the laser, the computer and many of the other innovations that have transformed modern society.

13. Much of this stance is based on the view that government is less effective in picking winners than the private sector. This stance misses the point. The issue is not picking winners, but identifying spillovers. In some cases industrialized policies were focused on shifting resources away from low-economic-return activities (such as speculative real estate investments) rather than towards specific high-return projects.

14. The mechanisms by which they did this are discussed at greater length in chapter 6 and are similar to those by which the multilateral development

banks can hope to have a stimulative effect on investments in developing countries.

15. The low returns often offered on these accounts suggest that safety and convenience may be a far more important consideration than high real returns in generating savings.

16. Beyond electricity generation, it is not clear how much of power should be public. For example, the transmission lines are likely to remain a natural monopoly (whether government-owned or privately owned and government-regulated).

17. Even there, new technologies (cellular, interactive cable) may soon make competition viable.

18. The older approach was linked to perceptions of a more closed economy. In a closed economy, material balance equations are satisfied through local production. With a lack of confidence in markets' forward-looking abilities, it was natural to turn to the government to provide the requisite check. In an open economy, any gap between supply and demand for tradeable goods can be resolved by expanding or contracting exports and imports. The older approach was also based on a perception of the development process that gave excessive emphasis to the accumulation of capital goods relative to the standard of living. The models of inter-temporal optimatization often pointed to a sequencing in development similar to that pursued by the Soviet economies.

19. Indeed, there is evidence, for example, that the Japanese development banks provided only a small fraction of total funds. The development banks did more than just provide direction; they provided monitoring services for loans. Their activities may have enhanced the likelihood of repayment.

20. And thus there will be a greater incentive for the borrower to fulfill conditionalities and commitments than with an ordinary investment bank. Multilateral development banks are in a better position to enforce sovereign guarantees than are most private lenders.

21. It is suggested sometimes that institutions arise when markets fail. Thus the absence of insurance markets gives rise to informal insurance institutions (such as the family). Some families may regulate behaviour, for example, providing assistance only for those who it has judged have made adequate efforts to help themselves. Note that there is no formal contract nor an explicit statement of what an "adequate level of effort" is.

22. They typically are designed to promote long-term relationships, for without such long-term relationships it is harder to establish trust. For instance, firms that have a steeply rising wage profile provide strong incentives for workers to stay with the firm.

23. Especially given the presumptions of courts, or of the sceptical, in interpreting the contract against the interests of the proposer.

24. These equity concerns play a role in the persistence of seemingly inefficient social arrangements. For instance, while unregulated use of commons can lead to overgrazing, the enclosures (which ensure efficiency) made those without access to land worse off. Proposals that on the face of it seem as if they represent Pareto improvements may be resisted because it is perceived (or feared) that they will change the future dynamics of the political process in ways that could adversely affect particular groups.

25. It is however, important to recognize that history is not only important for determining the evolution of institutions, but also for the equilibrium that emerges within an institutional structure. History and culture affect perceptions of what other participants do. When there are multiple equilibria, they affect the equilibrium that emerges.

26. We should further recognize that in the new information age the level of control required by authoritarian governments to stop the flow of information is such that it would almost inevitably stifle economic development.

27. Government actions can enhance confidence, for example, those that increase the franchise value of a bank and thus increase the likelihood that the bank will act in a trustworthy manner (to preserve its franchise).

28. In practice, those at the farm, factory and distribution levels in eastern Europe and the former Soviet Union, under the old regime, had great power to divert resources.

29. It should be noted that the banking community (as holders of long-term debt) may place a greater emphasis on controlling inflation relative to reducing unemployment than would the populace as a whole.

30. While this view is widely shared, the fact that health itself is not that closely linked to health care suggests that the more fundamental concern should be equality of health status, or opportunity to achieve adequate health status, rather than health care itself.

31. Though this incentive will be mitigated with information that allows medical practices to develop reputations concerning the quality of service provided.

32. Thus HMOs do not resolve the issue of inequality of access, except if there is a standard plan (at a standard cost) and no one is allowed to provide services beyond the standard plan. (Even then there may be some inequality, since plans may attempt to select a more healthy population, allowing them either to lower costs or provide additional services. An HMO located on the fifth floor of a building without an elevator will discourage clients with heart conditions, just as an HMO that has a plethora of sports doctors will encourage clients in good health.) Just as some hold it to be a fundamental principle that everyone should have equal access to health care, others hold it as a fundamental principle that an individual should be allowed to buy as much of any good as he or she wants. (As long as there is some elasticity of supply of health care services, additional purchases of health care services by a rich individual do not necessarily come at the expense of less health care services for the poor.)

33. Insurance also raises the problem of moral hazard. Since individuals do not bear the full cost of their care, they overconsume, in part by taking less care of themselves.

34. Formally speaking, there is a free rider problem here—the government cannot commit itself to not provide health services for those in need, regardless of whether they have resources. The problem is analogous to that of poverty among the elderly: the government cannot commit to not help the elderly who fail to save sufficient amounts during their working years to provide a decent standard of living in retirement.

35. In many developing countries a major issue is the imposition of fees for public sector health care services. Given the severe financial constraints facing most developing countries, it is natural that they look for fees wherever they can. Charging fees can increase the efficiency of resource utilization. But at the same

time that it reduces overconsumption by some, it may result in underconsumption (relative to an ideal health care standard) by others.

36. In practice, however, the question is often posed, do health problems arise because of actions undertaken by individuals? In some quarters there is concern that public provision of health care attenuates incentives for healthy living.

37. As in the case of health, supply is elastic so that extra consumption by some does not come at the expense of less consumption by others (at least in the long run). The issues concerning inequality in education and health care are not identical. Inequality in access to education can lead to social division and divisiveness and the perpetuation of poverty and elite classes.

38. In the United States the direct lending program has provided forms of loans (such as those that make annual repayments contingent on the individual's income) that the private sector has not, and it appears as if their overall lending costs are lower than those of the private sector. Again, a variety of institutional arrangements can be devised. One that leaves the lending activity in the private sector entails auctioning off the right to make the loans. This ensures that the premiums paid to private firms are not excessive.

39. We have touched on only one aspect of the public-private partnership in education. In several countries there is a debate about the role of the private versus the public sector in production. The debate typically involves issues that extend beyond efficiency. Advocates of private production argue that competition will enhance efficiency. Critics argue that education differs from conventional commodities in numerous ways, which make the standard competitive model inappropriate (for example, consumers are ill-informed about what they are buying; decisions are made not by consumers, but by their parents; in any locale, there are typically only a limited number of schools, so that competition is at best limited). Private systems may result in more social stratification, with adverse long-run implications for the economy. In developing economies the criticisms of public education often seem to have considerable force, yet the imperfections of competition in the education market raise more fundamental problems about the competitive market alternative.

40. One of the challenges of any change is that it affects different groups differently. Those who oppose change will always point to those who are adversely affected. Even though the gains to the winners are far greater than the losses to the losers, the losers will put up effective resistance. They may even resist when they are compensated for their losses. The compensation will typically be for only short-term losses, and they worry that it will eventually wither away, leaving them worse off. Societies that allow small, well-organized groups who lose from particular changes to sway decisions inevitably wind up with institutional ossification. It is too glib to say that "a rising tide lifts all boats". We know that is not necessarily true. Policies have to take into account those who are adversely affected. Still, an exclusive focus on equity as interpreted by the losers (which in many cases simply means preserving rents for those who currently enjoy them, for example, those from controlling a government monopoly) will in the long run result in everyone being worse off.

41. The central planning agency of the former Soviet Union.

42. One of the insights of some of the recent literature in this area is that such government interventions may even be incentive-compatible from the perspective of government; that is, it pays for government to follow through on its promises, even when it is not compelled to do so.

REFERENCE

World Bank. 1994. *World Development Report 1994*. New York: Oxford University Press.

INDEX